FESTIVALS OF THE JEWISH YEAR

A MODERN INTERPRETATION
AND GUIDE

Theodor H. Gaster

MORROW QUILL PAPERBACKS

FESTIVALS

of the Jewish Year

NEW YORK

First Morrow Quill Paperback Edition 1978

Copyright 1952, 1953 by Theodor Gaster

The writer is indebted to the Editor of *Commentary* for generous permission to reprint certain portions of this book which originally appeared in that magazine.

Printed in the United States of America.

3   4   5   6   7   8   9   10

Library of Congress Catalog Card Number 53-9341

ISBN 0-688-06008-0

TO RHODA STARR

CONTENTS

III
The Solemn Days

IV
Days of Sorrow

V
The Minor Holidays

VI
Sabbath

PREFACE

Nine out of ten people who pick up a book on the Jewish festivals are likely to put it down again in short order, in the not unreasonable belief that they will have heard it all before and that it will be but a repetition of what is readily to be found elsewhere. While the reader's eye is still on this first page, therefore, it may be well to reassure him that that is just what he is *not* going to find in the present book.

Here, the festivals, fasts and holy days of the Jewish year are going to be viewed in an entirely different light. We are going to regard them not as static institutions which came down more or less unchanged throughout the centuries, but rather as manifestations of a constantly evolving process, and we are going to interpret them in the light of that whole process, and not in the language and thought of any one or other particular epoch. In other words, we are going to consider them as parts of a continuing attempt to articulate certain broad universal truths, and we shall seek to discover, behind the varying forms of expression, just what those truths are.

We shall do this principally in two ways. First, we shall endeavor to trace the actual evolution of each festival, going back even beyond the Bible to its more remote and primitive stages. In such a perspective, we shall gain a clearer picture of what it really seeks to convey; we shall be able the better to recognize the permanent truth behind the changing forms, and to see more clearly how both the inner ideas and the outward expressions have been progressively crystallized and refined.

Secondly, we shall use the *comparative* approach— that is, we shall compare the customs and ceremonies of the festivals with those of other peoples, not for the purpose of diverting the reader with entertaining parallels, but in order to recover, behind the conventional traditional explanations, traces of earlier, more universal ideas which are nonetheless precious and pertinent for having been overborne and overswept in the onrushing tide of history.

At the same time, we shall not overlook the purely folk element of the festivals—the fact that the symphony consists not only in religious overtones but also in popular undertones, and that many of the things that people do on them are done not out of high-minded moral piety but simply because they have fun doing them.

Nor shall we be chauvinists. While we shall lay stress on the uniqueness of many concepts and on the distinctive character of many transformations, we shall also point out frankly and candidly what the Jews have borrowed or adapted from their neighbors. Firstly, this provides an effective illustration of the forces and influences which have in fact molded the development of the festivals; secondly, it is in any case scarcely credible that a people which has lived for nearly two thousand years in the midst of other peoples should have picked up nothing from them in the way of calendar customs and popular observances.

To be sure, on many points there can as yet be no certainty. Our information is incomplete, and we have often to fall back on tentative "reconstructions" and on more or less plausible conjectures. But such uncertainty attaches to all knowledge and to all science everywhere, and to insist on finality is to surrender the whole of the human adventure. "We know in part, and we prophesy in part"; no man can see the face of God, and live.

In the Jewish festivals, heaven and earth meet together. What is edifying is apparent enough, and there is no point in gilding the lily; what is crude is equally apparent, and there is no point in decrying human clay. We shall therefore avoid homiletics on the one hand, and apologetics on the other. This book is written primarily for the type of person—and his name is legion—who wants to know not so much the *how* as the *why* of the Jewish festivals, and who wants that *why* set forth in terms which will be intelligible and meaningful to him at the present day. To tell him simply that God commanded this or ordained that is to leave him high and dry; what he wants to hear, in the idiom of modern thought, is just what this whole idea of God-ordained institutions really means. He wants to hear not that the Jews are a Chosen

People, standing under special convenant with God, but what, in broad universal terms, this concept implies and what validity it possesses for our own times. He wants to know just what to do about the belief in miracles—whether, for example, he can conscientiously observe the Passover, if he denies that the waters of the Red Sea were parted; or whether he can subscribe to the commitment of the Covenant, if he rejects the story that it was concluded at Mount Sinai. He wants to know also whether the results of Biblical criticism and of historical research really invalidate his traditional faith. In short, he wants to know whether, and if so why, he should go on observing the traditional festivals rather than discard them as outmoded superstitions. This book tries to give him the necessary information and perspective in the light of which he may formulate his answer. It will not please everyone, and it will not try to. It will try only to be honest.

T. H. G.

FESTIVALS OF THE JEWISH YEAR

I

Backgrounds and Beginnings

ANCIENT IDIOMS
AND MODERN MINDS

*It is impossible to talk about Jewish festivals
without first saying something about Judaism
itself*

Judaism is the culture of the Jewish people—the quintessence of its collective experience throughout the ages. It is a term like *Hellenism* or *Americanism,* and does not imply any kind of rigid, authoritative creed.

This does not mean, however, that the Jewish people has not developed certain very distinctive ideas, or tenets, without which Judaism would today be altogether unthinkable; and two of these are, in fact, central to its whole existence. They are the ideas of the Torah and the Covenant.

Torah is a Hebrew word meaning guidance, or direction. In a more specific sense, it denotes the guidance and direction which God gives to man. This Torah is necessary for man, if he is to play his part in the general plan and purpose of the universe and to achieve therein his maximum fulfillment.

Judaism says that Torah is revealed continuously both in nature and in history. It has, however, to be properly interpreted, for if nature be misunderstood, or history misconstrued, man loses his bearings in the world, and the purpose of his creation is defeated.

Judaism bases its interpretation of Torah on the so-called Law of Moses—that is, on the moral and legal precepts contained in the first five books of the Bible. This document is regarded as the supreme authority for all human conduct, the written formulation of the divine will and plan.

Judaism recognizes, however, that Torah itself is dynamic, not static, unfolding itself continuously throughout the ages. It therefore insists that the interpretation of it is necessarily *progressive,* being achieved gradually through the insights and perceptions of successive generations. The Written Word (or Scripture), it maintains, has always to be supplemented by the Oral Tradition— that is, by the accumulated results of unremitting study. Moreover, such study is not the duty or prerogative only of professional scholars; it is part of the obligation of every Jew, an integral and essential element of his religious commitment, no whit less important than worship or observance.

At the same time, Judaism realizes that there can be neither uniformity nor finality to human knowledge and learning. It therefore imposes no formal dogmas, claiming always that God lies at the end, and not at the beginning, of the religious road. So long as they are based on serious study of the tradition, and take into due consideration the accumulated wisdom of the ages, differences of view and opinion among those who tread that road are freely admitted. "Both these and those," it is affirmed, "are words of a living God."

Torah applies to all mankind, but its special exponents are the Jews, the House of Israel.

According to Jewish teaching, Israel and God are bound to each other by a special contract, or Covenant, originally concluded at Mount Sinai and binding upon all generations. Under the terms of that contract, Israel has undertaken, in return for God's providence and protection, to serve as His witness in the world of men—that is, as a model society so organized and so conducted as to give practical realization to His Torah. Whatever its historical origins may be, the Jewish people is thus more than a fortuitous aggregation of individuals; it is a self-dedicated "kingdom of priests," committed to this holy task. As the sages put it, Israel has voluntarily taken upon itself what is at once a crown and a yoke.

Two thousand, or even twenty, years ago men did not express themselves in the same way as they do today. Each generation creates it own idiom, born of its own circumstance and environment. A modern man might say, for example, that someone has "gone off the rails" or "got the green light," or that a certain matter is "tied up in red tape"; but these phrases would have been quite unintelligible two hundred years ago and, for all we can tell, may be equally unintelligible two hundred years hence. As Mohammed said, "To every age its own book."

All of this is obvious enough, yet failure to realize it is today one of the greatest obstacles to the correct understanding and appreciation of Judaism and the Jewish festivals.

Confronted, for instance, with the statement that God conversed with Moses on the top of a mountain, or that He miraculously parted the Red Sea, or that He wrote a set of laws with His own finger, or that He concluded a special covenant with a particular people or that He formally prescribed the institution and ritual of seasonal feasts, modern man is apt to retort that these are ideas which belong to the world's childhood, which reflect views of deity long since superseded, and which can therefore scarcely serve as a serious basis for contemporary faith. He may, in fact, go even further and contend that the indentification of a particular code of laws with the eternal, immutable scheme of the universe is really an intolerable and intolerant attempt to force all human conduct into the strait jacket of a single arbitrary pattern; while the assumption that the Jews are a chosen people— the special and unique apostles of God—is a piece of arrogant chauvinism, smacking ominously of a *Herrenvolk* complex. Before going further, therefore, it may be well to deal briefly with these very common objections.

The overall answer to them is that a distinction must be preserved between what Judaism has to say and how it says it. When an ancient Hebrew said that God spoke with Moses on the top of a mountain, what he was really saying, in the only language then available, was that any code of laws which professes to set up a universal standard of human living must represent a link between the human and the divine—that is, must derive its authority from man's apprehension of what the basic scheme of the universe really is. Today, thanks to the progress of philosophy and theology, it is possible to express this idea in more rarefied, metaphysical terms; we can speak, for instance, of Natural Law as the ultimate source of human legislation, or of the general interpenetration of the punctual and the durative, the temporal and the eternal. But the fact that three thousand years ago, men used more primitive terms does not make the idea more primitive; at most, it makes the language antique.

By the same token, when we read in the sixteenth chapter of Leviticus that the ancient Israelites used to get rid of their sins every year by transferring them to a scapegoat, we must not at once conclude that because the procedure is primitive, so too is the underlying concept. Back of the crudity of expression, the grotesque *bizarrerie* of the actual ritual, lies the valid and valuable apprehension that sin is not merely a personal matter but impairs the effective vitality of society as a whole and that no society can take on new life unless and until the taint has been removed. It is this eternal verity, rather than the particular expression of it, that is really important.

So, too, when we come up against the ancient system of sacrifices and immolations, and when we find it bulking so largely in the traditional liturgy of the festivals, there is no need to dismiss it out of hand as a mere product of otiose, outmoded superstition. Here, again, it is only the medium of expression that is primitive; back of it lies the permanent human passion to achieve some sort of personalized contact with God, or a valid recognition of the fact that God, as the agent of Nature, cooperates in all human activities and is entitled to a share of what issues from them. The primitive happens to express these ideas by the belief that God can share a meal with men or that a certain portion of men's crops and livestock should be rendered to Him as a concrete payment for the help He gives. We, for our part, might envisage personal

contact with God in a less concrete and more mystical
fashion, and might think of the dedication of our selves
rather than of our possessions as the more appropriate
way of paying tribute to Him. But in both cases the
fundamental idea is the same; and it is this idea, rather
than the form of its articulation, that really counts.

Take, again, the familiar concept of the Messiah.
Many modern Jews, especially those of the Reform persuasion, reject altogether the traditional assumption that
the Jewish people is at present in a state of exile, waiting
for the restoration of its ancient glories under the sovereignty of an anointed king (Hebrew, *Messiah*), of the
line of David. They contend, on the contrary, that the
dispersion of the Jews from their original homeland, however calamitous it may have been at the time, was in
reality a furtherance of their historic mission to serve as
"a light to the nations," and that Judaism, far from being in a state of suspended animation, has in fact thereby
emerged from the local into the universal. But here,
once more, it is necessary to distinguish between the
basic notion and the form of expression. When a Jew
living in the Babylonian Exile wished to express the
idea of a future age of bliss, it was natural for him to do
so by envisaging a restoration of his national fortunes, a
triumphant reconstitution of his whilom state and temple.
The obvious symbol of such a triumph was the advent of
a conquering hero—a David *redivivus,* an anointed
prince. Today, no doubt, a more contemporary image
would be more natural, but the change would be one of
expression only. The Messiah is today simply a particular symbol for a general and perennial idea, and the
fact that this symbol sprang out of the conditions of a
distant past is completely unimportant. Indeed, our own
alternative image of the Golden Age issues, in precisely

the same way, out of ancient Greek mythology rather than out of our contemporary environment, while the French symbol of liberation during the Second World War was the cross of Joan of Arc! Viewed in this light, the Messiah is no more inappropriate as a symbol than are, for instance, Cupid, Santa Claus or the Minute Man.

In the same way, too, the idea that the Jewish people is at present in exile has by now transcended its national and political origins. What it really conveys today is that Jewish culture—outside of the very recent state of Israel —has become detached from any distinctive Jewish society and therefore lives, as it were, in a vacuum—constantly in danger of degenerating into a traditional heirloom instead of being a living and organic form of self-expression; of becoming, that is, a matter of conservation rather than of creation, something *in*jected into Jews rather than *pro*-jected out of them. The exile, it is important to note, has always been regarded in Jewish teaching as an exile of God no less than of Israel, and it is upon this aspect of it that the major emphasis is now placed. The Divine Presence has been withdrawn, and it is to the vision of that Presence—to the bleaching out of the world's slow stain—that Israel really aspires. Prayers for the return to Zion and the restoration of the Temple are thus, once again, but expressions of a wider sentiment in a narrower form.

Lastly, when the Bible says that the festivals are ordained by God and when it prescribes their rites and ceremonies in His name, all it is saying, *au fond,* is that the festivals are inspired and informed by man's consciousness of his relationship to the cosmic pattern and scheme. The same idea might be expressed today in a less anthropomorphic and legalistic metaphor; we might speak, for example, of the inworking of the divine or cosmic within us, and prefer to think in terms of inspiration and aspiration rather than of injunction and obedience. But the fact that our forebears used a different image in no way invalidates their basic concept, nor should we so press the language as to squeeze out the content.

Judaism retains these ancient forms of expression as a man retains his memories. His moods may change, his philosophy develop, his outlook undergo the most radical transformations, but all of them are inextricably interwoven with the body of experiences which he keeps in his mind and heart, with the scenes and moments of a lifetime, the impressions and associations which form the fabric of his spiritual being and which he cannot surrender without surrendering his identity. Nor is this merely a matter of nostalgic sentimentality. Judaism is a historical process, not a philosophical formula; its concepts and institutions therefore possess a durative rather than a punctual character, reflecting the spirit of the entire continuity rather than of any single moment within it. The language of Judaism is, in fact—like all language everywhere—a constantly evolving complex of old and new elements, the expression at once of the hereditary traits and of the acquired characteristics of a culture. There will always be certain features which are archaic and merely ornamental, and in every age there will be certain ideas which have not yet found adequate articulation. But language is an organic growth, and cannot be determined by rule of thumb or limited to the expression of the moods and passions of a single generation.

To take another analogy: even though its modern inhabitants may feel more comfortable in modern apartments, the ancient monuments of an ancient city are nonetheless part and parcel of its being; Jerusalem would not be Jerusalem, nor Athens Athens, nor Rome Rome, without the Wailing Wall, the Acropolis and the Forum.

Modern Jews are troubled also by the problem of *historicity*. The seasonal festivals and the fasts are geared to particular events in the past. If, therefore, the traditional record of those events can be challenged by Biblical criticism or by archaeological research, what happens to them? If, for example, it can be proved—or, at least, rendered probable—that the exodus of the Israelites from Egypt and their entry into Canaan never really took place in the form described in the Bible, what becomes of Passover, and should it then be discarded?

The answer is very simple. The historical events associated with the festivals are but illustrations of their basic themes, and it is not at all important if that illustration derive more from fanciful treatment than from factual record. If, for example, someone were to institute a festival revolving around the theme of human forgetfulness and its consequences, and were to use as an illustration the familiar story of King Alfred and the cakes, and even if it were supposed that the festival was the anniversary of that incident, it would not really matter one whit if the whole story should be proved a fiction. What we must learn to realize is that the legends connected with festivals are illustrations, not *raisons d'être;* the important thing is the permanent, continuous truth which those legends exemplify. Indeed, the assumption that the only validation of festivals lies in the factuality of their attendant legends is a piece of 19th-century rationalism which we ought to have outgrown. In all civilizations everywhere, festivals are "explained" and "justified" by myths and legends, and these are often cast in quasi-historical form. But the true origin of the festival does not lie in what is said about it, and to find the story unreliable impairs only the validity of the explanation, but not of the institution itself.

It must be remembered also that the recognition of purely folkloristic elements in the Biblical traditions in no way weakens the basic truth or authority of Holy Writ. For if the Bible is the word of God, it is just as much a word as it is of God, and that means that its divine inspiration is channeled and expressed through human speech and in the idiom of human thought. Myth, poetry, and imaginative fancy are part of that idiom. Moreover, we should be careful to draw the proper and necessary distinction between spiritual validity, or truth, and documentary fact. After all, there is no historical proof that Jesus was born on Christmas Day.

2

WHAT, WHY AND HOW

*The Festivals, fasts and holy days and their
place in Judaism*

The Jewish Festivals, fasts and holy days are a practical
expression of the Jewish commitment. However they
may each have begun, they are today welded together as
parts of a single consistent system and are subsumed to a
single consistent purpose. That purpose is to illustrate
the presence and activity of God in nature, history, and
the lives of men.

In the case of the festivals, the illustration from nature
is drawn from the succession and alternation of the
seasons, while that from history is furnished by particular
events in the career of the Jewish people. Each festival
thus possesses both a seasonal and a historical significance, and each carries both a universal and a particular
meaning. These several aspects are, however, skillfully

harmonized and made to run parallel, so that the same basic truth is conveyed simultaneously on two planes.

The seasonal festivals are three in number: *Passover* (Pesah), which marks the beginning of the barley harvest, in spring; *Pentecost* (Shavuoth), or the *Feast of Weeks,* which marks the end of it, seven weeks later; and *Ingathering,* or the *Feast of Booths* (Succoth), which celebrates the reaping of the summer fruits, at the commencement of autumn.

On the historical plane, these three festivals are associated with the Exodus of the Children of Israel from Egypt.

Passover, which represents the beginning of the harvest, commemorates also the beginning of Israel's national existence—that is, the actual release from bondage.

Pentecost, which represents the consummation of the harvest, after seven weeks of back-breaking labor, also commemorates the arrival of the Israelites at Mount Sinai after seven weeks of weary wandering, the Giving of the Law and—above all—the conclusion of the Covenant between God and His people.

Ingathering, or the *Feast of Booths,* which—on the seasonal plane—is an occasion when men dwell in booths or shacks during the reaping of the summer fruits, is interpreted historically to commemorate the perilous sojourn of the Israelites in the wilderness during their journey to the Promised Land.

The festivals serve as illustrations of how the Covenant has operated in history. Each of the events with which they are associated is therefore construed in terms of a reciprocal relationship between God and Israel. At the

Exodus, Israel faced the hazards of the desert, so God redeemed it from bondage. At Sinai, Moses went up to the top of the mountain; but God came down to meet him. And it was only because one generation had been prepared to die in the wilderness that God led its children to the Promised Land.

The three festivals were marked, in ancient times, by statutory pilgrimages to the sanctuary or Temple. They are therefore known in Jewish tradition as the three *pilgrim feasts.*

Passover and Ingathering were originally observed for seven days, the first and last of which were distinguished by solemn assemblies and by a total abstention from manual work and commercial activity. Pentecost, on the other hand, was observed for one day only; but this too was regarded as sacred and was marked by the same restrictions.

The festivals were geared to a lunar calendar, and their dates were therefore determined by observation of the preceding new moon. At the time of the Second Temple, the central authorities in Jerusalem used to send out messengers to distant communities as soon as that event had been reported and confirmed. The messengers, however, were often unavoidably retarded en route, with the result that they arrived at their destinations too late. To meet this difficulty, the practice grew up of adding an extra day to each festival to make sure that everyone would have a chance of observing it. This practice is still retained by Orthodox and Conservative Jews living outside of Palestine, so that for them Passover and Ingathering last for *eight* days, and Pentecost for *two.* Reform Jews, however, have reverted to the original Biblical usage.

In contrast to the festivals are the fasts. Modern scholars have sought to show that these, too, have also a natural, seasonal basis; but that basis has long since disappeared, and the fasts now possess only a historical character. They represent, as it were, the reverse of the coin; for while the festivals illustrate God's providence, the fasts exemplify His displeasure. They are therefore associated not with the triumph of the Exodus but with the disaster of the Destruction of the Temple, each fast commemorating a stage in that catastrophe.

The fast of the *Tenth of Tebet* celebrates the commencement of the siege of Jerusalem by the Babylonian army of Nebuchadnezzar.

The fast of the *Seventeenth of Tammuz* commemorates the first breach in the walls of the city.

The fast of the *Ninth of Ab* marks the date on which, according to tradition, both the First and Second Temples were destroyed, in 586 B.C.E. and 70 C.E. respectively.

The fast of the *Third of Tishri*—known as the *Fast of Gedaliah*—commemorates the assassination of Gedaliah, Nebuchadnezzar's viceroy in Judah.

These four fasts rank as half-holidays. They are distinguished by special features in the regular daily services of the synagogue, but abstention from work lasts only until noon. Moreover, they have today fallen into neglect, except among Jews of more orthodox persuasion. Reform Jews discard them on principle, holding that they are based on an outmoded conception of Israel's destiny and mission.

Over and above the festivals and fasts are the Solemn Days of *New Year* (Rosh Ha-Shanah) and *Yom Kippur*. These possess neither seasonal nor historical character, but illustrate the presence and activity of God from the world of personal human experience.

New Year is a development of the festival called in the Bible "the Day of Memorial." This festival fell on the new moon of the seventh month (Tishri), and it was only in later times, when that day was adopted as the official beginning of the festal cycle, that it became a New Year celebration. Its original purpose was to usher in the period of lenten abstinence and austerity which preceded the real commencement of the agricultural year at the Feast of Ingathering, and this continues to be its primary significance. New Year inaugurates the *Ten Days of Penitence,* during which, as the traditional fancy puts it, God holds assize in heaven and determines the destinies of men for the ensuing twelve months.

Here, too, the ancient calendarical device remains in operation, and New Year is consequently observed by Orthodox and Conservative Jews *for two days.*

The conclusion of the lenten period is marked by *Yom Kippur.* Described in the Bible as "a sabbath of sabbaths," this is the holiest day in the Jewish year. It is characterized by a rigorous fast from sundown to sundown and by services in the synagogue both on the initial evening and continuously throughout the day itself. Designed originally as a means of purging the community of all such material evil and disaster (e.g., sickness, plague, or blight) as might impair its prosperity during the coming year, it has developed into a day of atonement, on which both individual Jews and the House of Israel as a whole seek annually to regenerate their spiritual selves by the threefold process of self-examination, confession and repentance. On this day, says tradition, God finally "closes His books" and seals the ledger of human fates.

Lastly, the Jewish year is punctuated by certain minor holidays which have the character of popular celebrations rather than of sacred institutions. To this class belong: *Purim, Hanukkah,* the *New Year for Trees,* and the *Thirty-third Day of the Omer.*

Purim, or the *Feast of Lots,* falls on the fourteenth of Adar (roughly March) and commemorates the triumph of Esther and Mordecai in foiling the plot of Haman, vizier of King Ahasuerus (Xerxes), who sought to exterminate the Jews of the Persian Empire and who had selected that day *by lot* (Hebrew, *pur*) for the execution of his plans. The story is related in the Biblical Book of Esther, which is read in the synagogue as the "theme-text" of the occasion. Purim is regarded as the merriest day in the Jewish year and has taken on many of the features of Carnival and Shrove Tuesday celebrations.

Hanukkah, or the *Feast of Dedication,* which commences on the twenty-fifth of Kislev (December) and lasts eight days, commemorates the victory of the Maccabees over the forces of the Syrian monarch, Antiochus IV, and the cleansing and rededication of the defiled Temple in Jerusalem, in 165 B.C.E. The principal feature of the celebration is the lighting, every evening at dusk, of candles or oil lamps in commemoration of the reluming of the candelabrum in the sanctuary.

The *New Year for Trees* falls on the fifteenth of Shebat (February) and marks the date when, so it is said, the sap begins to rise in the trees of Palestine. It is customary on this day to eat of the fruit of such trees as grow in the Holy Land, and to recite a blessing over them. In modern Palestine, it has also become the custom to mark the occasion by planting new trees. There are, however, no special services in the synagogue and no special features of the liturgy.

The *Thirty-third Day of the Omer* (Lag[1] b'Omer), which likewise lacks any formal, ritual observance, marks what is virtually the middle of the *Omer,* or seven-week lenten period between Passover and Pentecost. Tradition asserts that the holiday commemorates the sudden termination of a plague which ravaged the disciples of the famous Rabbi Akiba in the first century C.E. This, however, would appear to be no more than a fanciful attempt to validate on historical grounds a folk festival which was really the Jewish counterpart of mid-lent ceremonies.

All of the Jewish festivals, fasts and holy days partake of the nature of *living experiences,* rather than of mere commemorations. They are based on the premise that the particular events with which they are associated are but so many historical illustrations of something that is essentially *continuous*—something in which all Jews participate throughout the generations. The Exodus from Egypt, for example, is conceived as an experience which transcends the actual moment of its occurrence; it is a *perpetual* adventure in which *all* Jews are involved at all times and in all places—a perpetual progress from bondage to freedom and from idolatry to the vision of God. When, therefore, a Jew celebrates Passover, he is performing an act of present commitment, and not merely indulging in picturesque reminiscence. Similarly, the Covenant at Sinai was concluded not only with those

. . . . .

[1] The word *Lag* is concocted out of the Hebrew letters *L G,* which have the numerical value of *thirty-three.*

who happened, at that particular moment, to be assembled at the foot of the mountain, but also—in an ideal sense—with all Israel forever. Pentecost therefore involves an annual reaffirmation of that bond, and is not merely a recollection of an event in the past. By the same token also, what the fasts really exemplify and epitomize is not this or that specific historical *event,* but rather a *continuing situation;* not, that is, the siege and fall of Jerusalem at the hands of the Babylonians and Romans, but the continuing detachment of Judaism and the Jewish people from their spiritual and cultural matrix—the fact that, ever since, both God and Israel have been in exile.

From this it follows that the festivals, fasts and holy days are of essentially *communal* character, the celebration of them being a collective performance, not an act of private, individual devotion. Indeed, even on Yom Kippur, free though it be of "national," historical associations, the point at issue is not only the shriving of personal sin or the spiritual regeneration of the individual, but equally the removal from the House of Israel of that collective taint and impurity which impedes and impairs the discharge of its mission as the continuous co-worker and witness of a holy God. This, in fact, is what is meant by the traditional view that the Jew who fails to observe the festivals not only neglects his obligation to God but automatically cuts himself off from his people.

3

OLD WINE
AND NEW BOTTLES

How Judaism transformed ancient festivals.
Sketch of the Jewish year

There are two ways of looking at the Jewish festivals:
the traditional way and the modern way.

The traditional way says that the festivals were first
instituted in the Law of Moses and are therefore
uniquely and peculiarly Jewish. The modern way says
that they go back to, or are borrowed from, more ancient
pagan ceremonies and that what is distinctively Jewish
about them is the manner in which they have been
transformed and reinterpreted.

The traditional way says also that the festivals were
ordained supernaturally by God, while the modern way
insists that they are the creation of man.

These two approaches are by no means so irreconcil-
able as might appear at first sight and as many people to-

day assume. For the truth is that the Bible itself nowhere assumes that the major festivals began with Moses;
all it does is to formulate, in the name of Moses, new
reasons why they should continue to be observed in
Israel. In the story of the Exodus, for example, the
previous existence of Passover is taken for granted, for it
is only because the Israelites so meticulously carry out
the time-honored regulations and dash the sacrificial blood
upon their doorposts, that the angel of Jehovah is able to
recognize their homes and pass over them when he comes
to smite the firstborn of the Egyptians. What the Mosaic
Law did was simply to relate the traditional rites to
that singular deliverance and to transmute them into perpetual reminders of it.

In studying the Jewish festivals, therefore, we must
always recognize two elements: the general and universal, and the particular and Jewish.

Archaeology, anthropology and comparative religion
support this approach, for they have in fact recovered to
us many arresting parallels to the Jewish institutions.
The ceremonies of the Mosaic "Day of Kippurim," for
example, with its purifications and lustrations, its confession of sins and dispatch of a scapegoat, find perfect
counterparts in the *kuppuru*-rites of the Babylonians on
the one hand and in the Ohoharahi celebrations of the
Japanese on the other, both of them likewise designed to
get rid of evil and contagion at the beginning of the
agricultural year. The inner content, however, is distinctive and unique; for the purpose of the Hebrew
procedure is not merely to remove impurity and blight
but annually to restore a dedicated people to the state of
holiness necessary to its mission: the Israelites had not
merely to be clean, but to be "clean *before the Lord.*"

Similarly, many of the things that were done in

ancient times at the Feast of Booths have abundant parallels elsewhere. Primitive peoples, for instance, commonly pour out water at this season as a charm to induce rainfall. There is therefore nothing at all unique in the outward form of the traditional Jewish ceremony described in the Mishnah as having been performed in Jerusalem at the great autumn festival. But the inner content is altogether distinctive. When the Jews poured out the water, they read into the rite a new and more spiritual meaning: for them, it symbolized the assurance that Israel would yet "draw water in joy from the wellsprings of salvation" (Isa. 12:3).

Often, too, the Jewish festivals served not only as a transformation of the more ancient practices but also as a pointed rejoinder to the contemporary beliefs of surrounding peoples. In Christianity, for example, Whitsun is the birthday of the Church, the day on which the Holy Spirit was poured out upon the original disciples at Antioch. In Judaism, the corresponding Feast of Pentecost became the anniversary of the Giving of the Law, when the presence of God was revealed not to a select few, but to *all* His people for all of time. Among the pagan Greeks, the winter solstice was the time when men and women danced on the hilltops, with blazing torches, in honor of Dionysus. Among the Jews, it became the occasion of the Feast of Dedication, when men lit lamps to commemorate the reluming of the candelabrum in the Temple. On New Year's Day, the citizens of ancient Babylon ceremonially reinstalled their god in his temple. Among the Jews, a universal God was figuratively re-enthroned as Lord of the world.

Nor, indeed, was it only in the case of individual festivals that Judaism offered significant alternatives and correctives to current modes of thought. Its distinctive genius is evident also in the underlying philosophy of the festivals as a whole. In Christianity, all of them are geared to the fundamental idea that God dies to save man; in Judaism, the dominant lesson is that man lives to save God.

It is in this transformation of the festivals, rather than in their original institution, that Judaism sees the work of God. When it calls the festivals a "divine ordinance," it does not mean—as is all too often supposed—that God ordained them "out of the blue" by the issuance of a sudden, supernatural fiat, nor that they are to be passed down unchanged until the end of time. It means only that the continuous process whereby primitive usages are constantly developed in the light of an ever-widening outlook and an ever-deepening insight is the result of the inworking within man of something larger than himself—of a cosmic, universal, eternal spirit which, for convenience, we image and personify as God. To be sure, the Bible tends to represent this process in terms of an instantaneous, transcendental revelation, but that, as we have already explained, is due simply to the limitations of a primitive idiom. The important thing is not what the Bible says, but what its expressions are really intended to convey.

The seeming contradiction between the traditional and modern approaches to the festivals is thus more apparent than real, more verbal than substantial; both are really saying the same thing in different terms.

It follows, then, that for a proper understanding of those festivals it is necessary to see them not only in terms of their Scriptural formulation but also—and more importantly—in the light of their entire evolution. For only thus can we fully appreciate their distinctive character and the unique contribution of Judaism to religious thought. Only thus can the divine revelation be truly apprehended.

There is also another reason why we must learn to look at the festivals in historical perspective, and that is that traditional rites and ceremonies often lag behind, or even run counter to, current patterns of thought, and therefore can be understood only if their original frames of reference are recovered. On the Feast of Booths, for example, it is customary, at one moment of the service, to point the *lulab*, or palm branch, successively to left and right and up and down, accompanying the action by the cry, *Hosanna*, "O save us!" To the average worshiper, this curious procedure is no more than a time-honored ritual gesture, without contemporary meaning or relevance. But once we see it in historical perspective, it holds a profound lesson. For the truth is that the gesture is simply a survival of primitive magical procedure by which the winds were summoned from all quarters at the beginning of the agricultural year, whereas the accompanying words are a ringing Jewish protest against such hocus-pocus—an affirmation of the fact that salvation and prosperity must be sought from God and cannot be "manufactured."

Similarly, it is only by studying them in historical perspective and wider context that the true significance of the sabbath or of Yom Kippur can be effectively brought home. For only then can we appreciate the distinctive genius of Judaism in transmuting a day of taboo into one of sanctified rest and in elevating physical evil into moral sin and mechanical purgation into spiritual atonement.

Then, too, it must be borne in mind that there are many valuable concepts and insights which tend to get lost in the historical shuffle—to be submerged, in any one or other generation, by purely temporary influences or fashions of thought. A modern American, for example, is apt to interpret the Passover ideal of freedom in terms of Western democracy, because that is the particular conception of freedom to which his environment has conditioned him. In so doing, however, he is likely to lose sight of the alternative Hebrew concept of voluntary dedication, the concept which makes Passover a supplement to, rather than a synonym of, the Fourth of July. It is only when we study the festivals in broad historical perspective that such submerged values come again to light, and that we are able to recognize those elements of the total picture that may momentarily stand in the shadow.

In the following pages we are going to try, in broad outline, to sketch the evolution of each festival, fast and holy day from its remote beginnings to the present day, to compare it with analogous institutions elsewhere and thereby to show not only how its outward forms developed but also how Judaism reshaped them and endowed them with new significance. To make the story intelligible, however, the reader should first have a picture of the rounded Jewish year.

The Jewish year is reckoned not by the sun but by the moon, and consists of 353 or 354 days. For civil purposes the year begins in spring; for religious purposes, in autumn. It is divided into the following twelve months:

Nisan (March-April)   Tammuz (June-July)
Iyar (April-May)   Ab (July-Aug.)
Sivan (May-June)   Elul (Aug.-Sept.)

Tishri (Sept.-Oct.)   Tebeth (Dec.-Jan.)
Heshvan[1] (Oct.-Nov.)   Shebat (Jan.-Feb.)
Kislev (Nov.-Dec.)   Adar (Feb.-March)

Every fourth year is also a leap year. A thirteenth month, known as Ve-Adar, "Extra Adar" (or Adar Sheni, "Second Adar"), is then added. This serves to adjust the lunar to the solar reckoning, and to prevent the harvest festivals from coming in time to fall outside of their proper agricultural seasons.

Passover and the Feast of Booths, it should be noted, commence at the first full moon of spring and autumn respectively. Other festivals and holy days, however, still preserve traces of more primitive calendarical systems. The weekly sabbath, for example, is quite independent of the phases of the moon, and reflects a method of measuring time in sequences of seven days; while the celebration of Pentecost seven weeks after the morrow of the paschal ceremony is a relic of the alternative convention of fifty-day spans. Similarly, the occurrence of Yom Kippur on the tenth of Tishri is a compromise between measurement by the moon and measurement by decans, the latter system also leaving a trace in the traditional rule that the paschal victim had to be selected on the *tenth* of the month, though slaughtered only on the eve of full moon (Exod. 12:3).

It should be observed also that in certain cases there is disagreement among the various legal codes of the Bible concerning the precise date of a festival or holy day. Thus, the Feast of Booths is variously dated to the "turn of the year" (Exod. 34:22)—that is, the autumnal equinox, "the time when thou hast gathered in from the threshing floor and vinepress" (Deut. 16:13), and as

· · · · ·

[1] Also called Marheshvan.

"the fifteenth day of the seventh month" (Lev. 23,39). Similarly, there is no accord about the date of Yom Kippur. This inconsistency reflects the fact that the codes were written in different ages and employ different systems of reckoning time.

Finally, it should be noted that, in the Jewish calendar, the day lasts from sunset. All festivals and holy days therefore begin on the preceding evening.

II

The Seasonal Festivals

*These are the appointed seasons of the Lord,
the holy convocations, which ye shall proclaim in their appointed season.*

LEV. 23:4

4

PASSOVER

The Festival of Freedom

The festival of Passover is known in Jewish tradition as the "Season of Our Freedom." Its central theme is Release. On the seasonal plane, it marks the release of the earth from the grip of winter. On the historical plane, it commemorates the exodus of the Children of Israel from Egypt. On the broad human plane, it celebrates the emergence from bondage and idolatry.

In each case, the release is accompanied by a positive achievement; it is not simply an escape. It is also a co-operative act between God and man. On the seasonal plane, Passover inaugurates the reaping of the new grain; man sows the seed, but God—or the cosmic power—provides the rainfall and sunshine which quickens it. On the historical plane, it commemorates the birth of the

Jewish nation: Israel was prepared to face the hazards of the wilderness, so God, in His providence, brought it to Sinai, gave it the Law, and concluded the Covenant. On the broad human plane, it celebrates the attainment of freedom and of the vision of God: man casts aside his idols and repudiates his ignorance and obscurantism, and in that very act God reveals His presence and imparts knowledge.

The three aspects of the festival run parallel to one another: the dark and dreary winter corresponds at once to the dark era of bondage and to the black night of ignorance, while the burst of new life in spring corresponds, in turn, to the flowering of Israel and the burgeoning of freedom.

Yet the freedom which is celebrated in the Passover festival is freedom of a special kind. Our own modern concept of freedom has developed through diverse channels and is today a fusion—or, perhaps, a confusion—of several originally distinct categories of thought. It is mixed up, for instance, with ideas of sovereign independence, personal liberty and democratic government; yet none of these ideas—however fervently Jews may today adhere to them—enters significantly into the Passover ideal. In Jewish tradition, freedom, in the modern sense, is scarcely a virtue; at best, it is an opportunity. What matters is *volitional dedication,* and it is this and this alone that forms the theme of the Passover story. If Israel had gone forth out of Egypt, but not accepted the Covenant at Sinai, it would have achieved liberation— that is, mere release from bondage—but it would not have achieved *freedom,* in the Jewish sense of the term. For the only freedom, says Judaism, is the yoke of the Torah; the only true independence is the apprehension of God.

The complex of ideas which today make up the Passover festival is the result of a long process of development and, more especially, of Judaism's inspired transformation of a primitive seasonal ceremony.

The nature of that ceremony is described in detail in the twelfth chapter of the Biblical Book of Exodus. At full moon in the first month of spring, we read, it was customary for every family to slaughter a lamb or goat at twilight and then, in the middle of the night, to eat it in common, along with unleavened bread and bitter herbs. The eating had to be done "in haste," and whatever portion of the meat remained unconsumed had to be burned ere break of dawn. Moreover, as soon as the slaughtering had been effected, a bunch of hyssop was dipped into the victim's blood, and a few drops were sprinkled with it on the doorposts and lintels of each house. The ceremony was known as *pesah*, and was followed immediately by a six-day festival, called the Feast of Unleavened Bread, during which no fermented food was allowed to be eaten, and the first and last days of which were regarded as especially sacred and marked by a total abstention from work.

Shorn of its later interpretations, this ceremony falls into a common pattern of seasonal festivals in many parts of the world. The essence of such festivals is to re-cement the bonds of kindred and community at the beginning of a new agricultural cycle. This is done by partaking of a meal in common—"breaking bread together"—for thereby a common substance is absorbed. The practice is well attested in antiquity. When, for example, persons or tribes entered into compacts with one another, as in the case of Abraham and Abimelech, or of Moses and Jethro, in the Bible, the agreement was usually sealed by eating together—a custom which underlies our own word *companion* (properly, "one who eats bread with another") and which survives also in the familiar usage of "having a drink on it."

On such occasions, however, it is not only *how* one eats but also *what* one eats that is important, for the food consumed is believed itself to impart new life and vigor. Accordingly, special precautions have to be taken to ensure that it is pure and free of putrescence, and in a Near Eastern country this means that it has to be eaten at once and "in haste," and not lie around in the sun. It means also that no fermented food may be absorbed with it, since fermentation is the result of putrefaction, and that bitter herbs must be eaten at the same time as an effective cathartic against any impurity that may inadvertently have been consumed.

Once the meal is finished, it becomes necessary to mark by some outward sign those who have participated in it and thereby entered into renewed ties with one another. The usual method of doing this is to sprinkle some of the animal's blood on the foreheads of all present or on the flaps of their tents or doorposts of their houses. This, for example, is the practice among the Amur Arabs of Palestine and at New Year ceremonies in Madagascar. Moreover, this sprinkling of blood serves a further purpose. In primitive societies, the family consists not only of its human members but also of its god. He, too, therefore is regarded as being present at the communal meal and as being bound by the bond which it cements. Accordingly, the mark of blood on the forehead or the doorpost affords a means whereby he may readily recognize those individuals or households with whom he has entered into a pact of friendship and protection. It thus becomes, in effect, a device for averting supernatural hurt.

The Israelites took over this primitive rite and gave it a meaning all their own, thereby relating it to their own historic experience and justifying its continued observance.

The Exodus from Egypt, they said, had coincided with the traditional *pesah* ceremony, and because their ancestors had so meticulously carried out the prescribed regulations and dashed the blood upon the doorposts of their houses, Jehovah had been able instantly to recognize His own protégés when He came to smite the firstborn in the land. All of the elements of the traditional ceremony were then fancifully explained as memorials of that momentous event. The unleavened bread recalled the fact that, in their hurried departure from bondage, there had been no time to wait for the dough to rise and the bread had therefore been baked without yeast, while the eating "in haste" commemorated the haste with which the departure had been made. Indeed, the very name of the festival (the original significance of which is obscure) was now connected ingeniously with the Hebrew word *pasah,* "skip," and taken to imply that, on seeing the sign of blood, God had "skipped" or *passed over* the houses of the Israelites and spared them from the plague.

Much of this explanation is, to be sure, historically frail. Modern scholarship has made it virtually certain that the Biblical narrative of the Exodus represents a foreshortened and anachronistic account of what really took place. In the light of historical and archaeological research, it has become increasingly improbable that all of the tribes of Israel, as they later existed, ever went down to Egypt or came out of it. It is now generally conceded that the confederation was of later origin and grew up gradually in the Holy Land after the Conquest, so that the story of a common ancestor who went down to Egypt with all his sons is as anachronistic as it would be to speak of "Uncle Sam" and his forty-eight children at the time of the Revolutionary War. Only a certain portion of what subsequently became the Children of Israel—according to some scholars, only the Joseph-tribes —ever went down to Goshen, and the conquest of Canaan was the result not of a single coordinated invasion but of the successive expeditions and gradual infiltration of various Hebrew tribes, which had begun before the Exodus and continued for some time after the arrival of the "redeemed" Holy Land.

Then, too, it must be borne in mind that the Biblical narrative is a *saga,* not a factual report, and therefore embellishes the record of events with all kinds of fantastic and legendary details drawn from the storehouse of popular lore. Moses' staff, for example, has parallels in the magical wands and weapons borne by heroes and deliverers in the folk tales of many nations; the miraculous parting of the Red Sea finds counterparts in the ancient Indian myth of Krishna's flight from the tyrannical King Kamsa and in the statement of various Greek writers that the Pamphylian Sea drew back and gave passage to the troops of Alexander the Great when they were marching against the Persian hosts of Darius III.

Nevertheless, even though the story of the Exodus cannot yet be confirmed from any extra-Biblical source, and although we may readily detect in it several obviously legendary traits, in broad substance it is indeed consistent with everything that we now know about political conditions in the Near East at the period in question. Historical records have confirmed that there indeed existed at that period, in virtually all parts of the Near East, a special class of persons (not, however, an ethnic unit) known as Hebrews, who did not enjoy full civic rights and who lived largely as mercenaries and freebooters, and who on several occasions made marauding raids upon Palestinian and Syrian cities. History also confirms that the land of Goshen (modern Wadi Tumilat), on the eastern confines of Egypt proper, had long been recognized as a free grazing ground or reservation for neighboring nomads, and it establishes that in the fourteenth century B.C.E. there was indeed a change of regime in Egypt which was unfavorable to aliens, for at that date the Hyksos, or Foreign Princes, who had been in control of the country for some two hundred years, were finally expelled and replaced by a native Egyptian monarch. Furthermore, we know that the new Pharaoh's successor, Ramses II (1298-32 B.C.E.) did indeed renovate for himself the abandoned Hyksos capital in the Delta and call it after his own name, and that he also built a store-city named Pithom, just as is described in the Bible. Lastly, an inscription of Pharaoh Merneptah (1232-24 B.C.E.), discovered in his mortuary chapel at Thebes, mentions the presence of the Israelites in the Holy Land in 1227 B.C.E.

Against this general background, it would seem not at all improbable that a particular group of Hebrews— what the Bible describes as the "family of Jacob"— should have migrated from the Holy Land to Goshen, to settle under the more favorable regime of the Hyksos; that it should at first have thrived and prospered but subsequently, after the fall of that regime, have been viewed with suspicion and enslaved; and that it should eventually have sought freedom by linking up with other Hebrews in a concerted attack on the Holy Land. And that, when the legendary trimmings are stripped away, is substantially the story related in the Bible. Nor, indeed, is it in any way remarkable that these events do not find mention in Egyptian records, for it must be remembered that to the Egyptians of the period, the Children of Israel were in no sense a formidable or important power, but merely a motley crowd of gypsies on a relatively distant reservation.

In Judaism, however, the story of the Exodus has long since been lifted out of a purely historical context. The Jewish attitude toward it stems from the premise that events transcend the moments of their occurrence —that anything which happens in history happens not only at a particular point in time but also as part of a continuous process and therefore involves as its participants not only a single generation but also—and more important—all who went before and all who follow after.

Take, for example, the American Civil War. What was secured by this conflict was not simply the Union of that particular day and age, but the Union *per se*, so that, in a wider perspective, both the Founding Fathers on the one hand and we ourselves on the other were also actively involved in it and personally shared in the victory which ensued. In exactly the same way, the Exodus of the Children of Israel from Egypt involved also both the patriarchs of the past and their children's children of the future, for it validated the mission of the former and determined the destiny of the latter.

It is this ideal Exodus—this Exodus detached from a mooring in time—that is really celebrated in the traditional Seder service on the first two evenings of the Passover festival.

The Seder—the word means simply "order of service" or "formal procedure"—is at once a substitute for the ancient paschal sacrifice and a fulfillment of the Biblical injunction (Exod. 13:8) to retell the story of the Exodus to one's children.

The principal feature of the ritual is the eating of various foods traditionally associated with the departure from Egypt. These are: *matzah,* or unleavened bread; bitter herbs (e.g. horse-radish), taken to commemorate the bitterness of servitude; and *haroseth,* a mixture of chopped apples, nuts, raisins and cinnamon, which symbolizes the mortar in which the Israelites labored while they built the store-cities of Pithom and Raamses (Exod. 1:11). Moreover, the meal is introduced by the consumption of parsley dipped in salted water. During the course of it, a minimum of four cups of wine must be drunk, recalling the four expressions used in Exodus 6: 6–7 to describe God's deliverance of Israel, viz., "I will *bring you out* from under the burden of the Egyptians, and I will *rid you* of their bondage, and I will *redeem you* . . . and I will *take you to Me for a people.*" In addition, besides the food actually consumed, the shankbone of a lamb and a roasted egg have to be placed on the table. The former symbolizes the paschal offering, while the latter is, in all probability, a later importation from pagan custom and, like the corresponding Christian Easter egg, exemplifies the beginning of life in spring.

There is a strict religious protocol about the manner in which the ritual foods are to be eaten. The *matzah,* for example, consists of three cakes placed one above the other and popularly known as "the priest, the Levite, and the Israelite." At the beginning of the service, the celebrant breaks the middle cake in half and sets one of the halves aside, wrapping it in a napkin. This, known as *afikomin,* is subsequently distributed among the company and constitutes the last thing eaten at the ceremony. The bitter herbs, in addition to being eaten separately, are also served in a "sandwich," between pieces of *matzah,* thereby carrying out to the letter the Biblical commandment (Exod. 12:8) which enjoins that unleavened bread and bitter herbs be eaten together as an accompaniment of the paschal meal. At the conclusion of the supper, an extra cup of wine is filled for the prophet Elijah who, it is believed, will come on Passover night to herald the final redemption of Israel. The main door of the house or apartment is flung open for a few moments to permit his entrance.

Those present at the Seder ceremony are expected to adopt a casual, reclining posture, symbolizing that of freemen at ancient banquets. In some parts of the world, however, everyone appears in hat and coat, with satchel on back and staff in hand, thus re-enacting the Departure from Egypt.

The narrative portion of the ceremony is known as the *Haggadah,* or Recital, and consists in a repetition of the Scriptural story of the Exodus, embellished by rabbinic comments and elaborations and rounded out by the chanting of psalms, hymns and secular songs.

The narrative is introduced by a series of questions *(Mah Nishtanah),* asked by the youngest member of the company: "Why is this night different from all other nights?" All that follows is regarded as the answer.

High points of the Haggadah are: the "Section of the Four Sons," the "Litany of Wonders," and the chanting of "Hallel."

The first of these is based on the fact that the Bible speaks four times of "thy son's" inquiring about the meaning of Passover, and each time poses his question in different terms. Once (Deut. 6:20), he is repre-

sented as asking, "What mean these testimonies and
statutes and judgments which the Lord our God hath
commanded us?" Another time (Exod. 12:26), he demands brusquely, "What means this service *of yours?*"
A third time (Exod. 13:14), he asks simply, "What is
this?" And a fourth time (Exod. 13:8), the question
is not even framed, but merely implied. This variation,
said the sages, is purposeful; in each case the form of
the question typifies the character and attitude of the
inquirer, who is respectively wise, wicked, simple and
too young to ask. Each must be answered differently, in
appropriate fashion.

The "Litany of Wonders" is a cumulative poem reciting the benefits conferred by God on Israel at the time
of the Exodus. Not only did He lead them out of Egypt,
but He also punished the Egyptians; not only did He
part the Red Sea, but He caused them to pass through
it dryshod; not only did He lead them to Mount Sinai,
but He gave them the Law; not only did He give them
the Law, but He brought them to the Promised Land;
not only did He bring them to the Promised Land, but
He built the temple in Zion. As each of these benefits
is recited, the company responds loudly with the word
Dayyenu, "Alone 'twould have sufficed us!" In all, fifteen benefits are enumerated, alluding, so the rabbis
said, to the numerical value of the Hebrew word *Yah,*
one of the names of God (cf. Exod. 15:2; Ps. 68:4).

The Hallel ("Praise") is the group of psalms, 113–
118, which is recited at all new moons and at all festivals and which is introduced by the word *Hallelujah,*
"Praise ye the Lord." In the present instance, they are
deemed especially appropriate, because one of the psalms
(Ps. 114) in fact describes events connected with the

Exodus. (These psalms, it may be added, were very probably the hymns intoned by Jesus and his disciples at the Last Supper.)[1]

Properly understood, the Seder ceremony is no mere act of pious recollection, but a unique and inspired device for blending the past, the present and the future into a single comprehensive and transcendental experience. The actors in the story are not merely the particular Israelites who happen to have been led out of bondage by Moses but *all* the generations of Israel throughout all of time. In an ideal sense, all Israel went forth out of Egypt, and all Israel stood before Sinai; and all Israel moved through darkness to the Presence of God, in the wake of a pillar of fire. Whenever the trumpets sound in history, they sound for all ages; and when the bell tolls, the echo lives on forever.

This is not a rarefied piece of modern rationalization. The conception of the Seder as an experience rather than a recitation runs like a silver thread through the whole of Jewish tradition and finds expression on every page of the Haggadah. "Every man in every generation," says a familiar passage (quoting the Mishnah), "must look upon himself as if he personally had come forth out of Egypt. It was not our fathers alone that the Holy One redeemed, but ourselves also did He redeem with them." Similarly, in the Litany of Wonders, it is not "they" but *we* who are said to have wandered for forty years and to have been fed upon manna in the wilderness, and finally to have reached the Promised Land. Everywhere the emphasis is placed squarely on the durative and ideal sig-

. . . . .

[1] Matt. 26:30; Mark 14:26. The English Bible renders, "When they had sung *a hymn*," but the Greek original would also permit the rendering, "When they had sung *hymns*."

nificance of the Exodus rather than on its punctual and historic reality. The Haggadah is the script of a living drama, not the record of a dead event, and when the Jew recites it he is performing an act not of remembrance but of personal identification in the here and now.

The Seder ceremony, said the sages, is valid only when the "bread of affliction" and the bitter herbs are actually before you. In a sense larger than they intended, these words epitomize its essential significance. *Wer nie sein Brot mit Traenen ass.* . . .

It may be said, in fact, that the central theme of the Seder is not—as commonly supposed—the Exodus from Egypt. That is merely its highlight. The central theme is the entire process of which that particular event happens to have been the catalyst. In Jewish tradition, the deliverance from Egypt is important only because it paved the way to Sinai—that is, to Israel's voluntary acceptance of its special and distinctive mission; and what the Seder narrative relates is the whole story of how Israel moved progressively from darkness to light, from the ignorance and shame of idolatry to the consciousness and glory of its high adventure.

All through the ages, the very structure of the narrative has evinced its purport. In ancient times it began, on a note of shamefaced humility, with the words, "At first our fathers were worshipers of idols," (or, in an alternative version: "A wandering Aramean was my father") and ended with the triumphant chanting of the Psalms of Praise. Today, even though later accretions have somewhat obscured this dramatic sequence, it still opens (in most parts of the world) with a reference to the "bread of affliction" and closes in a breathless and inspired climax with the defeat of the Angel of Death. Moreover, the very sentence which begins with the words, "At first our fathers were worshipers of idols," ends significantly with the proud affirmation: "But now the Presence of God has drawn us to His service."

The several features of the ritual and the several elements of the narrative in turn reinforce this sense of continuousness. For neither ritual nor narrative is the product of a single age or environment—a mere heirloom or museum piece passed down intact and piously conserved. On the contrary, some parts of each go back to the days of the Second Temple, while others are no earlier than the fifteenth century. Ritual and narrative alike are therefore dynamic, not static creations—virtual kaleidoscopes of Jewish history—reflecting in their growth and development the various phases of Israel's career.

The form of the meal, for example, with the reclining on cushions, the preliminary dipping of parsley in salted water, and the customary consumption of eggs as an hors d'oeuvre, reproduces the typical pattern of a Roman banquet, and one may even suppose that the recital of the narrative and the conclusion of the repast with the chanting of psalms may have been modeled after the Roman practice of having literary works read aloud at meals and regaling oneself afterward with choral entertainment. Indeed, it is not at all impossible that the initial invitation to the hungry and needy, and the prescription that at least four (originally, three) cups of wine must be drunk, are likewise of Roman origin. For the fact is that it was common Roman practice for "clients" to wait upon their patrons during the day in order to pay their respects to them; and for this attention they were often rewarded by a formal invitation to join the company at supper *(coena recta)*. Similarly, *pace* the traditional explanations of the three or four glasses of

wine, it is not without interest that a normal Roman dinner actually entailed a minimum of three cups—one for
the preliminary libation to the gods, a second for the
mutual toasting of the guests, and a third in honor of
the hosts or, under the Cæsars, of the emperor. (To be
sure, this minimum was usually exceeded; but so, too,
are the minimum three or four cups of the Seder!)

On the other hand, the *afikomin* is distinctly Greek,
although the term now bears a meaning quite different
from that which attached to it in Hellenic speech. The
Talmud says that "men must not leave the paschal meal
epikomin." This last word was really the Greek *epi kō-
mon,* a popular expression for "gadding around on
revels"—the common nightly pastime of the "gay blades"
of Hellas. The term, however, was subsequently misunderstood, and the sentence wrongly rendered: "Men
must not leave out the *afikomin* after the paschal meal."
The curious, unintelligible expression was then taken
to refer to some special condiment or "dessert" which
had to be served at the conclusion of the repast, and
thence arose the custom of distributing small pieces of unleavened bread and calling them *afikomin!*

Similarly, when the door is opened "for Elijah," we
are plunged at once into the Middle Ages, for the real
purpose of this act seems to have been to provide an effective rebuttal of the terrible Blood Libel which asserted
that Jews employ the blood of Christian children in the
preparation of *matzah.* The door was flung open so that
all might have a chance of beholding the complete innocence of the proceedings.

Lastly, the secular songs and ditties with which the
service now concludes and which constitute its most recent—though most familiar—feature take us straight into
Renaissance Europe. One of these songs, the famous

'*Ehad mi yodea*' ("Who knows one?"), for example, has been traced by students of comparative literature to a popular and widespread "counting-out rhyme," the earliest specimen of which appears in Germany in the fifteenth century. (In that earlier version, incidentally, the successive numbers refer to God, Moses, and Aaron, the three Patriarchs, the four Evangelists, and the five wounds of Jesus!) Similarly, the *Had Gadya* ("Only One Kid") finds its earliest prototype in a fifteenth-century German folk song, *Der Herr der schickt das Jockli hinaus,* though here again, the wide popularity of the song is shown by the fact that early versions of it have turned up in most European countries.

It should be observed also that, in Oriental lands, quite a different set of popular chants is appended to the Haggadah. The Sephardim, for instance, have many such chants written in the Ladino, or Judeo-Spanish, dialect current especially in the Levant, while elsewhere, Judeo-Arabic and Judeo-Persian songs are in use. The inclusion in it of those "native" compositions likewise bespeaks the true character of the Seder as an expression of the total, continuous experience of the Jewish people.

Even the illustrations which adorn the older editions of the Haggadah conspire to create a picture of the entire stretch of Jewish history. The "wicked son" (who balances on one leg from one Seder to the next) is simply a Roman centurion; the one who is "too young to ask," and who holds up his hands like a questioning child, is taken directly from an earlier print of a slave in supplication before Hannibal; while the store-cities of Pithom and Raamses, which the Israelites were compelled to build for Pharaoh, are the walled towns of fifteenth-century Europe! All the centuries seem, as it were to blend and blur.

Nor is it only in the accidental development of its form, or in the externals of the traditional "book of words," that the "continuous" character of the ceremony is evinced. Several of the poems which have been added to the narrative portion of the Haggadah revolve around the theme that Passover was the occasion not only of the deliverance from Egypt but also of *all* the main deliverances—and, indeed, of all the main events—in Jewish history. This, of course, is pious fiction, but the fact that it was invented shows that in the minds of successive generations of Jews the Seder has always exemplified a continuous and durative experience. Moreover, that experience is projected into the future as well as retrojected into the past. Every detail of the Exodus, it is maintained, foreshadows an element of Israel's ultimate redemption. In the words of a medieval hymn:[2]

They went from Egypt in the dead of night,
Yet was the glow of life their guiding light—
That glow which yet shall pierce the darkest skies
When God cries out, "Thy dawn is come! Arise!" [3]

. . . .

When that He did the sea from them divide
The waters were a wall on either side,[4]
So, when the new day breaks, the Lord shall keep
His word, and by still waters lead His sheep.[5]

On the final night of deliverance—the "night of vigil," as the Bible calls it (Exod. 12:42)—God will come to Israel as a lover serenading his beloved and eventually winning her as his own:

. . . . .

[2] From the poem, *"Pesah usheru be-or ha-hayyin le-or,"* by Jekuthiel bar Joseph, chanted in some synagogues on the eve of the eighth day of Passover.
[3] Isa. 60:1.
[4] Exod. 14:22.
[5] Isa. 40:10-11, 49:10.

O night of vigil and O witching hour,
When God rode forth from Egypt in His power!
The night shall come when He shall ride once more
As once he rode in those far days of yore.
But *we* with song shall fill that eventide;
To *us* He comes a lover to his bride.

O night of vigil and O witching hour!
Tho' God with darkness all the world o'erpower,
Lo, in His hand is day as well as night,
And over us shall break His morning light;
For ne'er that other night shall be forgot
When Abraham led his men to rescue Lot.[6]

. . . .

O night of vigil and O witching hour!
As once when steers would His poor sheep devour,
The Shepherd fought with them and lay them low,
So, as He rescued us so long ago,
He yet shall come, and this long night be done.
Deliverance cometh with the rising sun.

O night of vigil and O witching hour!
Tho' dark the earth and tho' the heavens lower,
This is the hour when God His tryst shall keep
With His beloved, rouse her from her sleep,
And, like a bridegroom leading home his bride,
Lead her in peace to Zion at His side.[7]

In another sense, too, the Passover story is a continuous experience. For if it is true that the punctual event
which it celebrates possesses also a durative character,
involving the children of all generations, it is equally
true that the particular historical occasion of the Exodus represents a situation which is in itself seemingly

. . . . .

[6] Cf. Gen. 14:10-16.
[7] From the poem *"Lêl shimmurim 'ôthô El hatsah,"* chanted in some synagogues on the first evening of Passover.

perpetual and which is by no means confined to a single
moment of time. In a larger sense, the villain of the
piece is not a particular Egyptian Pharaoh—Seti I or
Ramses II—but all the tyrants who have ever opposed
Israel at any time; the Sea of Reeds is not the particular Lake Timsah (or any other similar expanse of water)
which the Israelites had to cross on their way to Sinai,
but all the obstacles which Israel has ever encountered
throughout its career and which have yielded when the
emblem of God was lifted above them; the manna is
not the peculiar gum of *Tamarix gallica mannifera,* as
learned botanists assure us, but that divine sustenance
on which Israel has been fed continually while it has
been roaming the world's desert to the place of Revelation—that "bread of angels" which has to be gathered
afresh every morning and which (as the sages acutely
observed) tastes different to every man. And the journey through the wilderness, in the wake of a cloud
by day and a pillar of fire by night, is the eternal progress of Israel toward the Kingdom of God.

Nor is it only on the historical plane that this continuous significance of the festival is brought home. On the
seasonal plane, Passover marks the time when, in Palestine, the heavy rains of winter give place to the light
showers, or "dews," of spring; and for this reason special
prayers for "dew" are included in the morning service
of the first day. But this dew is not merely a blessing of
nature; it is also a symbol of God's beneficence toward
Israel both in the past and in the future. It is the dew
which was mentioned in Isaac's blessing upon Jacob
(Gen. 27, 28); to which Moses compared his final discourse (Deut. 32:2); which fell upon Gideon's fleece
as a sign that Israel would be saved from the Midianites
(Judg. 6:37-38). It is also the dew of rejuvenation and

resurrection—the "dew of youth" with which God anoints His Messiah (Ps. 110:3), and the "dew of lights" which, as the prophet says, will eventually fall on the "land of the shades" (Is. 26:19):

Behold, there is a word of God which saith:
"My dew shall fall upon the land of Death," [8]
And they that slumber now the long night through
Shall yet awaken with the morning dew.

.   .   .   .

Lily and rose shall blossom,[9] and the corn
Gleam in the valleys with the dew of morn.

.   .   .   .

Lo, angels shall unlock the treasuries
Of hea'n and pour the dewdrops from the skies;
And pilgrims wending to the festival
Shall see My dew upon Mount Hermon fall;[10]
And all the scattered shall come home again
Unto a land of corn and wine, where rain
Drops gently down from heaven,[11] and the Lord
No longer passes with a flaming sword.[12]

The Passover festival then has two basic messages for modern man. The first is that deliverance from the scourge of bondage and the night of ignorance lies just as much in his own hands as in God's. If it is true that God delivered Israel from Egypt "not by the hand of an angel, nor by the hand of a seraph, nor by the hand of any one man sent, but by His own glory and His own self," it is equally true that in the world of men it

.   .   .   .   .

[8] Isa. 26:19.
[9] Cf. Hos. 14:5.
[10] Cf. Ps. 133:2.
[11] Deut. 33:28.
[12] From the poem, *"Tahath elath 'opher,"* by Eleazar Kalir (IX cent.), recited in some synagogues as part of the Prayer for Dew.

is by the hands of men that His glory and His being can alone be revealed.

The second message of Passover is that deliverance is continual. "The festival is celebrated," says the Haggadah, in its answer to the "wise son," "because of that which the Lord did for *me*, when *I* came forth out of Egypt." And the wise son understands.

OMER DAYS

The seven weeks between Passover and Pentecost are known as the Days of the Omer. *Omer* is a Hebrew word meaning "sheaf," and the name derives from the Biblical commandment (Lev. 23:15) that from the day when the first sheaf of barley was offered to God in the sanctuary seven full weeks are to be counted until the final celebration of the harvest-home and the presentation to Him of the two loaves of new bread.

The counting, which commences on the second night of Passover, is performed in ceremonial fashion every evening at sunset. It is prefaced by a blessing recalling the Biblical ordinance, and is followed by the recitation of the Sixty-seventh Psalm ("The earth hath yielded her produce; God, our own God, is blessing us."). A prayer is also offered for the rebuilding of the Temple and the restoration of its ancient services.

The Omer Days are observed as a kind of Lent. At least during the earlier portion of them, it is not permitted to solemnize marriages, cut the hair, wear new clothes, listen to music or attend any form of public entertainment.

The traditional reason for the austerity is that it is a

sign of mourning, commemorating the fact that during this period of the year many of the disciples of Rabbi Akiba, the illustrious teacher of the first century C.E., were wiped out by the plague. This, however, is simply a historical rationalization of a far more ancient and primitive usage. The true explanation is to be found in the universal custom of regarding the days or weeks preceding the harvest and the opening of the agricultural year as a time when the corporate life of the community is, so to speak, in eclipse, one lease of it now drawing to a close and the next being not yet assured. This state of suspended animation is expressed by fasts and austerities and by a curtailment of all normal activities.[13]

Especially interesting in this connection is the ban on marriages—originally a method of showing that, at the time when the annual lease of life is running out, human increase also is arrested. Among the ancient Romans, marriages during May were considered unlucky. The poet Ovid declares flatly that such marriages will not last, and adds:[14] "If proverbs mean a thing to you, men say A wicked baggage is a bride in May." Moreover, this belief survives to the present day in many European countries. In Italy, for instance, it is regarded as inauspicious to marry in May because that month is "dedicated to the Virgin"; while a North Country rhyme current in Britain asserts that "If you marry in Lent,/You will live to repent." or, according to another version, "Marry in May—rue for aye." Similarly, in several parts of Germany, marriages in May are discountenanced, and a work on Kentucky superstitions, published as late as

. . . . .

[13] See below, pp. 53 ff.
[14] *Fasti*, V, 487.

1920, bears evidence that the notion has percolated also to the New World.

On the thirty-third day of the 'omer, known by the Hebrew name of Lag b'Omer,[15] the lenten restrictions are suddenly relaxed, according to some authorities, for twenty-four hours only; according to others, right up to the advent of Pentecost.

Lag b'Omer—which falls on the eighteenth of Iyar— is not regarded as a sacred occasion and is not distinguished by any special service in the synagogue; it is simply a folk festival. Various explanations of it are offered in Jewish tradition. It is said, for instance, that it commemorates the date when the plague which had been ravaging the disciples of Akiba suddenly ceased. This, however, rests on nothing more substantial than a misreading and misinterpretation of a passage in the Talmud. Alternatively, it is claimed that it marks the day when the manna first began to fall in the wilderness. But this flies in the face of Scripture itself, for, according to Exodus 16:13, that event occurred on the *sixteenth,* not the eighteenth of the month!

The true explanation, it may be suggested, is that Lag b'Omer had originally nothing whatsoever to do with the Omer period as a whole, but was simply a rustic festival which happened to fall within it. It is the equivalent of the European May Day.

This conclusion is borne out not only by the close correspondence of dates but also by the virtual identity of ceremonies.

. . . . .

[15] *Lag* is an artificial word made up of the Hebrew letters *L-G* which have the numerical value of 33.

It was customary on Lag b'Omer for children to go out into the woods and shoot with bows and arrows. Although this usage has fallen into desuetude in Western countries, it is still maintained in the Land of Israel. A popular ditty sung on the occasion runs as follows:

Up, and to the greenwood,
With arrow and with bow;
There the world is blossoming,
There the flowers blow.

There, on every branch and bough,
The little birds are seen;
And there, as far as eye can reach,
All things are bright and green.

Tradition gives various reasons for this custom. It is said, for instance, that it symbolizes the readiness of the Jews to take up arms against those who destroyed the Temple, or—even more fancifully—that it symbolizes the fact that the great second-century teacher, Rabbi Simeon ben Yohai, who died on the day, was so pious and virtuous that throughout his lifetime no rain*bow* ever appeared in the sky to portend disaster on earth!

The true explanation lies, however, in the common practice of shooting arrows at demons and evil spirits on days when they are believed to be especially rampant. May Day is preeminently one of these occasions, for, according to popular tradition, the preceding night—the so-called Walpurgis Night[16]—is the time of the witches' sabbath.

In Germany, it is common usage for country folk to go out into the woods on May Morn and shoot arrows; any-

. . . . .

[16] The name derives from Walpurgia, an English nun of the eighth century, who founded religious houses in Germany, and to whom the Church dedicated the day.

one who hears the noise from a distance is expected to cry out: "Shoot my witch away!" The most interesting example of the custom obtains, however, in the rural areas of England, where it takes the form of contests in archery in imitation of the exploits of Robin Hood. A fascinating description of these ceremonies as observed in the time of Henry the Eighth, is furnished by John Stow in his famous *Survey of London* (1603):

In the month of May, namely on May-day in the morning, every man, except impediment, would walk in the sweet meadows and green woods, there to rejoice their spirits with the beauty and savour of sweet flowers and with the harmony of birds praising God in their kind; and for example hereof, Edward Hall hath noted that King Henry the Eighth . . . in the seventh year of his reign, with Queen Catherine [of Aragon] his wife, accompanied with many lords and ladies, rode a-maying from Greenwich to the high ground of Shooters Hill, where, as they passed by the way, they espied a company of tall yeomen clothed all in green, with green hoods, and with bows and arrows, to the number of two hundred. One, being the chieftain, was called Robin Hood, who required the king and his company to stay and see his men shoot, whereunto the king granting, Robin Hood whistled, and all the two hundred archers shot off, loosing all at once; and when he whistled again, they likewise shot again, their arrows whistled by craft of the head, so that the noise was strange and loud, which greatly delighted the king, queen and their company. Moreover, this Robin Hood desired the king and queen, with their retinue, to enter the greenwood, where, in arbors made of boughs and decked with flowers, they were seated and served plentyfully with venison and wine . . . and had other pageants and pastimes.

Scholars have long pointed out that the familiar figure of Robin Hood is simply a transmogrified form of "Robin o' the Wood," chief of the hobgoblins and mischievous sprites. The seasonal ceremonies associated with his name are therefore nothing but distorted portrayals of the antics of these creatures and of the measures used to drive them away, at the beginning of spring.

In this connection, the use of the bow and arrow is of particular interest, for it is motivated by the idea that evil spirits should be given a taste of their own medicine, requited with their own weapons, it being a fairly universal belief that their principal means of attacking mortals is by hurling darts at them. In the Ninety-first Psalm, for instance, the pious Israelite expresses his confidence that Jehovah will deliver him "from the arrow which flieth by day, the pestilence that stalketh in darkness, the destruction that ravageth at noon"—all three of them well-known demons of Semitic folklore. Similarly, the anguished Job complains (6:4) that "the arrows of the Almighty are within me, the poison whereof my spirit drinketh up"; while in the Iliad of Homer (I, 43–49), Apollo sends plague upon the Achæans by shooting his arrows at them. In the same way, too, a man who was suffering from aches and pains was said in old English to be "elf-*shot*," and to this day the Germans call a "stitch" in the side a *Hexenschuss,* or "witches' shot." Moreover, the method of forefending these demons with their own weapons has several interesting parallels. At ancient Indian weddings, for example, arrows were shot to protect the bridal couple; and among the Bechuanas, the bridegroom discharges an arrow into the bride's hut when she leaves it on marriage.[17]

Of interest also is the fact that in the Lag b'Omer ceremonies, the children go with their bows and arrows not only to the greenwood but also to the *cemetery.* Here we have another link with May Day customs, for the

. . . . .

[17] A familiar equivalent is the custom of having bride and groom walk under an archway of crossed swords at military weddings.

fact is that dances and convocations in cemeteries were a common feature of the celebrations on that occasion. It is recorded, for example, in a medieval Scottish chronicle that in 1282 the priest of Inverkeithing himself "led the ring" in the village churchyard, the dancers being his own parishioners; and John Aubrey, the seventeenth-century English antiquary, informs us that, in his day, village lads and lasses used to dance in the churchyards not only on May Day, but also on *all* holy days and eves of holy days.[18] This curious practice goes back, of course, to the common primitive custom of communing with or propitiating the dead at major seasonal festivals.

In Palestine, Lag b'Omer is distinguished also by another celebration. On this day, it is said, Rabbi Simeon ben Yohai, the father of Jewish mysticism, passed from the world, after first revealing to his disciples the secrets of his mystic visions. In tribute to his memory, a pilgrimage is made, on the previous evening, to the traditional site of his grave in the village of Meron, near Safed. Since, however, the illustrious teacher departed this life in joy rather than in sadness, the anniversary of his death is celebrated as a festival, not as a day of mourning. Accordingly, the pilgrimage is followed immediately by the kindling of bonfires and by all-night singing and dancing. This latter celebration is known as "the *hillulâ* of Rabbi Simeon ben Yohai." *Hillulâ* is an Aramaic word (akin to the more familiar *hallelujah*), meaning "frolic" or "revel"; but, since it is also the technical term for wedding festivities, it is popularly interpreted, in this context, as referring to the mystic "wedding," or union, of all planes of existence which

. . . . .

[18] See Margaret Murray, *The God of the Witches* (New York, 1952), p. 107.

took place when the soul of the sage ascended to heaven

Here again, what we really have, under the guise of ι memorial exercise, is the last lingering survival of a typ· ical May Day ceremony. For the fact is that it is custo mary in many parts of the world to kindle bonfires at the end of April or the beginning of May as a means of forefending demons and witches at the moment when the cattle are first let out of the barn. In ancient Rome, for example, such fires were lit at the rustic festival of the Parilia, on the twenty-first of April; and in England, they are kindled at crossroads on St. George's Day (April 23).[19] Similarly, the Celtic festival of Beltane, on May 1, was marked by the kindling of fires, a custom still maintained in the Scottish and Irish Highlands; in Bohemia and Moravia, it is common practice, on the same day, to "burn out witches"; and in Sweden, "huge bonfires are built in every hamlet, around which the young people dance."

It is not, of course, to be assumed that the Jewish festival was actually borrowed from Europe. We are dealing solely with parallel phenomena. But the parallelism shows clearly that here too, as in the case of so many other festivals, Judaism has molded ancient clay into new shapes.

. . . . .

[19] Shakespeare alludes to this in a memorable passage of *King Henry VI* (I, 1, i, 153-154), where the Duke of Bedford, resolved to go to France and fight the Dauphin, exclaims: "Bonfires in France forthwith I am to make,/To keep our great Saint George's feast withal."

5

THE FEAST OF WEEKS

The Festival of the Covenant

In the Bible, the Feast of Weeks plays a somewhat minor role beside the major seasonal festivals of Passover on the one hand and Booths (or Ingathering) on the other. It is simply the end of the barley harvest, and its distinctive feature is the presentation to Jehovah (apart from special sacrifices) of an offering consisting, according to one version of the Law (Deut. 16:10), of whatever one feels prompted to give, or, according to another (Lev. 23:17), of two loaves made out of the new corn. The festival, we are told, is to take place a full seven weeks after the sickle has been first applied to the standing grain (Deut. 16:9).

It is easy to dismiss this early phase of the festival as nothing but the product of a crude, unsophisticated age, and to think one has explained the presentation of firstfruits by collecting parallels from other parts of the world, without stopping to penetrate to their significance. The truth is, however, that even at this primary stage, though the form of expression may be primitive, the underlying meaning of the festival is at once subtle and profound. Two ideas are combined, and each is capable of an extension and development of far-reaching import.

The first is based on the common Oriental principle that land belongs to him who "quickens" it, or brings it under cultivation. Since, it is here affirmed, the earth obviously depends for its fertility not only on the labors of men but also on the cooperation of God, who furnishes it with rain, wind and sunlight, He too is necessarily a part owner of it. The presentation of firstfruits is thus no mere token of thanksgiving or mere submissive rendering of tribute, although, to be sure, by a blunting of religious sensitivity, it may (and often does) degenerate into this. It is the payment to God of the dividend on His investment. To withhold that payment is an act not of impiety but of embezzlement.

Translated into broader terms, what is here proclaimed is that the relation between God and man is not one of master and servant but of mutually dependent partners in a joint enterprise of continuous creation. This idea gives new validity to human existence and at the same time provides a signal and momentous alternative to that more common conception which, projecting the image of God from the model of kings and magicians, regards Him merely as a supernal lord and benefactor of mankind. For the conventional attitude of subservience, worship and adoration there is substituted a concept of God which is at once more robust and more mystical and which, indeed, modern religion might do well to recapture.

The second idea which underlies this early phase of the festival stems from the fact that primitive man regards anything new and unused as being fraught with potential peril, much as an infant might regard a new toy. The firstfruits of the harvest (and likewise the firstborn both of men and of beasts) are therefore consigned to the gods or spirits so that the newness may be taken away and the rest thereby rendered "safe." The important thing, however, is not so much the *why* as the *how* of the ritual; the danger of a new thing is removed by bringing it into contact with some eternal being to whom it is *not* new, inasmuch as he transcends the limitations of our own temporal existence. Behind the symbolism of the primitive procedure, therefore, there lies once again a permanent, universal message: the only immunity against the terror of new things is to try to see them in the light of eternity, and the only protection against the perils of human existence is to dedicate the prime portion of it to God.

Thus, even in its rudimentary stage, the Feast of Weeks possessed its own spiritual values. For Judaism, however—especially after it had outgrown its Palestinian origins—these alone were not sufficient. The presence and activity of God had to be recognized at this season not only in the phenomena of nature but also, and on parallel lines, in some crucial event of history. Accordingly, in the first centuries of the Common Era, inspiration and ingenuity combined to produce the necessary development.

The Scriptural narrative states clearly (Exod. 19:1) that the children of Israel reached Mount Sinai in the third month, to the day, after their departure from Egypt. This, it was now argued, does not mean that a full three months elapsed, but only that the event took place *in the*

third month of the year, and in that case the giving of
the Ten Commandments might (with a little latitude
and fancy) be made to coincide with the Feast of Weeks.
The festival thus became the birthday of Israel, the anniversary of the day on which the Covenant had been
concluded between God and His people and the Law
first revealed. Such, ever since, has been its primary
significance; it is known, in fact, as "the season of the
giving of our Law."

The parallelism between the historical and agricultural aspects of the festival is far closer than might
at first be suspected, and is carried through with rare
ingenuity and resource. According to Jewish teaching,
the important thing about the session at Sinai was not
only the giving of the Law but also the receiving of it,
the two acts of offer and acceptance constituting a Covenant (or contract) between God and Israel. Here too,
therefore, the idea of collaboration is involved: if the
Law issues from God, its fulfillment lies with Israel.
Inspiration and aspiration, revelation and perception, are
the two sides of a single coin: on the one side is the face
of God; on the other, that of man. What Saint Theresa
said of the relation of the Christian to Christ was expressed by Judaism, many centuries earlier, in its concept of the covenantal partnership of God and Israel:
In the world of men, Israel is God's hands and feet and
eyes.

Nor is it only in this major respect that the natural
and historical aspects of the festival run parallel to each
other. For if the former marks the end of seven weeks'
collaboration between God and man in the reaping of
the material harvest, what the latter celebrates is the
end of a corresponding spiritual harvest, which began
with the deliverance from Egypt and reached its climax

with the conclusion of the Covenant. And just as the ingathering of the crops is the necessary condition of life and prosperity during the ensuing year, so the event at Sinai is the necessary condition of Israel's continuing existence and fortune. Moreover, if, in the primitive agricultural rite, man offers to God two loaves of the new bread as a symbol of cooperation, in the historical counterpart—by a fine and inspired inversion—God offers to man the two tablets of the Law.

Lastly, as the harvest is renewed from year to year, so too is the historic experience of Sinai. Jewish teaching (as we have pointed out repeatedly) is insistent on the point that the festivals are not mere commemorations. All the generations of Israel, say the sages, were released from Egypt, and all were present at the mountain. By this they did not mean, as is so often supposed, that all of time was telescoped into a single moment, but rather that a single moment was projected into all of time. Both the revelation of God and His covenant with Israel are essentially continuous and are no more confined to the single event at Sinai than is the process of nature to a single harvest.

The twofold character of the festival finds eloquent expression in the services of the synagogue: on the first day, the lesson from the Pentateuch (Exod. 19–20) deals with the promulgation of the Ten Commandments; on the second day, with the institution and observance of the Feast of Firstfruits (Deut. 15:19–16:17); while on both days an extra portion is read describing the special sacrifices which were anciently presented on this occasion (Numb. 28:26–31). The dominant theme is, however, the Giving of the Law. Interspersed throughout the morning prayers are elaborate medieval poems (*piyyutim*) in which the Scriptural account of that event is tricked out with all the embellishments of rabbinic fancy. The following extract, taken from the Ashkenazic liturgy for the first day, will serve as a fair specimen:

Loud rang the voice of God, and lightning spears
Pierced all the heavens; thunder shook the spheres,
And flames leaped forth; and all the angels blew
Their trumpets, and the earth was riven through.
Then all the peoples writhed, aghast and pale,
Like as a woman in her birth-travail.
And, lo, the mountains leaped and looked askance[1]
On little Sinai, and began to dance,
Certain each one that it would be the place
Which God would choose to hallow and to grace.
Like calves did Lebanon and Siryon leap,[2]
Bashan and Carmel like as frisking sheep;[3]
Tabor, too, and each high hill; but He
Who dwells on high to all eternity[4]
Looked not on them but on the humble mound,
And while that shame did all those hills confound,
To little Sinai bent the skies and came,
And crowned it with His mist and cloud; and flame
Of angels wreathed it. Then, amid the sound
Of thunder, under them that clustered round
Its foot gave forth His mighty voice; and they
Replied: O Lord, we hear and will obey.[5]
And when that they stood waiting, came the word,
That word that splits the rocks: I AM THE LORD.

Sometimes, indeed, the Law is made to recite its own "biography," as in the following passage from the same poem:

Ere that He stayed the heavens in the height[6]
I was firm-stay'd and stablish'd in His sight.

. . . . .

[1] Cf. Ps. 68:17.
[2] Cf. Ps. 29:6. [3] Cf. Ps. 114:4; Nah. 1:4. [4] Cf. Is. 57:15. [5] Cf. Exod. 24:7.
[6] Cf. Prov. 8:28.

Ere that in glory He the clouds bestrode,[7]
I was the vehicle on which He rode.

Ere that His stronghold in the vault He made,
I was the vault in which His power was laid.

Ere that His arm did first outstretch the sky,
A bracelet on that selfsame arm was I.

Ere that the sunlit welkin was His place,
I was well kindled by His holy grace.

And lo, He held me on His knees of old,[8]
Ere first the cloudmist did His feet enfold.

Moreover, a standard element of the traditional liturgy is the recital of rhymed versions (*Azharoth*) of the 613 commandments contained in the Pentateuch; while in Reform congregations it is customary also to "confirm" adolescents on the Feast of Weeks, the confirmands thereby pledging adherence to the Covenant which was then concluded with their forebears.

But it is not only as a historical event that the revelation at Sinai figures in the services of the festival. Supplementing the lessons from the Pentateuch are others from the Prophets, and in these the truth is brought home that inspired men *in all ages* can obtain a vision of God, and that the wonders wrought when Israel was delivered from Egypt will be repeated in the future when she is at last redeemed from the dark night of her present existence.

On the first day, the Lesson from the Prophets (*haftarah*) is taken from the opening chapter of the Book

. . . . .

[7] Cf. Ps. 68:5.
[8] An allusion to Prov. 8:30, which Jewish tradition renders, "Then was I beside him *as a nursling*."

of Ezekiel, where the prophet relates how, when he was "among the captives" in Babylon, he was granted a vision of the heavenly creatures adoring God in the firmament and how, by progressive stages, his vision penetrated to the very "Glory of the Lord" surrounded by the same radiance and holding the same promise as "the bow which is in the cloud in the day of rain." Similarly, on the second day of the festival, the lesson is taken from the great Prayer of Habakkuk (Hab. 3), in which that prophet, writing during the difficult days of the Assyrian Exile, recalls the historic revelation of God at the time of the Exodus and expresses the conviction that such deliverance will always be vouchsafed to His people and that the divine providence will never fail:

I have heard tell of Thee, Lord;
Lord, I have seen Thy work.
In the midst of the years revive it,
In the midst of the years make known
That even when Thou art raging
Compassion comes to Thy mind.

When from out of the Southland
God was about to come,
And the Holy One from Mount Paran,[9]
His splendor covered the heavens,
And the earth was filled with His sheen.
A glow there was as of dayspring;
Rays shot forth from His side;
While still in the darkness yonder
Lay hid the full force of His power.

Disaster went stalking before Him,
And Pestilence cleared His path.[10]
. . . . .

[9] Cf. Deut. 33:2. [10] An allusion to the ancient belief that major gods were escorted by *two* attendants.

He halted, and shook the earth;
Looked, and convulsed the nations.
Primeval mountains were split,
Old, old hills sank low,
And all the ancient highways
Were utterly effaced.
The tents of Cushan quivered;
Midian's curtains shook.

Thou didst tread the sea; Thy chargers
Were the surge of the ocean waves.[11]
Against the streams, O Lord,
Was it against the streams
Once more Thine anger was kindled?
Was Thy wrath against the sea,[12]
When Victory rode Thy chargers,
When Victory rode Thy wains?

Thy bow was made utterly empty;
Thou didst spend all the shafts of Thy quiver;
The streams gushed madly in uproar;
The earth was riven in sunder.[13]
The mountains saw Thee; they quailed;
The torrents overflowed;[14]
The deep gave forth its voice.
The sun forgot its station;
The moon stood still in the height,

. . . . .

[11] In the traditional text, this verse follows vs. 14, where it comes in awkwardly. I believe that its correct place is here. [12] An allusion to the ancient myth relating how Baal had once fought the rival power of the sea and streams. The myth is told on the cuneiform tablets recently discovered at Ras Shamra, in Syria; see my *Oldest Stories in the World* (New York, 1952), pp. 209 ff. [13] The traditional text of this verse is corrupt and unintelligible. The present rendering depends on the assumption that a few letters have accidentally dropped out. [14] i.e., the mountain-chutes (cf. Job 24:8). But many scholars think that the verse should read (by a very slight change in the Hebrew text), "The clouds poured streams of water," in accordance with the parallel passage in Ps. 77:18.

At the glint of Thy darts as they went,
At the lightning flash of Thy spear.

In fury the earth Thou bestrodest;
Didst thresh the nations in wrath;
Forth to the fray didst Thou sally
For the victory of Thine army,
The victory of Thy troops.[15]
Thou smotest the head of the wicked,
Didst smite him from top to toe;
Didst split the heads of his captains
As they like a stormwind rushed
To blow me away in their onset,
The while their war-song sounded
Like as [the roar of a lion][16]
At devouring the hapless unseen.

I have heard it; mine inwards tremble;
My lips have twitched at the sound;
Rottenness enters my bones,
And all my footsteps fail.

Yet now can I face with calm
The day of adversity,
The charging down of armies
That troop against me in force.

Here, too, the God of history is also the God of nature, and His bounty consists not only in the deliverance of His people from their assailants but also in the provision of increase upon earth:

• • • • •

[15] The English Bible renders, "For the salvation of *Thine anointed*," assuming that this means the king; but the allusion is to *warriors* who were customarily anointed before battle. [16] Here, too, it would seem that a few letters have dropped out; cf. Ps. 7:2; 17:12; Is. 5:29.

Though the figtree now be fruitless,
And produce be none in the vines,
Though the yield of the olive now fail,
And the field produce no food;
Though the sheep be cut off from the fold,
And no cattle there be in the stalls;
Yet I in the Lord will exult,
In the God Who saves me rejoice!

The Lord, the Lord is my substance;
He will make my feet like the hinds',
And will cause me yet to trample
Upon the backs of my foes!

The same message is conveyed also by the choice of the Sixty-eighth Psalm as the special "anthem" of the festival. For the purpose of that psalm (one of the most difficult and obscure in the entire Psalter) is, once again, to universalize the events of the Exodus and Revelation and to rehearse them as an assurance of God's continuing providence and bounty; and here, too, the divine salvation is said to be made manifest not only in history but also in nature:

O God, when Thou wentest forth before Thy people,[17]
When Thou didst march through the wilderness,
Earth trembled, and skies dropped rain
At the presence of the God of Sinai,
At the presence of Israel's God.

So, too, dost Thou alway pour
The shower of Thy bounties, O God,
On the people Thou callest Thine own;[18]

. . . . .

[17] Or, army. [18] Literally, "Thine inheritance"; cf. Deut. 32:9. "For Jehovah's portion is His people; Jacob is the lot of His inheritance."

And whene'er it hath waxen faint,
Thyself hast set it firm.

.   .   .   .

When Shaddai[19] went scattering kings,
It seemed as though dark Zalmon[20]
Had suddenly turned snow-white!
Mount Bashan, too, is a mount divine,
Yea, a cloud-capped mount is Mount Bashan.
Why, then, should ye look with envy,
                    ye cloud-capped mounts,
At the mountain which a god hath fancied
                    for his dwelling?
Surely, Jehovah too
Can take up an eternal abode? [21]

Lastly, the double-sidedness of the festival is brought
out by the custom of reading the Book of Ruth as a prelude to the afternoon service. For the two dominant features of this Biblical idyl are: first, that it plays against
the background of the barley harvest; and second, that
it relates how a woman who was formerly a pagan came
to embrace the faith of Israel and to throw in her lot
with Jehovah's people (1:16, "And Ruth said, Entreat
me not to leave thee and to turn back from following
thee, for whither thou goest I will go, and where thou
lodgest, I will lodge; thy people shall be my people,
and thy God my God."). The story thus epitomizes the
two main features of the Feast of Weeks: the ingathering of the harvest and the acceptance of the Law and
Revelation of God.

.   .   .   .   .

[19] Here the name of an ancient *pagan* god of Palestine.
[20] A mountain in Samaria (Judg. 9:48). The name means "dark," and the
reference is to some ancient myth, at present unknown, in which the god
Shaddai was said to have turned this mountain white as snow.
[21] The point of these lines, it would seem, is to indicate the superiority of
Jehovah's sacred mountain, viz. Zion, to those of the earlier gods of the
pagans.

In the early centuries of the Common Era a further element, scarcely less interesting, was injected into the celebration of the festival; it became, to a certain extent, a conscious counterbalance to the Christian festival of Whitsun, with which it approximately coincides.

In Christian tradition, Whitsun is the birthday of the Church, the anniversary of the date on which the Holy Spirit was miraculously poured forth upon the original disciples of Jesus. The event is narrated in the second chapter of the Acts of the Apostles, in the New Testament. At Pentecost, we read, ". . . they were all with one accord in one place. And suddenly there came a sound from heaven, as of a rushing mighty wind, and it filled all the house where they were sitting. And there appeared unto them cloven tongues, like as of fire, poised above each of them. And they were all filled with the Holy Spirit, and began to speak with other tongues, as the Spirit gave them utterance."

To this Christian version of Pentecost, Judaism now opposed its own. Not the Church, but the community of Israel had been founded on that day. Not to a select few, but to a whole people had come the revelation of God. Not over the heads of favored disciples had the tongues of fire appeared; ". . . . *all the people* saw the thunders and the flames" (Exod. 20:18). Not the astonished onlookers, but God Himself had spoken in a multitude of tongues; for, so the sages asserted, every word uttered from the mountain had been pronounced in seventy-two languages at the same time! Moreover, if Christianity emphasized at this season the figure of its resurrected saviour, Judaism replied by giving special prominence to that of David, the messianic king. The Feast of Weeks, it was maintained, was the anniversary of David's death. The Book of Ruth, which (as we have seen) was prescribed reading for the festival, ends with the genealogy of that monarch (4:13ff.); and on the second evening the pious would stay up late into the night reading the Psalms of David.

Nor this alone. If, according to the dominant faith, Christ would return at the end of days and fight the great Dragon of the Deep and bring renewed salvation to men, so too, in the equally fervent conviction of the Jews, would David or his scion appear to usher in the Messianic Age. In the twelfth century this belief found eloquent expression in the liturgy of the festival, for into the morning service of the first day, immediately after the reading of the first verses from the portion of the Law, there was introduced the famous Aramaic poem, *Akdamuth*. Written by a certain Meir ben Isaac Nehorai (probably of Orleans), this poem described, in highly fanciful terms, the ultimate victory of God over the monsters Leviathan and Behemoth, and the lavish banquet at which He would regale the faithful in heaven:

As maidens to the dance are led
God will lead them, and outspread,
Like viands at a royal feast,
Shall be the flesh of that fell Beast,
That raging monster of the sea
Who dared assail His sovereignty.
For when that monster coils and curls
And beats the angry sea and hurls
Defiance at his sovran Lord,
Unsheathed then shall be the Sword,[22]
And He that made him shall arise
And smite him, till that dead he lies.
The oxen on a thousand hills[23]
. . . . .

[22] See Job 40:19. [23] See Psalm 50:10.

Shall be our meat, the while He fills
Gleaming goblets crystalline
With that most rare and perfect wine
Which in His cellar He hath stored
Since first creation knew its Lord.

There is a remarkable similarity between the contents
of this poem and the description of the heavenly Jerusalem which is contained in the Book of Revelation in
the New Testament—a correspondence so close as to suggest the possibility that the Aramaic composition may
have been designed as a deliberate counterpart to the
Christian apocalypse. In the Book of Revelation, for example, we are told that the author was caught up "in the
spirit" and beheld "a throne set in heaven, and One
sitting on the throne" (4:2); while in the *Akdamuth*
we read how, on the eve of the first sabbath,

When all creation's work was done,
At twilight, with the setting sun,
In radiance God's Glory came
And sat upon a throne of flame.

In the Book of Revelation, we are informed that the
throne of God was surrounded by heavenly creatures
"having each six wings," who "had no rest day and
night, saying, Holy, holy, holy is the Lord" (4:6,8).
Similarly, the *Akdamuth* describes how

Flaming, six-wing'd seraphs sing
His praise, and through the welkin ring
Ceaseless, in a sweet accord,
The words: Thrice-holy is the Lord.

Besides the heavenly creatures, says the Christian book,
the throne is encircled by angels to the number of "ten
thousand times ten thousand, and thousands of thousands." Moreover, the heavenly creatures continually

prostrate themselves before God, offering to him "golden bowls full of incense, which are the prayers of the saints," the while the voices of the celestial choir resound "like the voice of many waters . . . as they cry, Hallelujah, for the Lord God omnipotent reigneth" (5:11, 5:8—9, 19:6). This picture is reproduced, with characteristic Jewish touches, in the Aramaic poem:

A thousand thousand angels throng
To serve Him and, a myriad strong,
The heavenly host each morning press
To make to Him their sweet address.

. . . .

God takes the prayers which forth have flown
From Israel's lips, and weaves a crown,
Or wears them for phylacteries
Between His everlasting eyes.

. . . .

Like as the surging of the deep
Through all the wide-flung heavens sweep
The thunders of the cherubim
As they His royal glory hymn.

Lastly, a prominent feature of the Christian vision is the picture of the New Jerusalem "coming down out of heaven from God, having the glory of God," gleaming like precious stones and bathed in celestial light, and graced by the presence of the Divine Bridegroom come at last to claim His bride and to summon the guests to the marriage supper (19:7—9, 21:10—11). The same picture reappears in the Jewish poem, where it is said that God will set up His marriage bower in Jerusalem, and entertain the righteous:

Lo, when the exiles He hath led
To Jerusalem, there shall be shed

Upon that city, day and night,
The splendor of His radiant light;
And silver-linèd clouds shall be
Spread o'er it for a canopy,
When He doth like a bridegroom ride
At last, at last, to claim His bride.
Then round about, on golden chairs
(Each one approach'd by seven stairs)
The righteous as His guests shall dine,
And perfect bliss shall be their wine;
And o'er their heads, for chandeliers,
Shall hang the radiance of the spheres,
A beauty which no lips can tell,
Whereon no earthly eye can dwell,
A starry glory which of old
No prophet's vision e'er foretold.
And they beside the Lord shall walk
In Eden's close, and softly talk
With him, and to themselves shall say:
This is He for whom alway
We waited through captivity;
This is our Lord, yea, this is He.

But it was not only in the loftier realm of doctrine
that the Feast of Weeks was influenced by contemporary
Christian lore. The usages of the Church (themselves
borrowed from earlier pagan custom) seem likewise to
have been imitated by the synagogue. In many parts of
Europe, for instance, it is customary to deck the churches
at Whitsun with wreaths and bunches of flowers; in
Catholic districts of Germany, even private dwellings are
adorned with green twigs on this occasion. In Italy, rose
leaves are often scattered from the ceilings of churches
during the progress of the services; they are popularly explained as representing the "tongues of fire" which the
original disciples beheld at Antioch when the Holy
Spirit descended upon them. Similarly, in Russia it is

(or was) customary to carry flowers and green twigs on Whitsun; and in many Latin countries, the festival is known as *Pascha Rosatum*. All of this appears to be but a Christian transformation of the ancient Roman festival of Rosalia, celebrated in the preceding month. At this festival it was the practice to adore Venus by decorating her images with roses.

Sometimes, indeed, the custom takes on a more sinister complexion. In Rumania, for instance, the festival is commonly known as *Rusaliile*. This, it is explained, is the name of three ancient princesses who were forced to remain spinsters. In revenge, they return to earth for three days each year to plague mankind, destroy the harvest and blow away the roofs of houses. During this period, no manual work may be performed, no one may smile, and children may not make faces. To exorcize the malicious ladies, branches of wormwood are placed under the pillow at night or worn in the belt!

The Jewish form of this common custom is to adorn the synagogue with flowers on the Feast of Weeks, and the lilies which are used for this purpose are sometimes taken (by an inspired sublimation) to symbolize that "lily of the valley" which, in the allegorical interpretation of the Song of Songs, is none other than Israel itself.

Another Pentecost custom which has its counterpart in Gentile usage is that of eating dairy dishes, especially those made with cheese. The usual explanation of this custom is fanciful enough. In Psalm 68—which is prescribed as the "anthem" of the festival—the mountain on which the Law was given is described (vs. 15) as "a mountain divine, a Bashan-like mount, a mount of *gabnunim*, a Bashan-like mount." The word *gabnunim* (which does not recur in this form elsewhere in Scrip-

ture) really means "gibbous, many-peaked," but it was
fancifully connected with the Hebrew *gebinah,* "cheese,"
the conception of a mountain made of cheese being a
commonplace of folktale. Accordingly, it was maintained
that the eating of cheese was a reminder of the giving of
the Law at this season! In reality, cheese and dairy
dishes are eaten at this time because the festival has a
pastoral as well as an agricultural significance. Thus, at
the analogous Scottish celebration of Beltane, on May
1, dairy dishes are commonly consumed, and churning
and cheese-making are a common feature of spring harvest festivals in many parts of the world. In Macedonia,
for instance, the Sunday before Lent is known as
"Cheese Sunday"; in several districts of Germany cheese
and dairy dishes are (or were) standard fare at Whitsun.

That such usages are extremely ancient is shown by
the fact that at the Roman rural festival of Parilia (April
21), which fell at the same time of year as marks the
beginning of the barley harvest in Palestine, milk and
must were drunk, and the image of the pastoral god
Pales was sprinkled with the former. Moreover, that a
rite involving the seething of a kid in milk was part
of the Canaanite prototype of Pentecost is strongly suggested by the fact—noted already by Maimonides—that
in two passages of the Pentateuch (Exod. 23:19, 34:26)
where this practice is prohibited to the Israelites, it is
somehow connected with the offering of firstfruits; and
the rite of seething a kid in milk seems actually to be
mentioned in a recently discovered Canaanite text possibly designed for a spring festival.

If, however, anthropology and comparative religion
throw light on many features of the festival, there is one
which still remains a puzzle, namely, its precise date. In
the earlier code of the Pentateuch, it is said, quite

vaguely, that it is to take place seven full weeks after the beginning of the harvest. This is the kind of vague and general dating which one would naturally expect in a primitive agricultural society unconscious of a fixed and stable calendar. Later, however, the date is given more precisely: the festival is to be celebrated seven full weeks "after the morrow of the sabbath" (Lev. 23:15).

Scholars have long disputed the meaning of this term. According to the Sadducees and the Samaritans, the word "sabbath" is here to be taken literally and refers to the first sabbath in Passover. Pentecost would therefore always fall on a Sunday. The Pharisees, on the other hand, contended that "sabbath" was but a loose term for "festival," and this interpretation has prevailed in Jewish usage. The counting of the fifty days therefore begins with the second day of Passover.

A novel view was put forward, some fifty-five years ago, by the distinguished Jewish Assyriologist, the late Morris Jastrow. According to this scholar (later followed by many others), the original meaning of the word *sabbath* was "full moon," i.e., the moment when the moon comes, as it were, to a stop (Hebrew: *shabat*), its waxing changing to waning. Jastrow supported this view by reference to an Assyrian calendar now in the British Museum, where the term was applied to the fifteenth day of a lunar month. Since Passover in fact begins at full moon, "the morrow of the sabbath" would denote, quite simply, the second day of the festival. The objection to this is, however, that there is no evidence to prove that the term *sabbath* regularly bore this meaning. All that is really implied by the statement in the Assyrian calendar is that in a given month, on a particular occasion, the sabbath (in whatever sense we take it) happened to coincide with the full moon, not that this was the standard term for that event.

Lastly, an ingenious theory has recently been propounded by Professors Julius and Hildegarde Lewy. According to these scholars, the ancient Semites used more than one calendar, and for practical purposes these had often to be accommodated to one another. One of the prevalent systems was to reckon time by pentacontads, that is, in stretches of fifty days, while another was to reckon by lunar months. The two methods were reconciled by regarding the interval between the end of a pentacontad and the next new moon as a "vacant" period, outside the ordinary calendar. Such a period would have been called "sabbath" or standstill, and the reference to "the morrow of the sabbath" would be a relic of this ancient computation.

Whether this theory is right or wrong, further discoveries alone will tell. In the long run, except to professional students of antiquity, this is not particularly important. What matters is not the origin of the festival, but the meaning and value which it has acquired in the course of its subsequent history. And these are values which transcend any single date or, for that matter, any single epoch.

6

THE FEAST OF BOOTHS

The Festival of Ingathering

Corresponding to the festival of Passover in spring is the Feast of Booths *(Succoth)* in autumn. This, too, begins at full moon in the first month of the season; this, too, is a harvest festival; and this, too, is observed for eight days. Moreover, just as Passover marks the beginning of the summer dews, so Booths marks that of the winter rains.

The original name of the festival was Feast of Ingathering *(Asif);* it celebrated the ingathering of summer crops and fruits, and the close of the agricultural year. The date was at first variable and indefinite; the feast took place whenever the harvest happened to be in (Deut. 16:13). Later, however, when the year came to be determined on an astronomical basis, the Feast of Ingathering was made to begin either at the autumnal equinox (Exod. 34:22) or at full moon in the appropriate lunar month. The latter system is the one which has prevailed in Jewish practice.

The Feast of Ingathering was really but the concluding stage of a longer festive season, the three principal moments of which were: *(a)* the Day of Memorial; *(b)* the Day of Purgation; and *(c)* the harvest-home. The two former stages are now represented respectively by New Year, on the first day of the lunar month, and by the Day of Atonement, on the tenth. Prefaced by these two solemn occasions, on which all noxious and evil influences are ceremonially removed, the Feast of Ingathering marked both the successful issue of the preceding year and the "clean start" of the one which followed. It was therefore regarded as the most important of all the seasonal festivals, and came to be known as *"the* festival" *tout court.*

The principal features of the celebration were: *(a)* the actual reaping of crops and fruits and the bringing in of the vintage; *(b)* the performance of special ceremonies designed to induce rainfall; *(c)* the custom of dwelling in booths *(succoth)* or trellis-roofed cabins throughout the period of the festival. Of these usages the most important was the last, and it was this that gave the feast its popular name.

The booths were originally functional in character; they were simply the wattled cabins in which the harvesters and vintners were wont to lodge during the time of the ingathering. Such booths, made of plaited twigs of carob and oleander and roofed with palm leaves, are still used in the Holy Land throughout the period (from June to September) when the reaping is in progress, and it is in this sense that the word *succah* is usually employed in the Hebrew Bible.

The primitive ceremonies for inducing rainfall can be deduced only from a later survival in the days of the Second Temple. The Mishnah tells us that on every day of the festival a golden flagon was filled from the neighboring pool of Siloam and carried to the Temple in gay procession. Delivered to the officiating priest, it was then poured into a silver container, the spout of which was trained upon the altar.

This ceremony, known as the Water Libation *(Nissuch Ha-mayim)*, has abundant parallels in other parts of the world, and is based on what is known as "sympathetic magic," that is, on the primitive notion that things done by men may induce similar actions on the part of nature or "the gods." Lucian of Samosata, writing in the second century C.E., records an analogous practice performed twice yearly in the pagan temple at Hierapolis (Membij), Syria; while at Ispahan, in Iran, there is (or was) an annual ceremony of rain-making which consisted in pouring water on the ground; and in many parts of modern Palestine, rogations for rain, accompanied by the ceremonial drenching of a little girl known as "Mother Shower," are a common element of folk usage in early spring. Interesting also is a more remote parallel from the Mara tribe of northern Australia. In time of drought, the local magician besprinkles himself with water and scatters drops of it on the ground; this, it is believed, will induce rainfall.

The Mishnah likewise preserves the record of another magical ceremony which would seem to go back to the primitive observance of the festival. On the evening of the first day, we are told, men repaired to the precincts of the Temple in Jerusalem and lit huge candelabra in the Court of the Women. "Men of piety and good works" danced in front of them, waving burning torches, while a throng of Levites, standing on the fifteen steps which divided the Court of the Women from that of the Israelites, furnished accompanying music. At the Nicanor Gate stood priests, holding trumpets. At cockcrow, they ascended the steps and sounded a series of prolonged and quavering blasts. When they reached the gate which leads out to the east, they turned their faces westward, in the direction of the Temple building, and cried: "Our forefathers, when they were in this place, turned their backs to the Temple of the Lord and their faces toward the rising sun in the east [cf. Ezek. 8:16], but we— our eyes are turned toward the Lord."

This ceremony—known as the Rejoicing at the Beth Ha-Shoebah—was originally a magical rite, its purpose being to rekindle the decadent sun at the time of the autumnal equinox and to hail it when it rose at dawn. Such a ceremony is likewise recorded by Lucian, and a Christianized survival of it may be recognized in the Festival of the Cross *(Maskal)* still observed by the Ethiopian Church on September 26. Elsewhere, however, it is usually combined with the idea of burning up all evil and harmful influences at the start of the agricultural year. Thus, at Fez and amid the Berber tribes of Morocco, it is customary to light bonfires on the rooftops on the festival of 'Ashura, the Mohammedan New Year, and for children and unmarried men to leap through the flames while they say "We have shaken out over thee, O bonfire, the fleas and lice and sickness both of body and of soul!" The same custom obtains also in Tunis. Analogously, an ancient Babylonian text which describes the ceremonies of the New Year festival refers to the custom of tossing firebrands in the air; Ovid tells us that the Romans leaped over fires and raced through the fields with blazing torches at the beginning of the

year. To this day, bonfires are a standard feature of
Halloween ceremonies in most parts of Europe, and
Halloween was, of course, the eve of the ancient New
Year.

For Israel, this purely agricultural aspect of the festival was not enough. Like Passover and Pentecost, so too
the Feast of Booths had to possess a historical as well as a
seasonal significance; it had to exemplify the presence of
God not only in the world of nature but also in that of
event; and it had in some way to symbolize and epitomize Israel's continuing covenant with Him.

The transformation was accomplished by an ingenious
device: the traditional booths were interpreted as a reminder of those in which the ancestors of Israel had
dwelt when they wandered through the wilderness on
their journey from Egypt to the Promised Land! The
festival thus became a logical sequel to Passover and
Pentecost, which commemorated respectively the escape
from bondage and the conclusion of the Covenant at
Sinai. Moreover, by themselves dwelling in booths at
this season, each successive generation of Jews could be
said to be sharing in that experience and thereby endow-
ing it with a perpetual character.

This interpretation was, of course, purely fanciful;
the cold fact is that people who wander through deserts
live in tents, not booths, wood and green leaves being
unavailable except at rare and intermittent oases. To be
sure, the point is not really important; the "myth" which
is woven around a traditional institution is usually more
indebted to fancy than to fact, and its validity lies not in
its historical accuracy or authenticity but in the transcendental truths which it focuses and conveys. Nevertheless, throughout the ages Jewish scholars and teachers

felt a little uneasy about the story of the booths in the wilderness, and alternative interpretations were therefore propounded.

It was observed, for instance, that in sundry passages of the Bible, the word *succah*—or, more precisely, its masculine equivalent, *sok*—serves, by poetic metaphor, to denote the temple of God in Jerusalem, and that both the First and Second Temples are said expressly to have been dedicated at the Feast of Booths. This at once suggested that the seasonal booths might be regarded as a symbol of that holy habitation. The idea finds repeated expression in the traditional liturgy of the festival. Typical is a medieval hymn chanted during the morning service of the first day, in which a sustained contrast is drawn between the heavenly and earthly tabernacles. The poem is full of recondite allusions and quaint conceits, but its general spirit and tenor may perhaps be conveyed by the following partial and paraphrastic rendering:

Where flaming angels walk in pride,
Where ministers of light abide,
Where cavalries of heaven ride,
Where souls have rest at eventide,
    There, 'mid the sapphire and the gold,
    God's tabernacle rose of old.

Yet here, as in a mead aflower,
Here, as in a bridal bower,
Here, where songs of praise and power,
Wreathe Him, every day and hour,
    Here, in an earthly booth as well
    His glory did not spurn to dwell.[1]

. . . . .

[1] *Az hayethah hanayath sukkô,* by Eleazar Kalir; Adler-Davis, *Tabernacles,* p. 212.

In the same way, in a poem recited on the eve of the second day, the ruined Temple is likened to a booth fallen to pieces:

Thy tabernacle which is fallen down
Rebuild, O Lord, and raise it once again!

Alternatively, the succah was given a continuing historical meaning by being identified with the protective providence of God, spread like a pavilion over His chosen people. Says the same poem, in reference to the Exodus from Egypt:

Thy cloud enfolded them, as if that they
Were shelter'd in a booth; redeem'd and free,
They saw Thy glory as a canopy
Spread o'er them as they marched upon their way.

And when dryshod they through the sea had gone,
They praised Thee and proclaimed Thy unity;
And all the angels sang the antiphon,
And lifted up their voices unto Thee.
     "Our Rock, our Savior He"—thus did they sing—
     "World without end the Lord shall reign as King!" [2]

Whatever meaning be given to it, Jewish tradition insists that the seasonal succah must be in every sense a true booth; no mere token substitute will do. Specifications are laid down clearly in the Mishnah. The succah must not be lower than five feet, nor higher than thirty; and it must possess at least three sides. It may not be roofed with matting or burlap, but only with lightly strewn leaves or straw. It must be exposed to the elements and to a view of the stars. Moreover, since the task of erecting it is regarded as an essential part of the commandment, no permanent structure may serve.

. . . . .

[2] *Yephi ananechâ*, by Jehiel ben Isaac (XIIIth cent.); Adler-Davis, p. 218.

The duty of eating and sleeping in the succah is incumbent upon all adult males; women and minors alone are exempt. Since, however, it is often impossible to observe this rule in modern cities, modifications of it have been introduced. According to some authorities, at least one meal must be taken in the booth each day and each night of the festival; according to others, it is sufficient if one eats in the succah on the first night only. In either case, nothing must be done to lessen the discomfort or even hardship which may attend the observance; rain water, for instance, may be baled out only if it "threatens to spoil the gruel"!

But the booth was not the only feature of the earlier pagan festival which the genius of Israel transformed and transmuted. The Biblical commandment ordains that "ye shall take you, on the first day, the fruit of a goodly tree, palm-branches, foliage of leafy trees, and willows of the brook, and ye shall rejoice seven days before Jehovah your God" (Lev. 23:40). What is envisaged is evidently no more than the carrying of a gay bunch such as is borne by revelers at harvest festivals in many parts of the world. The most obvious example is, of course, the European maypole, in spring, for although this was later conventionalized as a single beribboned post set up on the village green, it was originally a green bough carried by each of the revelers in token of nature's revival. In Cornwall, England, for example, doors and porches used to be decked on May Morn with boughs of sycamore and hawthorn; in Sweden and in parts of Alsace boys and girls used to march around the villages carrying festive bunches. Nor are such usages unattested in ancient times. At the beginning of spring, it was customary in ancient Greece for children to make the rounds of houses in the manner of modern carol singers, bearing a leafy bough and chanting an appropriate ditty; and the carrying of wands (*thyrsoi*) wreathed with fresh leaves and topped with pine cones was a prominent feature of the winter festival of Dionysus. Moreover, on a Cretan seal dating from the second millenium B.C.E., suppliants of a female deity are portrayed bearing flowering wands; while the prophet Ezekiel, satirizing the pagan "abominations" performed in Jerusalem during high summer, observes significantly, *"The rod has blossomed*—arrogance has flowered" (7:10).

In Jewish tradition, however, the festive branch and bunch (called *lulab*) was invested at once with a historical as well as a seasonal significance. The various ingredients of the bunch—somewhat arbitrarily identified as the beautiful but scentless palm branch, the beautiful and fragrant citron *(ethrog),* the humble but sweet-smelling myrtle, and the simple, unprepossessing willows—were taken to symbolize the characters and virtues of the ancient patriarchs, and when they were carried in procession around the synagogue during the morning services of the festival, this was regarded as a memorial of the circuits which the priests used to make around the altar on the Feast of Booths. Moreover, the ceremony came to be accompanied by the chanting of *hosha'anoth*—that is, of poetic litanies punctuated by the refrain *Hosanna* (O save us!), and to this day these litanies are associated specifically with incidents in the lives and careers of the patriarchs and of other ancestral worthies.

On the first day, God is invoked to remember all those incidents which involved the number one, e.g., the fact that Abraham had been the *one* true believer in his generation; that Isaac had been delivered from sacrifice

by the substitution of "*one* ram caught in a thicket"
(Gen. 22:13); that Moses had transmitted to Israel
the *one* true Law. On the second day, reference is made
to Abraham's journey to Mount Moriah in the company
of *two* servants (Gen. 22:3); to Isaac's having been
the ancestor of *two* great nations; to Jacob's having
acquired the parental blessing by dressing *two* kids for
his aged father (Gen. 27:9); and to Moses' having
brought down from Sinai *two* tables of stone. On the
third day, the litany alludes to the *three* angels whom
Abraham entertained (Gen. 18:2); to Moses' having
formed a triad with Aaron and Miriam; and to his having
divided the people into the *threefold* division of priests,
Levites and Israelites.

Dexterously, and sometimes even tortuously, the same
scheme is carried through for the remaining days of the
festival. On the seventh day—known as *Hoshanna Rabba,*
or the Great Hosanna—for example, when seven circuits
are made, not only do these commemorate the seven
worthies, Abraham, Isaac and Jacob, Moses and Aaron,
Phineas and David, but they also serve to call to mind
the first seven days of the world; the seven lambs set
apart by Abraham in his covenant with Abimelech at
the well of Beersheba (Gen. 21:28); the seven years
of famine endured by Jacob; and the seven-day festivals
ordained by Moses.

Thus, although in itself not so readily capable of
historicization as is the succah, the lulab is nonetheless
securely wedded to the historical interpretation of the
festival.

The same process was applied also to the ceremony of
the Water Libation. All that now remains of the ancient
rite is the custom of offering special prayers for rain on

the eighth day of the festival, the cantor or precentor being usually attired for the occasion in the same long white robe *(kittel)* which he wears on Passover during the recital of the prayers for dew and which he also dons on New Year and the Day of Atonement. These prayers, however, have been thoroughly integrated with the historical aspect of the festival. The rain is besought in the name of such ancestral heroes as Abraham, Isaac, and Moses, and God is invoked to remember all those moments of their careers in which water played a part. The following lines from a medieval poem embodied in the Ashkenazic (German-Polish) liturgy will serve to illustrate the pattern: [3]

Remember him whose heart outflowed to Thee
Like water; unto whom Thy blessing came
That he should thrive and flourish like a tree
Beside a stream; whom Thou didst save from flame
And water; that his offspring might abide
Like seed which grows the running brooks beside.

Remember him whose birth was heralded
By angels, when his father washed their feet
With water; [4] who his blood would fain have shed
Like water; [5] whom his servitors did greet
With tales of water found where none before
Had e'er been sighted in the days of yore. [6]

Remember him who from the river deep
Was drawn; of whom the seven maidens said:
"Water he drew for us and gave our sheep
To drink;" [7] who through the torrid desert led
    . . . . .

[3] *Zechor ab* by Eleazar Kalir; Adler-Davis, p. 138.
[4] Compare Gen. 18:1-4.
[5] i.e., when he was destined for sacrifice on Mount Moriah (Gen. 22).
[6] Compare Gen. 26:19-22, 32.
[7] i.e., the seven daughters of Reuel (or Jethro); cf. Exod. 2:16-18.

Thy people and, himself for this accurs'd,
Struck water from the rock to slake their thirst.

At the same time, the Jewish genius insists that history is a living and continuing experience, and not
merely a remembrance of things past. The ceremony is
therefore wedded also to the present and immediate situation of the Jewish people, for the poem concludes:

Remember them for whom Thou didst divide
The sea, and sweet the bitter waters make;
Whose children's children, beaten and decried,
Pour out their blood like water for Thy sake!
Turn Thou to us, O Lord, and make us whole;
For lo, great waters swirl about our soul!

As in the case of Passover and Pentecost, so, too, in
that of the Feast of Booths, the seasonal and historical
aspects of the festival are made to run parallel, so that
the same truths may be expressed concurrently on two
different planes. The essential point about the festival,
alike in its seasonal and in its historical aspect, is that
what it celebrates is not an achievement but a prospect,
not something finally accomplished but something which
has been but begun and the consummation of which lies
in the future. On the seasonal plane, the Feast of Booths
marks the ingathering of the harvest and the onset of the
rains; but the harvest is consumed only in the ensuing
months, and when the festival actually takes place, none
but the first token drops of rain have yet fallen. Similarly, on the historical plane, the festival commemorates
not the actual entry of the Israelites into the Promised
Land but the fact that, in the sure and certain hope of
it, they wandered in a wilderness for forty years, pro-
tected only by the shelter of fragile booths.

All of these ideas are caught up and reflected not

only in the poems and hymns interspersed throughout the liturgy, but also—and more strikingly—in the lessons from the Law and the Prophets which are appointed to be read during the morning services.

On the first and second days of the festival, two portions are read from the Law. The first is taken from that section of the Book of Leviticus (22:26—23:44) in which the seasonal feasts are ordained. It is here that the succah is explained as a memorial of the booths in the wilderness, and it is here too that the carrying of the festive bunch is prescribed. The other portion is taken from Numbers 29:12-16 and describes the special sacrifices offered in the tabernacle and the temple on the first day of the feast.

The Lesson from the prophets is the fourteenth chapter of the Book of Zechariah. The ostensible reason for this choice is that the prophet there foretells how, in days to come, "every one that is left of all the nations that came up against Jerusalem shall go up from year to year to worship the King, the Lord of Hosts, and to keep the feast of booths" (vs.16). It would appear, however, that there is really far more behind the selection than this single passing allusion to the festival; for the fact is that throughout the chapter the prophet seems to be playing on the characteristic phenomena of this season, as if he were delivering a sermon especially geared to the traditional ceremonies. Thus, when he says that "on that day . . . there shall be a singular kind of day (it is known to Jehovah), not day and not night, for at evening time there shall be light" (vs.7), it is not difficult to recognize in his words a projection into mythology of the autumnal equinox at which the Feast of Booths anciently took place (cf. Exod. 34:22). Similarly, when he goes on to predict that "in that day, living waters shall go out from Jerusalem . . . in summer and winter it shall be" (vs.8), and that "upon those of the families of the earth that go not up to Jerusalem to worship the King, the Lord of Hosts, there shall be no rain" (vs.17), he is painting a picture of future times in terms of the seasonal conditions which obtain at the Feast of Booths, for that festival falls at a period of the year in which rain is still scarce and the beds of the rivers have not yet been replenished and the earth is moistened chiefly by the "perpetual streams."

The same tendency to project the features of the festival into a picture of the future age also characterizes the lessons chosen for the intermediate sabbath. The portion from the Law (Exod. 33:12—34:26) describes the conclusion of the Covenant at Sinai and ends by relating to it the observance of the three great seasonal festivals. The portion from the prophets, however (Ezek. 38:18—39:16), deals with the war which Jehovah will wage at the end of days against Gog and Magog. At first sight, it is difficult to see why the latter passage should have been selected, for it would seem to have no ostensible bearing upon the Feast of Booths. If, however, we look more closely, an extremely interesting fact emerges: the details of the doom which awaits the opponents of Jehovah can readily be construed as a projection into future times of several leading features of the autumn festival. It is said, for instance, that Jehovah "will *rain* upon Gog and his hordes . . . *torrential rains*" (38:22); and this message would, of course, have had peculiar significance when it was recited at the festival, which, in fact, inaugurated the rainy season and on which, according to a belief recorded in the Mishnah, "the world is judged through water." Similarly, the prophet declares that Jehovah "will send fire on Magog"

(39:6) and that "those who dwell in the cities of Israel will go forth and make fires of the weapons and burn them" (39:9); and these words would likewise have sounded with particular effect upon the ears of people who were actually performing the rite of kindling fires for the Rejoicing at the Beth Ha-Shoebah. Moreover, when the prophet further describes how Jehovah "will appoint for Gog a place of burial in Israel" where "he and all his multitude will be buried" (39:11), it might be possible to detect an ironic allusion to the common pagan custom of burying and subsequently disinterring at this season little dolls and puppets representing the god (or goddess) of fertility who was believed to die and be resurrected from year to year.

On the other hand, the portion from the prophets selected for the second day strikes an entirely different note. This describes Solomon's dedication of the First Temple on the Feast of Booths (I Kings 8:2-21). Its primary purpose is thus to drive home the lesson that the seasonal booth is but a symbol of that holy habitation— a lesson which also informs the selection for the eighth day, when, as a supplement to Deut. 15:19—16:17 (the laws of the seasonal festivals), the continuation of that passage, containing Solomon's prayer on the occasion, is recited (I Kings 8:54-66).

There were, of course, some features of the earlier pagan festival which did not lend themselves so readily to reinterpretation and which were therefore discarded or survived only in extremely attenuated form. The fire rites, for instance, disappeared entirely, since it was contrary to Jewish belief to imagine that men could rekindle the sun or in any way influence the course of nature. Similarly, all that now remains of the festival's original connection with the equinox is the custom of solemnly blessing the sun on the Feast of Booths every twenty years or so, when the lunar and solar cycles happen to be completed at about the same time.

On the other hand, there is one ancient "functional" rite which has indeed survived almost unaltered, though so different a meaning is now read into it that its original purport can no longer be recognized. This is the custom of "beating hosannas"—that is, of taking extra twigs and beating off their leaves upon the lectern during the recital of the Hosanna litanies on the seventh day. The conventional explanation of this practice is that it symbolizes the frailty of human lives, which fade and fall "thick as autumnal leaves which strew the brooks in Vallombrosa." The truth is, however, that it harks back to a primitive and fairly universal belief that the willow is a symbol of fertility and to the consequent custom of beating people with branches of that tree in order to induce potency and increase. Throughout Europe, for example, "Easter smacks," administered in this fashion, are a characteristic feature of the great spring festival. Thus, in Croatia, those who attend church on this occasion "beat health" into one another with rods of willow, while in several parts of Germany and Austria the same practice obtains on St. Stephen's Day (December 26) or on Holy Innocents' Day (December 28); and in Russia it is (or was) common on Palm Sunday. In ancient Greek ritual, at the major seasonal festival, human scapegoats were beaten with squills of willow or *agnus castus* in order, at one and the same time, to beat *out* sterility and beat *in* fecundity. Nor, indeed, was this beating always confined to human beings; the poet Theocritus informs us that in times of drought the youths of Arcadia used to smite the statue of the god Pan.

It must be confessed that of the three seasonal festivals which punctuate the Jewish year, the Feast of Booths has suffered most from the conditions of modern life and that, for all the tenacity of its observance, it is the one which possesses for the modern Jew the least contemporary relevance.

The first reason for this is purely practical. Traditionally, as we have seen, the principal feature of the festival is the erection of the succah in the precincts of one's own home. This was intended not only to commemorate the experience of the ancient Israelites but also to provide their living descendants with a means of sharing in it. In most modern cities, however, this is obviously impossible, and the conventional substitute is a communal succah set up in the courtyard of the synagogue. But this involves not only a curtailment of the traditional rite but also an attenuation of its significance. In the first place, the element of personal labor and construction disappears altogether; the succah is put up by paid employees or professional contractors. Second, although the matrons of the congregation may indeed foregather, a few days before the festival, to deck the structure with fruits and flowers, in cities where most people live in apartments rather than in private houses these do not, as a rule, represent offerings from their own gardens or orchards, but are simply bought for cash at the local greengrocer and florist. Last, a perfunctory visit to the succah after the synagogue service is obviously no substitute for actually living and sleeping in it: what should be a reproduction of ancestral hardship becomes mere attendance at a social function, and the succah itself is reduced to an artistic showpiece. Small wonder, then, that the festival loses its personal immediacy.

The other reason for Succoth's decline is ideological.

Passover and the Feast of Weeks, though geared to particular events in the past, epitomize and focus elements
of Judaism which continue in the present—namely, the
progressive mission and adventure of Israel, its persistent
struggle for freedom, and its special Covenant with God.
In this continuous adventure, in this struggle and in
this Covenant, every Jew in every generation is personally involved, so that observance of these festivals is a
direct personal experience, part and parcel of his own
individual life, and not a mere act of pious remembering.
The Feast of Booths, on the other hand, seems (apart
from its seasonal significance) to be moored and an-
chored to a single specific event, to the particular situation of a particular group at a particular moment of
time. At a distance of more than three thousand years
and miles, the modern Jew finds it difficult to recognize
in the incident of his forefathers' sojourn in booths anything in the nature of a continuing experience which he
can personally repeat—especially when the historicity of
that event is itself more than doubtful. Once again,
therefore, the festival degenerates into a mere survival.

Viewed in the proper light, however, the Feast of
Booths can indeed possess a continuing significance no
whit inferior, and in fact complementary to, that of the
other seasonal festivals. For if Passover and the Feast of
Weeks exemplify, in the stories of the Exodus and the
Covenant, the trials, achievements, and obligations, first
of Israel and then of mankind in general, the transcendental theme of the Feast of Booths is the persistent
hope and confidence without which all such trials are
insupportable, all such achievements impossible, and all
such obligations unacceptable. Thus interpreted, the festival is pertinent not only to every generation but also
to every individual. For every individual can at once rec-

ognize in it an experience which is paralleled in his own life; every individual knows that the only sure sustainment of labor is hope, and that the Promised Land is reached only after years of wandering. Thus, too, it becomes clear why the dominant note of the festival is joy and not austerity, why the Biblical commandment enjoins especially that "thou shalt be altogether joyful" (Deut. 16:15), and why the Feast of Booths is known in Jewish tradition as "the season of our rejoicing."

THE FEAST OF AZERETH
THE REJOICING IN THE LAW

The Feast of Booths is followed immediately by a festival which is called in the Bible by the name *Azereth*. The meaning of this term (conventionally rendered "Solemn Assembly"), and hence the original significance of the festival, is quite uncertain, no explanation of it being given in the Scriptural text. In the Book of Deuteronomy, however, it is applied also (16:8) to the last day of Passover, and in the Mishnah to the Feast of Weeks, while its Arabic equivalent is today the current term for Easter. It must therefore have applied in the first place to some feature of the seasonal celebrations common alike to the vernal and autumnal harvests. What this feature was can only be guessed, but seeing that the root of the word *azereth* normally means "restrain," it is not impossible that it originally denoted a day of abstinence and austerity which marked the end of the reaping and the real beginning of the new agricultural cycle.

The Festival of Azereth coincides in part with the extra day which was added to the Feast of Booths in the time of the Second Temple. Since, however, it is really an independent festival, it is itself observed by orthodox and conservative Jews for *two days*.

The second of these days is known as the festival of the *Rejoicing in the Law* (Hebrew, *Simhath Torah*).

On the eve of the festival, all but one of the sacred scrolls of the Law are paraded in procession around the synagogue, members of the congregation alternating in the privilege of shouldering the precious burden. At the head of the procession march children waving flags inscribed, in Hebrew, with the words, "Flag of the camp of Judah," or carrying poles surmounted by scooped apples in which candles are inserted. The latter are fancifully supposed to symbolize the Law which "enlighteneth the eyes."

In the morning, the last and first portions of the Pentateuch are read respectively by two members of the community known as the Bridegroom of the Law and the Bridegroom of the First Portion. Throughout the service, these two bridegrooms hold the sacred scrolls in their arms, and when they are summoned to the rostrum to read their portions, the choir strikes up with a gay song of welcome.

The privilege of serving as "bridegroom" on this occasion is greatly coveted, and in many congregations it is sold at auction on a preceding sabbath, the proceeds going to charity or to the maintenance of the synagogue.

The institution of Simhath Torah is not attested earlier than the eleventh century, and appears to have originated in western Europe. It was inspired by the fact that the annual cycle of Pentateuchal readings in fact begins anew on the following sabbath. The more ancient custom was, however, to read the Law in the synagogue in *triennial* cycles, and this explains why the festival is of comparatively recent origin.

Nor is it by any means the universal practice to have *two* "bridegrooms." In Eastern rites, as also in Rome, the same person reads both the last and the first portion, while elsewhere the honor is shared by *three* members of the congregation.

The whole ceremony is really a mystical imitation of the wedding service, and symbolizes that marriage of Israel to the Law which the ancient exegetes read into the Biblical Song of Songs and which served as one way of expressing the Covenant relationship. The bridegrooms, for instance, are attended by "bridesmen"— counterparts of the modern "best man"—who sit beside them and assist them. The procession with the scrolls is very probably an imitation of the common wedding custom of walking seven (or three) times around the bridal couple, a custom which was originally motivated by the idea of forming a closed circle in order to prevent the assaults of demons. Moreover, while the procession is moving around the synagogue, it is customary in some parts for bystanders to pelt it with nuts, in imitation of an ancient practice common especially at Roman weddings. According to some authorities, this was a fertility charm; but the more probable explanation is that the nuts were designed to hit the invisible demons and evil spirits who were believed to be hovering around the bridegroom and bride, ready to work mischief upon them.

Not impossibly, the custom of celebrating the Rejoicing in the Law as a *wedding* was inspired by the idea of sublimating to a more spiritual plane the common folkusage of staging a mock wedding at harvest festivals, this ceremony representing the union of natural forces for the production of the year's fertility.

A special feature of the service is the fact that on this day children under the age of thirteen—that is, children who have not yet attained religious majority—are called collectively to the reading of the Law. The way in which this is done is that after the conclusion of the regular Lesson, an adult member of the congregation (usually one distinguished by learning and piety) is summoned to the rostrum. The precentor then repeats the final verses of the Lesson, while all the children stand behind him, a large white praying-shawl *(tallith)* being spread over their heads like a canopy. When the adult escort recites the customary blessings before and after the reading, the entire congregation joins in. At the end of the reading, the rabbi turns to the children and pronounces a special blessing over them, repeating especially the words uttered by Jacob when he blessed Ephraim and Manasseh (Gen. 48:16): "The angel who hath redeemed me from all evil, bless the lads."

The regular service of the synagogue is interspersed with special chants and hymns celebrating, in fanciful terms, the Giving of the Law. One of the most familiar of these (of unknown authorship and date) describes how all the angels gathered around the throne of God, expressing their amazement when the mortal Moses ascended Mount Sinai to receive the tablets of stone. The following is Israel Zangwill's spirited and famous rendering:

The angels came a-mustering,
  A-mustering, a-mustering
The angels came a-clustering
  Around the sapphire throne.

A-questioning of one another,
  Of one another, of one another,

A-questioning each one his brother
  Around the sapphire throne.

Pray, who is he, and where is he,
  And where is he, and where is he,
Whose shining casts—so fair is he—
  A shadow on the throne?

Pray, who has up to heaven come,
  To heaven come, to heaven come,
Through all the circles seven come,
  To fetch the Tórah down?

'Tis Moses up to heaven come,
  To heaven come, to heaven come;
Through all the circles seven come,
  To fetch the Tórah down! [8]

This poem is chanted to a rousing melody at the conclusion of the procession with the scrolls of the Law. Its real purport is to emphasize the cosmic significance of the event at the mountain—the fact that even the heavenly host participated in it.

Another poem on the same theme, written in a somewhat more literary vein, also deserves quotation. It comes from the pen of Amittai ben Shephatiah, who lived at Oria, Italy, in the tenth century and revolves around the Biblical verse (Isa. 6:3), "Holy, holy, holy is the Lord of Hosts," the solemn recitation of which forms a central and sacred moment in every synagogal service:

Through the heavenly casements
  A gentle music rings;
Through the clear and cloudless sky
  Sounds a low, soft melody
And all the welkin rings:
    Holy, holy, holy is the Lord of Hosts.

· · · · ·

Hithkabezu mal'achim; Adler-Davis, p. 203.

The rainbow in the firmament
  Is shot with colors three,[9]
And in those threefold tints and flames
The glory of the Lord proclaims,
  A threefold litany:
    Holy, holy, holy is the Lord of Hosts.

Enoch, who from mortal flesh
  Was turn'd by God to flame,[10]
Sits like a teacher in the height,
Imparting to the Sons of Light
  The song which they declaim:
    Holy, holy, holy is the Lord of Hosts.

The while the Angel of the Law
  Takes in his hand the fire,
And as he wreathes a crown with it,
To crown the words of Holy Writ,[11]
  Sings with the heavenly choir:
    Holy, holy, holy is the Lord of Hosts.

And he who is the Prince of Storms,
  Whose winds do rage and roar,
Repeats in every thunder-crash,
Retells in every lightning flash,
  The threefold message o'er:
    Holy, holy, holy is the Lord of Hosts.

All the great lights of heaven,
  Bear and Orion bright,
Proclaim the constancy of Him

  . . . . .

[9] The basic colors of the spectrum are three: red, blue, and yellow.
[10] It was a common medieval belief that Enoch, the patriarch who "walked with God, and was not, for God took him" (Gen. 5:24), was turned into the fiery angel, Metatron.
[11] Rabbinic fantasy asserted that the Law was originally written by God "in black flame upon white flame," and that every letter of it was surmounted by a fiery crown.

Whose light ne'er darkens nor grows dim
    Nor ever fades from sight:
        Holy, holy, holy is the Lord of Hosts.

The curtain-folds of heaven
    Are hung with tinkling bells;
When they by morning winds are stirred,
A music of the spheres is heard,
    As each one rings and tells:
        Holy, holy, holy is the Lord of Hosts.[12]

   . . . . .

[12] *Eshnabê shehakim;* Adler-Davis, p. 246.

III

The Solemn Days

7

NEW YEAR

The Day of Remembrance
The Ten Days of Penitence
Blow the horn at the new moon,
At the appointed season, for our feast-day . . .
Psalm 81:3

Among primitive peoples, there is usually no such thing as a fixed and definite year. They reckon time in variable and irregular cycles, from any one natural event to its recurrence. Moreover, some of them do not even go as far as that, but recognize only brief spans—times of heat or cold, rain or drought, sowing or reaping—which they do not add together into a continuous stretch. As civilization proceeds, however, the need is felt for some more regular and uniform system, and at this point people begin to reckon time from easily observable astronomical events—from the solstice or equinox, from the new moon nearest to sowing or reaping, from the early rising of Orion or the Pleiades, and so forth.

The ancient Hebrews had two principal systems.

They reckoned the year from the new moon nearest to the beginning of the barley harvest in spring, or to the ingathering of fruits, in autumn. The former—the new year of Nisan—did not survive as a formal religious occasion, but was used only for legal and calendarical purposes. The latter, however—that of Tishri—was adopted as the beginning of the festal year and now ranks, beside Yom Kippur, as one of the two great solemn days of the Jewish faith.

In the Bible, the first of Tishri is called simply "the Day of Memorial," but what this term meant is not known for certain. A prevalent opinion among scholars is that it refers to a public *commemoration of the dead;* for, as we have seen, it is standard belief of primitive peoples that the dead return to rejoin their descendants at the beginning of the year, or are especially called to mind on that occasion. Moreover, the Hebrew word rendered "memorial" is actually employed in other Semitic languages to denote such a commemoration. Be this as it may, in its modern development New Year is the Day of Remembrance. On New Year's Day, man remembers the beginning of the world; God remembers the deeds of His creatures; Israel remembers its special function as His witness, and recalls the successes and failures of its mission.

But such remembrance is not merely an excursion into the past. The central theme of New Year's Day is the power of Memory itself. Memory defies oblivion, breaks the coils of the present, establishes the continuity of the generations, and rescues human life and effort from futility. It affords the only true resurrection of the dead. The act of remembering is thus in itself redemptive. If, on the one hand, it involves a chastening assessment, it involves, on the other, a comforting reassurance. New

Year's Day is at once a day of judgment and a new beginning. If it looks backward, it does so only on the way forward; and its symbol is the trumpet of an eternal reveille.

Judaism brings out the message of the day with vivid and remarkable effectiveness, by ingeniously developing and reinterpreting all the customs and myths traditionally associated with it from primitive times. Primitive peoples have no conception of the continuity of time. They regard it as a series of leases annually or periodically renewed. On the basis of this conception, Judaism regards New Year's Day not merely as an anniversary of creation but also—and more importantly—as a renewal of it. The world is reborn from year to year—even, in an extended sense, from day to day and from minute to minute—and the primary message of the festival is that the process of creation is *continuous*, that the breath of God moves *constantly* upon the face of the waters, and that the light is *continually* being brought out of darkness. Nevertheless, if there is a new creation every moment, it is not a creation out of nothing; no moment is self-contained, but each emerges from its predecessor. The deeds of the present are thus the raw material of the future, and this means in turn that virtue and merit are not merely the ornaments of those who evince them, but are also the seeds of their children's prosperity. In the traditional Jewish phraseology, the original virtue of the patriarchs is eternally redemptive and insures the welfare of their descendants, even outweighing the latter's defects.

Primitive peoples believe also that New Year is a time when the order of the world is re-established and when the fates of men are determined for the ensuing twelve months. In ancient Babylon, for example, it was commonly supposed that at this season the gods met in conclave in the principal shrine of the city and not only fixed the movements of the heavenly bodies and established the alternation of the seasons for the ensuing twelve months, but also reviewed the deeds of individual human beings and settled the destiny of each. Judaism inherited or took over the idea, but it gave it a new and significant twist. The Jewish people had lived through too much adversity to credit the belief in summary, unrelenting condemnation or peremptory doom; there was always, it maintained, the Last Chance, the merciful loophole. The review which took place at New Year, it said, was not finally concluded until Yom Kippur, and, in the meanwhile, "prayer, penitence and charity might avert the evil decree." New Year thus became a day of warning rather than of judgment. If, in the end, there was condemnation, it was a condemnation pronounced reluctantly, rather than in vengeance; man had forced the unwilling hands of God. What was now represented as inevitable was not divine retribution, but divine mercy. As a medieval New Year hymn expresses it:

O constant God, when Thou dost us arraign,
If Thou shouldst plumb the depths, if Thou shouldst drain
The cup, would there be any to remain?

Didst Thou not deign, O Lord, for Thine own sake
Thy fury and Thy wrath from us to take,
No deed of ours could intercession make.*

But this mercy of God was not wholly an act of grace; it was also a fulfillment of His obligation to Israel under the terms of the Covenant. For the moment God started to remember and count up the deeds of His people, He

. . . . .

* *El emūnah be-'orchechâ dîn,* by Eleazar Kalir; Adler-Davis, *New Year,* p. 145.

had perforce to recall also the many occasions on which
it had indeed proved faithful to that bond and on which
it had qualified for the promised providence and protection by "passing through fire and water for the sanctification of His Name."

The "remembrance" which takes place on New Year's
Day thus becomes inseparable from the memory of the
Covenant, and it is an act performed by each of the
partners to it: God remembers His debt to Israel in
respect of its trust and devotion, and Israel remembers
that only by reason of such devotion is it entitled to claim
the divine favor.

The point is brought out in traditional lore by associating with New Year's Day two pertinent stories
from the Bible, in the one of which man performs and
God promises, and in the other of which man promises
and God performs. The former is the story of how
Abraham prepared to sacrifice Isaac in obedience to the
command of God, and how his piety was rewarded not
only by the eventual sparing of his son but also by the
assurance that his seed would be multiplied "as the
stars of heaven and as the sand which is upon the shore
of the sea" and that "in it all the nations of the earth
shall be blessed!" This incident, which, as it were, al-
legorized the perpetual role of Israel, was said, by a
pious fiction, to have taken place at New Year, and the
story was selected as the Lesson from the Law on the
second day of the festival.

The other tale which was fancifully associated with
the occasion was that of the birth of the prophet Samuel,
a tale in which the promise of service made by Hannah
at once impelled the reciprocal grace of God: "And
Hannah was in bitterness of soul, and she prayed to the
Lord, and wept sore . . . and she said: 'If Thou

wilt remember and not forget Thine handmaid, and if
Thou wilt give unto Thine handmaid a son, then I in
turn will give him to the Lord all the days of his life'
. . . And Eli answered and said: 'Go in peace, and the
God of Israel will grant thy petition which thou hast
made to Him.' " The birth of the prophet is likewise
said to have taken place at New Year, and the tale is
recited as the Lesson from the Prophets on the first day
of the festival.

To primitive peoples, New Year, or the beginning of
a new month or season, is a crucial and critical time, when
demons are thought to be especially rampant, eager to
inflict mischief and harm. To scare them away it is
customary in most parts of the world to beat drums,
sound gongs, blow trumpets, crack whips and generally
create pandemonium. In Japan, for example, the advent
of New Year is heralded by troupes of dancers who go
from house to house and, on being admitted, proceed to
make a furious noise by rattling bamboo sticks. This is
regarded as an effective method of clearing out malicious
spirits. Similarly, in some parts of Scotland, parties of
boys parade through the villages, on New Year's Eve,
encircling every house three times and setting up a
deafening din for the purpose of expelling demons and
witches, while in the neighborhood of Zurich, Switzer-
land, and in the Falkenau district of Germany, it is (or
was) the common practice for boys and girls to pace the
streets on New Year's morn beating drums and kettles
and blowing whistles. In Cornwall, England, March 1
—the beginning of the old Celtic year—was likewise
"cracked in" with whips, while the general practice of
noise-making indeed survives (though the reason has long
since been forgotten) in our own New Year's Eve celebrations.

Here again, Judaism took over the traditional usage and invested it with a new and more spiritual significance. The blowing of the ram's horn (Hebrew, *shofar*) —which had, in fact, taken place *at every new moon*— was taken to recall those moments in Israel's history when it had heard, in more than a physical sense, the notes of the clarion. It recalled the trumpets and thunders at Sinai, sounds which, as the Scripture says (Exod. 19:19), "grew ever louder and louder" and which, far from being a means of repelling hostile forces of nature, revealed their cooperative presence at the Giving of the Law and the Conclusion of the Covenant. Moreover, since, in Jewish teaching, memory always looks forward as well as backward, the blasts of the *shofar* came, by a fine "twist" of the primitive conception, to prefigure the great day when, as the prophet had foretold, God himself would drive out the powers of darkness, "blow the ram's horn, and come with the whirlwinds" (Zech. 9:14). Nor this alone, it was interpreted also as a symbol of the Last Trump and as the rallying call of Israel in its eternal battle for the Kingdom of God.

Lastly, primitive people believed that at New Year, when their supreme gods defeated the forces of chaos and thereby reasserted their dominion, they were formally reinstated as sovereigns of the world and exacted renewed allegiance. In Babylon, for instance, an essential feature of the New Year celebrations was the recital (possibly also the enactment) of the story which related how, at the beginning of the present dispensation, the national god Marduk had engaged and defeated the monstrous Tiamat, a divine marplot, together with all her confederates. In reward for his triumph, the high god Anu had consigned to him the "tablets of destiny" and other insignia and had ordained that he be ensconced in a palace especially built in his honor. The palace in question was identified with Esagila, the great temple of Marduk in Babylon; and annually, at the New Year festival, the image of the god was paraded through the city and finally installed in that sacred edifice.

Similarly, among the Canaanites, Baal, god of rainfall and fertility, was said to have acquired "kingship eternal" by vanquishing the rebellious Lord of the Sea (alias Leviathan), who claimed dominion over the earth; and as a reward for his prowess, he, too, was enthroned in a palace especially built for him on the sacred "Mountain of the North." The tale of his victory, subsequently developed into an elaborate poem recently discovered at Ras Shamra, on the north coast of Syria, was very probably recited at the autumnal festival which inaugurated the season of the rains and marked the beginning of the agricultural year.

In the same way, too, it would appear, the God of the Hebrews was thought to have done battle against demon and dragon and thereby to have insured the world order and His own supremacy. For there are several passages in the Bible which allude—albeit cryptically—to a primeval combat between Jehovah and Leviathan (or the Dragon of the Sea), [1] and it is significant that both of His temples in Jerusalem were in fact dedicated at the autumnal festival of Ingathering, [2] and that the prophet Zechariah refers expressly to pilgrimages made on that occasion for the purpose of paying homage to "the King, the Lord of Hosts." [3] Indeed, some scholars have suggested that psalms which begin "Jehovah is become king" (or "The

. . . . .

[1] e.g., Isa. 27:1, 51:9-10; Hab. 3:8; Ps. 74:13-14; 93; Job 9:13, 26:12-13.
[2] I Kings 8:2; Neh. 8:13-18.
[3] Zech. 14, 16.

Lord reigneth")[4] were originally designed for recitation at the New Year festival.

Judaism translated this ancient myth into the present tense: God was *continually* doing battle against the forces of chaos, *continually* fighting His way to Kingdom, *continually* asserting His dominion, and *continually* enthroning Himself as sovereign of creation. At New Year, when the world was annually reborn, that sovereignty was evinced anew, but it was the consequence of a continual, not of a particular triumph; and the palace in which He was enthroned was not an earthly dwelling, but rather nature itself, and the hearts and minds of men. Thus, although the more grotesque features of the myth were discarded, its essential message was conserved, and remained attached to New Year's Day as one of its cardinal features. The Sovereignty of God is a dominant theme of the occasion, reiterated constantly in the services of the synagogue. Indeed, the sounding of the ram's horn has been brought into direct connection with it, for one of the meanings which is today assigned to that practice is that it symbolized the fanfaron before a king.

All of the varying aspects of the day, as they are conceived in Jewish thought, are epitomized in the great formula which is inserted, on New Year, into the recital of the Eighteen Benedictions—one of the staple elements of all Jewish services, viz.: "Remember us for life, O King who delights in life; inscribe us in the Book of Life, for Thy sake, God of life." Here is the remembrance; here is the kingship; here is the judgment. But here is also the resonant, dominant note that New Year is a new beginning, and that on this day all these things coalesce into a triumphant affirmation of life.

. . . . .

[4] e.g., Pss. 93, 97.

The lesson of New Year is imparted, in Judaism, not by mere abstract formulation but by concrete symbolism in the service of the synagogue. The essential feature of that service is the blowing of the shofar, or trumpet. The instrument is usually fashioned out of ram's horn, and the name *shofar* itself properly refers to horned sheep; in point of law, however, the horn of any clean *(kosher)* animal may be used, with the exception of the cow or calf, for that—it is held—might serve to recall the disgraceful incident of the Golden Calf. The shofar may not be painted, but it may be embellished with carved designs. It is usually curved, symbolizing (as one of the sages observed) the natural posture of the humble and contrite.

The blowing of the shofar demands considerable skill, and for this reason the services of a trained expert (known as the *ba'al teki'ah,* or "trumpeter") are usually enlisted. Nor are the notes sounded at random or in an arbitrary manner; they are duly prescribed by tradition, and there may be no deviation from the established order. There are three basic sounds. The first, called *teki'ah,* or "blast," is a short bass note ending abruptly. The second, called *teru'ah,* or "trump," is a long, resonant blast. The third, called *shebarîm,* or "quavers," is a series of trills.

The shofar is blown during the morning service of the day, except on the Sabbath, when it is omitted. It is first sounded after the reading of the Lesson from the Prophets, the congregation remaining seated. The ceremony is introduced by the chanting of the Forty-seventh Psalm, selected on account of the verse, "God is gone up with a fanfare, the Lord to the sound of the ram's horn." This is followed by a short prayer and by two blessings. The first praises God for ordaining the blowing of the trumpet; the second, for "keeping us alive and sustaining us and enabling us to reach this season." It is customary for the *ba'al tekî'ah* to cover his head with the praying-shawl *(tallîth)* while performing his office. When the blasts have been sounded, the congregation chants the verse (Ps. 89:15) : "Happy the people who know the trumpet sound; these walk, O Lord, in the light of Thy face."

The blowing of the shofar is repeated four times more during the service. These blasts occur during the cantor's repetition of the statutory "Standing Prayer," so that on these occasions the congregation rises. The first time it is sounded to celebrate God's kingship; the second time, "for remembrance"; and the third time to bring to mind all those events both past and future which are linked, by the authority of Scripture, with the blowing of the ram's horn. On each occasion, ten Biblical verses are recited dealing respectively with each of these themes.[5] The excerpts are known as "Kingship-verses" *(Malkiôth)*, "Memorial-verses" *(Zichrônôth)* and "Shofarverses" *(Shôfarôth)*, and form the keynote of the entire service.

Finally, the blowing is repeated once more toward the end of the service.

But it is not only in the notes of the shofar that the message of the day is conveyed. Interspersed in the order of service are a number of hymns and devotional compositions designed to reinforce it. One of these, which has acquired especial fame, is the poem entitled, from its initial Hebrew words, *"U-netanneh Tokeph"*

· · · · ·

[5] Typical "Kingship-verses" are: Num. 23:21; Deut. 33:5; Ps. 93:1; Isa. 44:6; Zech. 14:9. "Memorial-verses" include: Gen. 8:1; Exod. 2:24; Ps. 106:45; Jer. 2:2; Ezek. 16:60. "Shofar-verses" are: Exod. 19:16, 19; Ps. 47:6, 81:4, 98:6; Isa. 18:3; Zech. 9:14.

(Let us rehearse the grandeur). This poem—which is repeated on Yom Kippur—recites the grandeur and majesty of the great Day of Judgment, when the sovereignty of God is reasserted from year to year and when He sits upon His heavenly throne to judge both the hosts on high and the families of mankind upon earth:

A sudden hush, a trumpet blast—
The angels quail and are aghast;
"The Judgment Day is here," they cry,
"The Judgment on the hosts on high!"
(For there's no minister of light
Untarnish'd in the Judge's sight.)

And all that roam the earth below
Like sheep before their shepherd go,
Filing past him to the fold,
Counted, number'd, reckon'd, told.
God declares and God decrees
When Fate's abhorrèd shears to these
Shall come; and with His mighty hand
Sets upon their souls the brand.
. . . .

Dust are men, to dust return;
With their souls their bread they earn—
Fragile vessels, wither'd grass,
Fading flowers, shades that pass,
Drifting clouds, and winds that blow,
Dust-specks, dreams that wingèd go.
But Thou, eternal King sublime,
Thy days and years outdistance time.
Thron'd above the cherubim,
Who can all Thy glory limn?
Who the mystery proclaim
Hidden in Thy hidden Name?
Yet Thy glories cover us,
For Thy Name is over us.

Legend asserts that this poem was written in the tenth century, by a certain Amnon of Mayence, who had been ordered by the archbishop of that city to abjure his faith. Amnon asked for three days in which to think the matter over. When, however, he failed to appear at the end of this period the archbishop had him arrested, and Amnon then begged that his tongue be cut out for having given a false undertaking. The archbishop replied, however, that the punishment should more fittingly be visited upon his feet, which had failed to convey him. Amnon's toes (and likewise his fingers) were therefore amputated.

The New Year festival had now come around, and Amnon, dying of his wounds, requested that he be carried into the synagogue. As the cantor was about to intone the solemn words of the Sanctification ("Holy, holy, holy is the Lord of Hosts"), which form a cardinal element of the Standing Prayer, Amnon stayed him, saying, "Pause, that I may sanctify the most holy Name." He then began to recite the poem *U-netanneh Tokeph*, and when he came to the words, "Yet Thy glories cover us, For Thy name is over us," he, too, passed into the hands of the heavenly Judge.

Scholars have long ago pointed out that this story lacks historicity and that it is probably based on a medieval Christian legend associated with a certain St. Emmeram of Regensburg. Nevertheless, it has retained such a hold upon the imagination of Jews throughout the ages that it has acquired a kind of reality which transcends the prosaic limitations of fact.

Another theme which finds constant expression in the New Year hymns is the immutability of God and the mortality of man. An excellent specimen of this genre is the poem *Ammiz Ha-menusse'* written in the tenth century by Simeon ben Isaac ben Abun of Mayence, which contrasts the status of the heavenly King with that of earthly princes. The following extracts, somewhat freely translated, will serve to convey its general tone and tenor:

King in the world of light—
    Austere, exalted He,
    Above all powers that be,
        All things by His command are made and known.
    Uplifted high and proud,
    He raiseth up the bow'd;
        'Tis He that setteth kings upon the throne.
                    Eterne His reign.

.   .   .   .

King in the world of light—
    The cloud-mist is His screen,
    He strides the flames between,
        And drives his cherub-chariot thro' the sky.
    Stars in their courses shine
    To light the way divine,
        And shimmering sparks proclaim that He is nigh.
                    Eterne His reign.

.   .   .   .

Kings in the world of blight—
    Grow old and faint and slow,
    Down to the Pit must go,
        Down to the slime and slough must they descend;
    After the world's spent riot,
    Into the grave unquiet,
        Into the weariness withouten end.
                How long their reign?

Kings in the world of blight—
    Lo, at the end of all,
    Sleep on their eyes shall fall,
        And slumber o'er their eyelids shall be sprent.
    Folds of obscurity

> Their winding-sheet shall be,
> And grey oblivion all their cerement.
> > *How long their reign?*

A further prominent feature of the devotions is the ceremony of "falling *kor'im*," or performing the act of prostration. Although this was common in the time of the Temple, Jews are today forbidden to kneel in worship. On New Year and the Day of Atonement, however, an exception is made; and a high point of the service is the moment when the entire congregation kneel and fall upon their faces as the cantor intones the ancient words said in tradition to have been composed by Joshua himself upon his entry into the Promised Land:

We bend the knee *(kor'im)* and prostrate ourselves and make acknowledgment before the supreme King of Kings, the Holy One, blessed be He, who stretched out the heavens and laid the foundations of the earth, whose glorious throne is in the heavens and the home of whose majesty is in the loftiest heights.[6]

It is customary, during the morning services of the festival, for all adult males to wear a long white cloak known as a *kittel*. This cloak is also worn on the Day of Atonement and likewise at the Seder ceremony of the Passover and during the recitation of the special prayers for dew and for rain on that festival and on the Feast of Booths respectively. It is a symbol of purity, and in this garment the pious Jew is both married and buried.

In the afternoon of the first day of New Year (or of the second day, if the first happen to fall on the sabbath), it is the practice of orthodox Jews to repair to the

· · · · ·

[6] The "dignified" Spanish and Portuguese Jews, however, in an effort to preserve the "decorum" of public worship, omit this ceremony altogether.

nearest body of flowing water and there recite in Hebrew
the closing words of the biblical Book of Micah, viz.:

God will again have compassion upon us;
He will tread our iniquities under foot;
And Thou wilt cast all their sins into the depths of the sea.

Thou wilt show faithfulness to Jacob, mercy to Abraham,
As Thou hast sworn unto our fathers from the days of old.

The ceremony is called *Tashlich,* from the Hebrew word
for "Thou wilt cast"; and while the verses are being
recited, it is customary to shake crumbs from one's pock-
ets into the water.

The custom is first attested in the fifteenth century,
and it is explained by tradition in a purely homiletic
manner. According to one view, the sight of water on
New Year's Day is intended to recall the fact that the
world was created out of watery chaos; while another insists that the purpose of visiting flowing streams is to
observe the fish and thereby to be reminded that, in the
words of the Preacher, mankind is "as the fishes that
are caught in an evil net" (Eccles. 9:12). Yet a third
interpretation sees in the custom an allusion to the
ancient legend which relates that when Abraham was
speeding to Mount Moriah in obedience to the divine
commandment to sacrifice his son Isaac—an event which
was said to have taken place on New Year's Day—Satan
interposed a turbid stream to impede his progress. The
patriarch, however, would not be stayed, but strode
through it undaunted!

The true origin of the ceremony is probably to be
found, however, in the common custom of throwing sops
to the spirits of rivers on critical days of the year. The
Romans, for example, used to cast straw puppets into the
Tiber at the Ides of May; in European folk-usage, such

offerings are (or were) often made to Rhine, Danube, Rhone, Elbe and Neckar on New Year's Eve. The Jews would thus have adopted the custom from their Gentile neighbors, reinterpreting it in accordance with their own outlook and tradition.

DAYS OF PENITENCE

It is a common human instinct to want to begin the new year with a clean start, and from time immemorial men have had the custom of devoting a few preliminary days to a general purification and, more especially, to the performance of rites designed to remove evil and blight. Our own practice of "spring cleaning" is one survival of this usage, for in ancient times the year began in spring. Another is our word *February*, for this derives from the Latin *februatio*, the technical name for the general scouring and cleansing which took place for a full month before the beginning of the Roman year.

In Morocco, the new year month of Muharram is still marked by special restrictions; and the custom is also well attested among primitive peoples. In Cambodia, for example, the first seven days of the year are a period of solemn austerity, during which no business may be transacted, and all litigation must be suspended. Similarly, in the Malay Peninsula, special taboos are imposed for three days before the reaping of the rice crop; while the Natchez of Mississippi fast for three days, and the Mao of Manipur observe a four-day "lent" before the harvest.

There is, moreover, another factor which contributes to the idea that the days immediately preceding the new year are somehow "abnormal," and that is that among peoples who reckon time by the moon, eleven or twelve days are often inserted between one formal year and the next in order to harmonize the lunar and solar calendars. These days are naturally regarded as being "outside time," and are therefore marked by a suspension, or deliberate inversion, of normal activities. A survival of them may be seen in the European "Twelve Days" between the winter solstice (December 25) and the Old New Year (January 6), a pagan institution which was later Christianized with special reference to the alleged birthday of Jesus on the one hand and to the Feast of Epiphany on the other.

The Jewish counterpart of this usage is the ten-day period of penitence, which begins at New Year and ends on Yom Kippur. Judaism, however, has refined and spiritualized the traditional institution; for the ten days are dedicated not to outer but to inner cleansing—i.e., to the regeneration of the souls of men. They are regarded as a kind of annual "retreat," and although they do not rank as formal holy days, they are distinguished by an abstention from all pleasures and amusements and by concentrated self-scrutiny and introspection. In Jewish teaching, however, penitence is more than mere negative regret; it is positive reform. The Hebrew word so rendered means properly "return," and what is involved is an active return of the aberrant human soul to the highway of the Torah, the route mapped out by God.

Jewish tradition has its own fanciful way of expressing the significance of the Ten Days of Penitence. On New Year, it is said, God opens three books. The first contains the names of the virtuous and pious, who are inscribed forthwith for life and blessing during the ensuing twelve months. The second contains the names of the irremediably wicked and impious; these are inscribed forthwith for death and disaster. In the third, however, are written

the names of the "betwixt-and-betweens"; these are given
a chance to determine their own fates, for the record is
not sealed until twilight on Yom Kippur.

The Ten Days of Penitence are not formally prescribed in the Bible, but the institution of Yom Kippur
on the tenth of the month, and the analogy of the
primitive usages which we have already cited, would
suggest that the real agricultural new year, at the Feast of
Ingathering, was preceded, from very early times, by
such a period of austerity and purgation. Moreover, it is
not without significance that the corresponding New
Year ceremonies of the Babylonians in fact lasted for
ten days, the "visiting deities" leaving the city and
returning to their native shrines on the eleventh of the
month.

At the present day, the principal outward observance
of the period is the recital of special supplicatory psalms
and prayers every morning at dawn. These are known as
Selihoth, "prayers for forgiveness," or (less commonly)
as *Bakashoth,* "petitions." [7] The form of these services is
by no means uniform everywhere, for in every country
where Jews lived—perhaps even in every community—
the basic nucleus of quotations from Scripture was
tricked out by the poetic compositions of local virtuosi.
Some of these date back as far as the seventh century;
others are much later and allude, in their entreaties for
divine pardon, to the sufferings endured by the House

. . . . .

[7] In the Sephardic, or Spanish and Portuguese tradition, Selihoth are recited also throughout the preceding month (except on sabbaths), and the
ram's horn (*shofar*) is sounded daily. Moreover, more pious Ashkenazim,
or German-Polish Jews, commence the recital four days before New Year,
the reason being that they observe a half-day fast throughout the penitential period and wish to compensate for the fact that the law does not
permit them to fast on the two days of that festival, on the intervening
sabbath and on the day immediately preceding Yom Kippur.

of Israel at the time of the Crusades. Despite the variety of form, however, certain motifs are constant. The grace of God is always besought by virtue of His express assurance to Moses that He is a "Lord merciful and gracious . . . forgiving iniquity, transgression and sin, and ready to acquit the guilty" (Exod. 34:5-7, 9).[8] The repetition of these words, as a prelude to the formal confession of sins, is, in fact, a statutory element of the service in all of its many recensions. The words form the climax to an ancient hymn in which God is portrayed as a benevolent king ready at all times to overlook and forgive the rebelliousness of his subjects:[9]

O King, Whose throne is mercy,
    And love is all His way,
Who overlooks His people's sins
    And makes them pass away,
Who sheds His pardon freely
    On them that err and stray;
Who on all flesh and spirit
    His charity bestows,
And claims not from His subjects
    The debt which each one owes;

Lord God, Thou didst reveal to us
    Thy virtues three and ten
When that Thy servant told them o'er,[10]
    . . . . .

[8] This, by an inspired exegetical twist, is how the ancient Jewish sages interpreted the words usually rendered: ". . . and He will not by any means acquit the guilty." (It is probably correct, for the Hebrew word *lô'* rendered "not," may be regarded in this verse as a later distortion of the archaic *lū* meaning "verily, indeed.")

[9] *El Melech yosheb.* Pool, *New Year,* p. 18.

[10] The English Bible represents the "thirteen attributes" as having been declared *by God to Moses,* when He passed before him. The Hebrew text, however would permit the interpretation that *it was Moses who thus addressed the Presence;* and this view can claim added support from the fact that such ecstatic proclamations of the Divine qualities are, indeed, the

The meekest of all men.
Remember then the solemn pledge
Which in that utterance lay;
Remember then Thy holy word
Upon this holy day:

*And the LORD came down in the cloud, and stood with him
there, and he called on the name of the LORD. And the
LORD passed before him, and he cried: The LORD, the
LORD, merciful and gracious, long-suffering and abundant
in lovingkindness and truth, keeping mercy unto them of
the thousandth generation, forgiving iniquity, transgression
and sin, and ready to acquit the guilty.* [Exod. 34:5-7, 9]

An equally constant element is the listing of occasions (drawn mainly from Scripture) in which God is
said to have answered the prayers of His servants in
moments of seeming desperation. This serves at once
to remind God of the merit of Israel's forebears, and
Israel of the mercy of God. A versified version of this
litany, attributed to the illustrious Hai Gaon, head of the
academy of Pumbedita (939-1038 C.E.), is chanted by
Sephardic Jews at the beginning of the synagogal service
on the eve of Yom Kippur. Though scarcely distinguished
by poetic inspiration, it possesses especial interest as being, apparently, the earliest example of rhyme in Hebrew
literature:[11]

O hear my voice, Who hearest prayer,
Who hearest voices everywhere,
Whose works are great, Whose deeds are rare,
Unsearchable, beyond compare;
Whose wisdom and eternity
And might surpass all things that be.

---

earliest form of Semitic prayer, surviving in the familiar formula of
Islam: "God is great, God is merciful," etc.
[11] *Shema' Koli.* Pool, *Day of Atonement,* p. 23.

A God of mercy, God of grace
Benign and good, He doth efface
Our every human faltering
As it were but a trivial thing;
By Whom all things were duly wrought
The which the patriarchs had sought;
Who Joseph from the pit set free,
From charnel house to high degree;
Who heard His people's anguished cry
And rescued them from slavery;
Who split the sea, His folk to save,
And drowned their foemen in the wave;
Who answered Moses' anguished plea
By showing glories yet to be;[12]
Who, when Aaron waved incénse,
Stayed the desert pestilence;[13]
Who, when Phineas did slay[14]
The guilty, did the plague allay;
Who Joshua and Eli heard,
And Hannah and her mumbled word;[15]
Who Samuel to success did rear,
And saved the mother nigh to bear;
Saved Solomon from all alarms,
And David when he sang the psalms;
Who for Elijah sent the flame,
To put the priests of Baal to shame;
Who did not spurn Elisha's cry,[16]
Nor Hezekiah, near to die;[17]
Who answered Jonah in the main
And brought him forth to land again;
Who saved the three intrepid men,[18]
And Daniel from the lions' den;

• • • **:** •

[12] Exod. 33:12 ff.
[13] Num. 16:17 ff.
[14] Num. 25:1-8; Ps. 106:30.
[15] I Sam. 1:9 ff.
[16] II Kings 6:17 ff.
[17] Isa. 38.
[18] viz., Shadrach, Meshach and Abednego; Dan. 3:12-20.

Who answered Esther, Mordecai,
And turned their grief to revelry;[19]
Who answered Ezra, that great scribe,
And all the Maccabean tribe;
Who answered Honi with His grace
When he his magic ring did trace
And called upon His holy name,
Standing in that ring of flame;[20]
Who answers every pious prayer,
Whereso, whenso men repair;
Who answers ships upon the main,
And them that toss on beds of pain,
And them that stray through desert ground,
And them whose hands and feet are bound;
Who answers all who call and cry
And come to seek His clemency.

The lowliest of the low, I pray,
Take my every sin away;
Give me length of days to see,
Thou Who hearest every plea.
Give me all my heart's desire;
Be my prayer as altar-fire;
Be my prayer before Thine eyes
As the ancient sacrifice.

Hear my voice, Who hearest prayer,
Who hearest voices everywhere!

At the same time, though the piety of his remote
ancestors provides the Jew with a special claim upon the
consideration of God, it does not necessarily counterbalance his own and his contemporaries' obvious defec-

. . . . .

[19] Esther 9:22.
[20] Honi (Onias), known as the "circle-drawer," was a famous teacher of
the first century C.E. He was credited with having once induced God to
send rain in a time of drought, by drawing a circle, standing in the center
of it, and praying; Talmud, Ta'anith 23ᵃ.

tion from that high standard, and therefore does not eliminate the need of penitence and regeneration. As one of the most famous of the "supplications" expresses it:[21]

*A*ll they that kept the faith are passed away,
*B*y their own virtue girded for Life's fray;
*C*hampions they were that stayed the crumbling wall,
*D*iverted doom when it was nigh to fall;
*E*ncircling ramparts, when that trouble came,
*F*ortress and bastion; they allayed the flame
*G*od's wrath had kindled; for their sake the Lord
*H*eld back His anger. Though no single word
*I*ssued from out their lips, in silence they
*K*new in the language of the heart to pray.
*L*ike as a father's heart, the heart of God
*M*oved for their sake, and He withheld the rod.

*N*ow, for our sins, all these from us are ta'en;
*O*ur sins have put them from us and our stain.
*P*assed to their rest are they, but we—but we
*R*emain to bear the grief and agony.
*S*talwarts who healed the breach, repaired the wall,
*T*hey all are perished, faded are they all;
*V*anished are they whose virtue moved His grace,
*W*hile we go wandering from place to place,
*Y*et find no healing, till, with weary feet,
*Z*ealous at last His mercy to entreat,
*W*e come unto the turning of the road,
*A*nd in His house lay down our heavy load.

Sometimes the poems play dexterously upon selected verses of the psalms. Thus, in a tenth-century composition by Solomon ben Judah ha-Babli,[22] the familiar words, "The voice of the Lord cleaveth[23] flames of fire" (Ps. 29:7) are developed into the thought:

. . . . .

[21] *Anshê emūnah abadū.* Pool, *New Year,* p. 21.
[22] *Eyn mî yikra be-sedek.*
[23] Actually, we now know that the Hebrew word formerly rendered "cleav-

Thy voice, O Lord, doth cleave out tongues of flame
To purge our dross, remold our stubborn frame.

Similarly, the assurance that "With Thee is the fountain
of life; in Thy light do we see light" (Ps. 36:9) becomes
the basis of the entreaty:

Fountain of life, all life doth well from Thee;
Lighten our eyes; Lord, hearken to our plea!

Nowhere, however, has the spirit of the penitential
days found finer expression than in the verses of the celebrated medieval poet, Moses ibn Ezra (*ca.* 1070-1138),
where the soul is portrayed as a weary, overburdened
wanderer coming suddenly and unexpectedly, at this season, within view of the hostelry of God:[24]

Not in the casual caravanserai,
But where Thy doors stand open, thither, Lord,
I turn to seek my rest; when I draw nigh,
Do Thou give welcome with a kindly word.

Lo, I am bowed beneath the heavy load
Of stubbornness, and I am gone astray;
Perverseness is the guide upon the road,
And Sin it is that speeds me on my way.

A vagrant weary and forespent am I,
Whom Mischief beckons onward all the day
And drives, and lo, his promise is a lie,
For nightfall brings no rest, but new affray.

Lord, wake me from the dreams of this long night;
Wake Thou my tired spirit, and fulfill
The dream of Thy redemption. Let the light
Of morning shine from yonder clouded hill.

---

eth" (or "heweth out") really means "flashes forth," as it is indeed translated in the revised standard version.
[24] *Mi-bêth meloni.* Pool, *New Year,* pp. 58 ff.

Pious Jews fast until noon during the Days of Penitence. An exception is made, however, on the intervening sabbath and on the day immediately preceding Yom Kippur.

The intervening sabbath is known as Sabbath *Shubah.* *Shubah* is a Hebrew word meaning "return," and the name is derived from the opening of the Prophetic Lesson (Hos. 14:1-10) selected for that occasion, viz.,

Return, O Israel, until the LORD thy God;
For thou hast stumbled in thine iniquity.
Take with you words,
And return unto the LORD;
Say unto Him: "Forgive all iniquity!"

At the end of this lesson it is customary also to repeat the words of the prophet Micah (7:19-20), in which, as always in Jewish teaching, the mercy of God is portrayed as a fulfillment of His Covenantal obligations, more especially as a reward for the piety and fidelity of the ancient patriarchs:

He will again have compassion upon us
    Will tread our iniquities under foot;
Yea, Thou wilt cast all our[25] sins into the depths of the sea,
    Keeping faith with Jacob,
    Trust with Abraham,
As Thou didst pledge to our fathers
    From days of old.[26]

. . . . .

[25] The English Bible, following the traditional Hebrew text, reads *"their* sins," but this is simply a scribal error, duly corrected in all of the ancient versions.
[26] In some congregations, Joel 2:15-17 is also read, viz.: "Blow the ram's horn in Zion, proclaim a sacred fast," etc. This is taken to refer to the impending Yom Kippur.

On the day immediately preceding Yom Kippur, the rigors of the penitential period are somewhat relaxed, and the emphasis shifts perceptibly from the inward process of shriving sin to outward procedures for clearing offenses. On that day, it is a common practice among "orthodox" Jews to present themselves, after the morning service, before a duly ordained rabbi or before an impromptu court of three laymen and to recite a solemn formula abjuring all personal vows which have been made during the preceding year and which they now regret. Such abjuration in no way affects agreements contracted with another person, nor is it intended to provide an escape from serious pledges made to God. Renegation of the latter is a sin, and for the former the consent of the second party is required. The ceremony is intended only to enable the devout soul, at the end of its penitence, to present itself before God on Yom Kippur without being burdened by responsibility for non-fulfillment of such rash and intemperate vows as a man may make to himself in moments of bravado or despair. It is, in fact, part of the general process of beginning the year with a clean slate.

Jewish popular custom knows also of two more primitive methods of "clearing the slate" before Yom Kippur.

The first, which has long since been discarded in Western countries, is the ceremony known as Scourging. Ancient Jewish law prescribed that certain offenses—especially those for which no other penalty was laid down—were to be expiated by flagellation. Accordingly, it used to be the practice among pious Jews to repair to the synagogue on the day before Yom Kippur and there submit themselves to a token form of this punishment at the hands of a specially appointed official. However repugnant this custom may seem to modern tastes, it should be borne in mind that, in actual performance, it was not so much a crude punitive act as a gesture of voluntary humiliation—an essential element of penitence and atonement.

The other popular ceremony connected with the Penitential Period was that of *Kapparah,* or Ransom. This was simply an attenuated form of the scapegoat ritual prescribed in the Bible (Lev. 16) as part of the service of Yom Kippur. Before sunrise, on the preceding day, each family took a cock and a hen. After reciting appropriate Biblical verses (Ps. 107:10, 14, 17-21; Job 33:23-24), the master of the house twirled the cock three times around his head, meanwhile exclaiming, "This is in exchange for me; this is instead of me; this is as ransom for me." Each male member of the family then repeated the gesture in turn, while the women, led by the mistress of the house, did likewise with the hen. The two birds were then slaughtered and given to the poor, or sold on their behalf. The purpose of this rite was, of course, to transfer all potential evil and blight from human to animal victims. In general spirit, it may be compared with the procedure described in the Book of Leviticus (14:1-7, 53) for removing the contagion of leprosy.

Throughout the ages, this custom has been condemned by leading Jewish authorities as savoring of heathenish superstition, and it is now virtually extinct in Western countries.

8

YOM KIPPUR

The Day of Atonement

Yom Kippur, the holiest day of the Jewish year, is at the same time the most persistently misundertood of Jewish institutions. To nine out of ten Jews, it is "the Day of Atonement," and its purpose is to provide an opportunity year by year, of obtaining divine forgiveness of sin by means of appropriate penitence and prayer.

The traditional devotions of the day serve, indeed, to encourage this impression, for they are couched throughout in terms of entreaty to a celestial Judge about to pass sentence on wayward man. Favorite images are those of the suppliant hammering on the doors of heaven, and of the prisoner pleading desperately for his life.

The fact is, however, that this conventional view represents but a half-truth. The ultimate purpose of Yom

Kippur, as the Bible states expressly (Lev. 16:30), is not merely to cleanse men of sin, but to cleanse them *before the Lord*—i.c., to wipe out, year by year, "the world's slow stain," to restore them to that state of wholeness and holiness which is a condition of their fulfilling their function in the world and of serving as effective co-workers of God. The whole process of introspection, confession and atonement, the so-called "affliction of soul," with which the day has come to be identified, is, in the final analysis, simply a means to an end—the removal of an initial impediment.

Moreover, the regeneration which Yom Kippur is designed to accomplish is effected from within, not from without—by man's own effort, not by an external power. It is the inevitable result of his strenuously fanning into flame that divine spark which is always and innately within him but which usually lies smothered beneath the dust of his mortality. To put it another way, God works *within* man, not *upon* him; and the whole picture of the heavenly tribunal, with God as the presiding magistrate and man as the defendant craving His pardon, is nothing but a survival of outmoded mythology, an unfortunate, if picturesque, relic of that more primitive stage of thought wherein man was conceived as the vassal rather than the partner of God, and wherein the triumphs and defeats of his spiritual adventure were reduced to terms of rewards and punishments. Taken as poetry, this traditional imagery may be useful and convenient; taken literally, it is dangerous distortion.

For Israel, this annual process of regeneration possesses a special significance. Israel is committed by the Covenant to serve as the special steward of the Torah, the agent and exemplar of the divine dispensation in the world of men. Wholeness and holiness are condi-

tions of that commitment: "Ye shall be holy unto Me;
for I the Lord am holy, and have set you apart from the
peoples, that ye should be Mine (Lev. 20:26). Any
diminution of them—any tarnishing of the divine by the
corruption of the human—is therefore not only an
individual offense, a blot on individual character, but
also a breach of the Covenant, a positive impediment to
the discharge of its obligations. Conversely, any individual enhancement of them is at the same time a contribution to the collective endeavor.

For this reason, Yom Kippur is a public institution as
well as a private experience. The confessions which
are recited on this day are couched, significantly enough,
in the first person plural; and what is envisaged is a
purification not only of individual souls but also of the
whole House of Israel.

THE BIBLICAL RITUAL

From the historical point of view, it is the collective
character of the day that is at once its oldest and its
most important element.

The earliest account of Yom Kippur that we possess is
in the sixteenth chapter of the Book of Leviticus, where
it is said to have been instituted by Moses in connection
with the tabernacle erected in the wilderness. Although
this account seems in fact to have been written centuries
later, the ceremonies which it describes are all premised
on primitive modes of thought and therefore not improb-
ably go back to a remote antiquity.

The ritual is performed by the high priest (called
"Aaron"), and its purpose is to purify priests, laymen
and sanctuary once a year. The purification is conceived, however, in physical rather than spiritual terms,

and consists in the performance of elaborate rites designed to remove taint and contagion. The measure adopted include ablutions (vss. 4, 24, 26, 28); sacrifices (vss. 5-6, 11, 15); fumigations (vss. 12-13); aspersions of sacrificial blood (vss. 14-15, 18-19); and changes of raiment (vss. 4,23); and culminate in the dispatch into the desert of a scapegoat to whom the collective sins of the community have been previously transferred (vss. 10, 20-22).[1] The Hebrew term for such eliminatory procedures is *kippurim,* and it is from this that the day derives its name. Although, to be sure, the confession and shriving of sin bulks largely in the program, sin, at this level of thought is considered primarily as miasma, and *yôm kippurim* is thus a day of purgation rather than of *atonement.*

The general form and spirit of this ritual can be readily paralleled from other parts of the world. Perhaps the best instances come from Babylon and Japan respectively. On the fifth day of their ten-day New Year festival, the ancient Babylonians performed a rite which they called *kuppuru,* or "purgation." A ram was beheaded, and its body was rubbed against the walls of one of the main chapels of the temple, in order thereby to absorb any latent impurity. Head and trunk were then tossed into the river, the officiating priest and the slaughterer being sent into the desert or outside the city, there to observe a quarantine until the end of the celebrations. At the same time, the temple and its precincts were

. . . . .

[1] The goat is said (vss. 8, 10) to be consigned to Azazel, but the meaning of this term is unknown. According to some Jewish authorities, it is the name of a rock off which the animal was hurled; according to others, it is the name of a demon who was believed to inhabit the wilderness. The ancient versions, however, tried to explain the word from the Hebrew *ez ozel,* "goat which departs," and from this interpretation comes the conventional *scapegoat,* i.e., "escape-goat."

aspersed with holy water and fumigated; while on the following day, the king—as the vessel and steward of the communal life—was required to make confession of his sins, and a condemned criminal was paraded through the streets and beaten about the head as a human scapegoat.

The Japanese ceremony—called *Ohoharahi,* or "Great Purgation," takes place in every Shinto temple throughout the land on June 30 and December 31, the last days respectively of the two major seasons into which the year is divided. The ceremony is performed, in the name of the Mikado, by a member of the priestly clan of the *nakatomi,* and consists in a formal confession of sins (especially those committed by officials) and a symbolic banishment of them. The sins are reeled off in a lengthy catalogue and are banished by being transferred to such objects as rags, rice stalks or animal hides, which are eventually thrown into the river. Alternatively, everyone provides himself with a life-sized paper doll *(kata-shiro)* on which he writes his name and the year and month of his birth. These are rubbed against the body and breathed on, so that each penitent's personal sins may be transferred to them. At the end of the ceremony, the dolls are tied together in bundles and thrown into the streams, while the deities of mountain torrents, winds and tides, and—finally—of the nether regions are bidden to carry them away.

Nor is it only in general spirit that the Hebrew ceremony conforms to a fairly universal pattern. Its several details likewise possess abundant analogies elsewhere. Thus, the prescription that the high priest must first bathe and put on clean garments goes back to the primitive notion that moral impurity takes a physical form and attaches both to the person and to the clothing. In Peru, for example, penitents had, after confession, at once to don fresh raiment, and the same practice still obtains in the Brahman ceremony of *avabhrta* which concludes the annual expiatory rite known as *varunapraghasa*. Similarly, in the Orientalizing cults of the late Roman Empire, penitents used to immerse themselves in the waters of the Tiber; in Mexico, adulteresses are often obliged to change their clothes after making confession.

The use of fumigation as a means of purging impurity likewise reflects common primitive usage and likewise goes back to the idea that moral defection implies physical uncleanness. In India, newborn children are often fumigated from the impurities of that other world whence they have come into this, and in the Avesta —the scripture of the ancient Iranians—it is prescribed that the house of a dead person must be similarly treated in order to remove the miasma of death. In the same way, too, the Greeks used to fumigate their dwellings as a means of keeping off witches; and in the apocryphal Book of Tobit (8:3) the archdemon Ashmedai is driven away by smoke.

Common is also the rite of sprinkling blood, though its precise significance is disputed. According to some scholars, the purpose was *negative*, viz., to remove "bad blood," and in support of this view it is pointed out that "blood-letting" as a means of releasing impurity is indeed common among many primitive peoples, e.g., the Bechuana of Central Africa, the Yuchis of South America, the Aztecs of Mexico, and various tribes in China, Peru, Nicaragua and Guatemala. Other scholars contend, however, that the purpose of the rite was *positive*, viz., symbolically to infuse "new blood" into that which had become tainted and impaired. Whichever of the two interpretations we adopt, it is plain that this element of the ceremony reflects a primitive usage which was indeed

already little more than a survival at the time when our
account was written.

As for the public confession of sins a few examples
will suffice. In ancient Peru, each of the major agricultural festivals was preceded by a public recital of misdeeds committed by members of the community; and the
same procedure is still observed, once a year, by the
Kagaba of Sierra Nevada, the Orondanza (an Iroquois
tribe), the Bechuana, the Ojibwa of Lake Superior, and
by several other North American Indians. In most cases,
the confession is recited by the headman or chief priest
on behalf of the assembled people.

The practice of transferring sin or evil to a scapegoat
is world-wide, and the discussion of it fills a bulky
volume of Sir James Frazer's *The Golden Bough*. We
may therefore content ourselves with but two representa-
tive examples, the one ancient and the other modern.
At the ancient Greek festival of Thargelia, held in May,
two human scapegoats were ceremonially scourged out
of the city—a misshapen man or condemned felon for
the male, and a deformed woman for the female population; while among the Garos of Assam, a goat and
monkey (or bamboo rat) are sacrificed annually as vi-
carious bearers of sin and evil, in order to insure prosperity for the coming year.

Sometimes, too, this rite is performed not at a fixed
season of the year but at an occasional moment of crisis,
when the continuance of life or fortune seems to be
threatened by some conscious or unconscious infringe-
ment of the moral order. Thus, it is customary among
Malagasy whalers to observe an eight-day period of purification and to confess their sins to one another before
embarking on a fishing expedition. Among the Caffres
of South Africa, whenever a man is critically ill, it is the

practice to take a goat, confess over it the sins of the entire kraal and then turn it loose on the veldt. Similarly, when calamity strikes the Dinkas of the White Nile, they load the evil upon a sacred cow and drive it across the river.

The essential thing about all these ceremonies is that they are designed not for the benefit of individuals but of society and, indeed, of mankind in general. Their object is not to regenerate the souls of transgressors but to repair the harm which their transgressions inflict upon the commonweal. They are orientated from the standpoint not of the sinner but of that which is sinned against, not of the offender but of the offended; and that is why they are public, communal procedures rather than mere private personal experiences.

The customary confession of sins, for example, is not an act of individual atonement but an element in the process of collective purgation; it is simply an inventory of the several taints and impurities of which the community has to be disencumbered.

It is in this way, too, that the rite of the scapegoat is really to be understood. Unfortunately, the term has been greatly abused in recent years—especially by publicists and political propagandists—and the belief has grown up that a scapegoat is simply someone whom you blame for your own mistakes and who is made to bear the burden of them. This, however, distorts the whole meaning of the institution. The essential point about the scapegoat is that it removes from the community the taint and impurity of sins *which have first to be openly and fully confessed*. There is no question of transferring to it either blame or responsibility; the sole issue is how to get rid of the miasma of transgressions which one freely acknowledges. In the case of private individuals, this can be accomplished by a process of personal contrition, repentance and regeneration, but in that of a community the problem is far more complex, for there can be no assurance that every single person will indeed undergo that process; latent impurity may therefore remain, and the taint of one affects all. There is thus only one method of securing clearance, namely, to pronounce a *comprehensive,* blanket confession of sins and to saddle the *comprehensive* taint upon some person, animal or object which will be forcibly expelled and thereby take it away. This and this alone is the real purpose of the rite.

Nor is it only for the benefit of man that these periodic rites are performed. In primitive thought, the actions of men very largely determine the course of nature. If, by their remissness or misconduct, they impair the harmony or upset the equilibrium of the universe, the sun will not recover its strength after the winter, the rains will not fall in due season, there will be no increase of crops or cattle, and eventually the whole of creation will go to rack and ruin. Accordingly, the removal of impurity, the clearance of sin, and what we may call the "rehabilitation of impaired holiness" are regarded as necessary conditions for the maintenance and continuance of the world order, and it is equally in this spirit and conviction that they are periodically undertaken.

On a purely literal level of interpretation, one might say that these rites are simply a form of communal "spring cleaning" or, at best, a means of removing the consequences of breaking taboos. But such interpretations, though all too common, merely scratch the surface; they describe rather than explain. What is really involved, what conditions the taboos in the first place, is the deeper sense that where holiness is sullied, there, too, is life itself impaired, and that no continuance can be expected unless and until the taint is removed. Behind these periodic ceremonies of purgation and elimination there lies a consciousness—as Gilbert Murray has expressed it—that "man, though he desperately needs bread, does not live by bread alone, but longs for a new life, a new age . . . not stained by the deaths and impurities of the past."

Into the ancient, time-honored ceremony Israel read a new meaning. The essential thing about it became the fact that it had to be performed "in the presence of the Lord." This means that it was no longer a mere mechanical act of purgation, a mere riddance and dispatch of impurity. The people had now to be cleansed not for themselves but for their God: *before Jehovah shall ye be clean* (Lev. 16:30). Sin and corruption were now regarded as impediments not merely to their material welfare and prosperity but to the fulfillment of their duty to God and of their obligations under the Covenant. If the dispatch of the scapegoat could serve to expel the actual contagion, it had still to be supplemented by an act of expiation before Jehovah; a sin-offering, too, had to be presented.

Moreover, the waving of frankincense, which had originally been but a means of fumigation, was now interpreted as designed to interpose a smoke screen between the glory of God, hidden behind the Veil, and the mortality of the high priest: "He shall place the incense, in addition to the fire, before Jehovah, that the cloud of the incense may cover the veil which is upon the (ark of) the testimony, and that he may not die" (Lev. 16:13).

Translated into broad terms, what the Israelite transformation affirmed was that impairment of holiness not

only impeded the prosperity of men but also inflicted
injury upon God. For to the extent that a man was
tainted and sullied, he lost his effectiveness as an instrument of, and partner in, the divine plan. Accordingly,
when once impurity had been introduced either into a
human being or into anything dedicated to the service of
God, more was necessary than a mere removal of it;
something had also to be done to make restitution to God,
or, at least, to repair the damaged relationship with Him.
Not only *ex*piation but also *pro*pitiation was now required; not only the scapegoat but also the sin-offering.

This conception revolutionized the entire approach to
evil. For loss of holiness, or moral turpitude, was now
no longer a matter of mere personal and communal degeneration nor was its consequence mere personal misfortune; it was *a crime against the Kingdom of God,* and
the expiation of it therefore involved atonement as well
as purgation. The dominant motif now changed perceptibly from mere disinfection and decontamination to
reconciliation and truce with God. The entire frame of
reference was enlarged. What was now sought through
the traditional rite was not only clearance but also *forgiveness;* evil was something which had to be shriven as
well as repaired, and repentance became not only a
process of inner rehabilitation but also a positive "return" to the service of God.

Nor this alone. The Israelite development of the
ancient ritual also brought home another important and
universal truth. Even the high priest, for all his elaborate
purifications and for all his entry, this once in the year,
into the very holy of holies itself, could not behold the
full glory of God, which remained hidden behind a
cloud of smoke. What is here affirmed, albeit in primitive terms, is that the attainment of holiness can be, at

best, but partial, and that, given the limitations of human existence, the religious quest can never actually reach its goal, its value and validity lying in the search itself. The religious adventure consists essentially in a continuous effort *to reach beyond,* but the making of this effort, far from being futile, itself expands the nature of man to its maximum extent. Moreover—and this is supremely significant—the cloud which is finally interposed between the glory of God and the mortality of man is not the dense, black smoke of the mundane but the thin vapor which issues from two handfuls of incense and from a few coals taken off the altar itself.

THE TEMPLE RITUAL

So long as the Temple stood in Jerusalem, the Day of Atonement was mainly a temple celebration. The manner of its observance during the time of the Second Temple is described in detail in a special treatise of the Mishnah, entitled *Yômâ,* or "The Day."

Particular care was taken to insure that the high priest would not incur impurity during the preceding night, thus rendering himself unfit to perform the ceremony. He was kept awake by Scriptural readings and expositions, and whenever he seemed inclined to doze, younger members of the priesthood would crack their finger joints beside him or force him to pace up and down on the cold stone.

The ceremony of dispatching the scapegoat was carried out in particularly picturesque fashion. As soon as the lots had been cast, the goat which fell to Azazel was marked by a crimson thread tied around its head. The task of leading it away was assigned to a member of the priesthood on the grounds that, however disagreeable it might be, this was still a sacred office and should therefore not be delegated to a layman. A special causeway was constructed for the purpose, in order to prevent the heathen from laying hold on the animal and trying to use it for the expiation of *their* sins. The goat was taken to a ravine some twelve miles outside of Jerusalem, the journey being divided into ten stages, each but the last marked by a booth. For the first nine stages the officiant was accompanied by dignitaries of the city, but from that point on he had to travel alone. When he reached the edge of the ravine, he divided the crimson thread, tying one part of it to the rock and the other between the horns of the goat. Then he pushed the animal from behind till it went rolling down, "and," says the Mishnah, "ere it reached half-way, it was broken to pieces." The officiant then returned to the last booth and remained there in quarantine until nightfall, the successful conclusion of the ceremony being indicated to the high priest in the Temple by the waving of towels from easily visible lookout posts.

An equally important feature of the ceremonies was the recital of the Confession. A prescribed formula was used. When he offered the sin-offering for the priestly household, the high priest pressed his hands upon it and proclaimed: "O God, I have committed iniquity, transgressed and sinned before Thee, I and my household. O God, forgive the iniquities and transgressions and sins which I have committed and transgressed and sinned before Thee, I and my household, even as it is written in the Law of Thy servant Moses: 'For on this day shall he make atonement for you, to cleanse you of all your sins; ye shall be clean before Jehovah'" (Lev. 16:30). The same formula was likewise repeated over the scapegoat except, of course, that the guilty persons were then identified as the entire House of Israel. In each case, when he came to the final word of the Scriptural quotation, the high priest pronounced it as it was written, instead of substituting for it the usual reverential paraphrase "the Lord" *(Adonai)*. This utterance of the otherwise ineffable name was, in a sense, the high point of the entire service. "When," says the Mishnah, "the priests and the people who were standing in the courtyard heard the Ineffable Name issuing from the mouth of the high priest in purity and holiness, they bowed and prostrated themselves and fell upon their faces and said: Blessed be the name of Him whose glorious majesty endures for ever!"

But there was also, curiously enough, a gayer side to the Day of Atonement. On that day, the Mishnah tells us,[2] it was customary for the girls of Jerusalem to dress up in spotless white finery and to go out and dance in the vineyards in order to attract suitors. As the young men gathered around them, they would raise their voices and chant: "Lift your eyes, pick your prize;/ Care for race, and not for face!" and they would quote the Scriptures (Prov. 31:30) to prove that, since "charm is deceitful and beauty vain," it is inner virtue, and not outward grace, that should count in choosing a bride!

This ceremony, so utterly incongruous with the general spirit of penitence and austerity, is probably to be explained as a survival in popular usage of the common primitive practice of mass-mating around the time of harvest. The idea behind this practice is that such mating promotes the fertility of mankind and even the fecundity of the earth at that annual moment of crisis when the collective life of the community and of the

. . . . .

[2] *Ta'anith* IV, 8.

world seems to hang in the balance. Thus—to cite but
a few instances—among the Hereros of German Southwest Africa and among various Bantu tribes, mass-mating
and sexual promiscuity are obligatory at specific seasons of the year; and the Garos of Assam encourage men
and women to consort together at certain major agricultural festivals. Similarly, in some parts of the Ukraine,
couples copulate openly in the fields on St. George's
Day (April 23) in order to promote the growth of the
crops; and at Arçal and Santo Tirso in Portugal they
perform the rite of *rebolada* or "rolling together" before the reaping of the flax in May. The familiar Classical legend of the rape of the Sabine women probably
reflects this usage, for the incident is said to have taken
place at a festival (possibly the Consualia) in August;
and such may also be the basis of the Biblical tale (Judg.
21:16-23) relating how the men of Benjamin carried
off the women of Shiloh on the occasion of a seasonal
celebration.

There are many attenuated survivals of this custom in
European and Oriental folklore. In certain parts of England, for instance, girls may be lifted up and kissed with
impunity on May 15; and at Hungerford, in Berkshire,
the second Thursday after Easter is "hocking day" when
the "tutti-men" go about the streets lifting up or "hocking" (cf. German *hoch,* "high") the women and exact-
ing a kiss from each. A more usual form of attenuation,
however, is the belief that certain days are auspicious
for selecting husbands or wives. Thus, in some parts of
England, St. Roch's Day (August 16) is especially favored for this purpose, while elsewhere St. Luke's Day
(October 18) is similarly regarded. In the same way, too,
it is the custom in Spanish Galicia for girls to repair
at harvest time to a duly selected barn, where their ar-

dent swains attend upon them; while among the Thompson River Indians of British Columbia, husbands and wives are chosen at a seasonal festival held in the so-called "spring house." It is such an attenuated form of the primitive institution that is to be recognized, in all likelihood, in the usage mentioned in the Mishnah.

THE SYNAGOGUE SERVICES

When the Temple was destroyed in 70 C.E., and sacrifices came to an end, the traditional Day of Purgation necessarily underwent a profound change. The taint and corruption which were anciently removed, from year to year, by the almost mechanical ritual of the scapegoat and the sin-offering, had now to be purged by a process of personal catharsis, involving the successive stages of contrition, confession, reform and absolution. At the same time, the *collective* character of the institution remained paramount. When the community declared in the statutory confessions of the day, "we have robbed, we have slandered, we have committed adultery," it was their collective conscience that was speaking, and what they were acknowledging were not merely individual misdeeds, but collective defilement of their character as an "holy nation and a kingdom of priests."

In this there was no inconsistency, for Israel never elevated the collective to the status of an independent, transcendental entity. It was but the aggregate of individuals. The taint which had to be removed might be one that infected the entire community, but it was entailed and occasioned by individual misdeeds and could be removed only by individual regeneration. This conception has endured to the present day. The Jew who attends the synagogal services on Yom Kippur is not

merely attending a public exercise but actively participat-
ing in a collective effort; and it is upon such individual
participation that the success of the collective enterprise
depends.

The Day of Atonement is described in the Bible as "a
sabbath of sabbaths" (Lev. 16:31). It is marked by a
rigorous fast—an interpretation of the Biblical command
to "afflict your souls" (ibid.)—and by abstention from
all work and normal occupations from sunset to sunset.
The fast may be broken, and the abstention from work
infringed, only in case of serious illness or where life is
imperilled. The preceding evening and the whole of the
day are devoted to religious services in the synagogue,
and more pious Jews even spend the intervening night
reciting psalms, engaging in meditation, or studying the
treatise of the Talmud relating to the holy day.

In most communities—though, curiously enough, not
in Jerusalem—the prayer-shawl (tallith), which is normally worn only in the morning, is also worn at the
afternoon and evening devotions, and it is a common
custom for the rabbi, cantor and married men of the
congregation to don the long white robe of purity (kittel) which eventually serves also as their shroud. The
latter may not be embellished with any form of orna-
ment, especially not with a golden neckband, for this
would recall the idolatry of the Golden Calf. It is likewise customary to cloak the scrolls of the Law in white
mantles, to deck with a white curtain the "ark" or closet
in which they are contained, and to spread white cloths
over the cantor's reading desk and the pulpit. For this
reason the day is sometimes known as "the White Fast,"
in contrast with "the Black Fast" of the Ninth of Ab,
when the synagogue is draped in mourning.

Pious Jews remove their shoes, or wear felt slippers,

and remain standing from the beginning until the end of the services.

Throughout the day, the ark of the Law is kept open and the cantor is flanked by two honorary assistants *(seganim)* ready to lead the prayers, should he fall sick or falter.

The devotions begin, a few minutes before sunset, with a solemn declaration pronounced from the rostrum by the rabbi and two of the more learned members of the congregation, each holding a scroll of the Law in his arms and each covering his head with the prayer-shawl. Constituting themselves an *ad hoc* rabbinical tribunal, they announce that "with the consent of the Court on High and with the consent of the court below, with the knowledge of God and with the knowledge of the congregation, we declare it permissible to pray alongside of transgressors." The formula is repeated three times, the three men uttering it in unison. Its purpose is to invite even the most recalcitrant Jew to return to the fold on this sacred day and at the same time to absolve his brethren from the normal duty of keeping him at arm's length. It is believed to have originated at the time of the Spanish Inquisition, and to have been designed to permit forced converts to rejoin their brethren, albeit clandestinely, on this sacred day.

All but one of the scrolls of the Law are then removed from the ark (for the ark may never be left entirely empty) and carried in procession to the rostrum. When they are all assembled, the cantor begins the service proper with the chanting, to a traditional South German melody of the sixteenth century, of an Aramaic formula called from its opening words *Kol Nidrei* ("All vows"). This is simply a more elaborate form of the abjuration made during the preceding afternoon (see

above, p. 133). It has come down to us in two versions.
The older version, adopted by the Sephardim, is *retro-active*, referring to all vows contracted from the previous
to the present Day of Atonement; the more modern,
adopted by the Ashkenazim, is *prospective*, referring to
all vows which may be contracted between the present
Day of Atonement and the next. The formula is recited
three times: first, in a whisper; then in a somewhat
louder voice, and finally, in clear, resonant tones, symbolizing the initial trepidation and gradually developing
confidence of the suppliant who approaches the throne
of God. The recitation must begin while the sun is still
on the horizon, and must be timed to end when it has
finally sunk.

The formal abjuration of vows *(Kol Nidrei)* appears
to have originated in the Orient at some time between the
sixth and tenth centuries, but the recital of it was con-
sistently opposed by the highest rabbinic authorities and
was not permitted in the seats of the leading academies
on the grounds that it might encourage the charge that
Jews forswear their obligations in advance or subsequently revoke them. Because anti-Semites have indeed used it to bolster such an accusation, the recital of
it has now been discontinued by modern Reform congregations. At the same time, those who defend the custom have repeatedly pointed out that the formula refers
only to vows *which have been forgotten,* since, according to the express statement of the Mishnah, those which
are indeed remembered cannot be annulled even by
the Day of Atonement but, once made, must be faith-
fully fulfilled.

When the scrolls have been returned to the ark, the
regular evening service begins. In this case, however, it
is expanded by the inclusion of special penitential prayers

(*Selihoth,* see above, p. 125) and by the recital, first privately and then publicly, of the great confession of sins.

The Confession *(Viddui)* is the primary feature of the Atonement liturgy, and is included in each of the services of the day. It consists in an alphabetical catalogue of sins coupled with prayers for pardon. The Confession is essentially *collective,* and is couched throughout in the first person plural, e.g. "*We* have trespassed, *we* have erred," etc.

There are two forms. The one, known as "the Minor Confession" *(Viddui ze'irâ),* contains, as a rule, but one Hebrew word for each letter of the alphabet, e.g., we have *a*ggressed, *b*etrayed, *c*heated, *d*efamed, *e*rred ... *i*ntrigued, *l*ied, *m*ocked, etc. It is first recited silently, then repeated aloud and in concert; and it is customary to cover the head with the prayer-shawl and to beat the breast as each of the sins is named.

The other form, called "the Major Confession" *(Viddui rabbâ),* contains *two* complete sentences for each letter of the alphabet. Each sentence is introduced by the phrase: "For the sin which we have sinned in Thy presence," and the whole is punctuated at regular intervals by the refrain:

For all of these, O Thou forgiving God,
Pardon us, and shrive us, and forgive!

The scheme may be best conveyed by the following excerpts:

> *For the sins which we have sinned in Thy presence*
> through *b*lindness of judgment,   through *b*lasphemy of tongue;
> through carnal *c*oncupiscence,   *c*landestinely or *c*learly;

*d*esignedly, *d*eliberately,   through open *d*eclaration;
through *e*xploitation of others;   through *e*ncitement of lust;

    •   •   •   •   •   •   •   •

through *i*mpurity of mouth,   through *i*ncontinence of speech;
*k*nowingly, unknowingly,   through *k*neeling to base instinct;
through *l*ying and deceiving;   through *l*aying hands on bribes;
through *m*ockery and *m*alison;   through *m*alice and *m*alevolence;

    •   •   •   •   •   •   •   •

through *v*enomous *v*endettas,   through *v*oiding *v*ows . . .
For all of these, O thou forgiving God,
Pardon us, and shrive us, and forgive!

This catalogue is followed in turn by a further listing
of sins according to the traditionally prescribed punishments, e.g., presentation of a guilt-offering, burnt-offer-
ing, or sin-offering; submission to forty stripes; extirpation; extirpation and death; death from God; and death
at the hands of an earthly tribunal. The key to this list
is to be found in the Law of Moses and in two special
treatises of the Talmud dealing respectively with the
penalty of stripes (Makkoth) and of extirpation (Kerit-
oth). Thus, according to Leviticus 19:21, a guilt-offering is due in certain cases of rape, and, according to
Numbers 6:12, when a nazirite breaks his vow and
partakes of strong drink. Similarly, according to the
Mishnah, forty stripes are prescribed for such crimes as
incest, sacrilege, entering the temple in a state of impurity, eating leavened food on Passover, working on
the Day of Atonement, and tattooing upon one's person
the symbol of a heathen god; while extirpation is decreed
for gross immorality (Lev. 18:29), use of force (Num.
15:30), dedicating one's seed to Moloch (Lev. 20:5),
practicing sorcery (Lev. 20:6), desecrating the sabbath (Exod. 31:14), and neglecting the duty of circumcision (Gen. 17:14).

Of special interest is the comprehensive reference to

sins committed "knowingly or unknowingly," for this formula is characteristic of liturgical confessions everywhere. Thus, in the penitential psalms of the ancient Babylonians, the suppliant not infrequently asks pardon for "the sin which I know and the sin which I know not"; while in one of the hymns of the ancient Indic Rig Veda, the god Varuna is entreated to "cancel all those sins which we have committed as if in jest, knowingly and unknowingly," and similar expressions occur both in Greek inscriptions from Asia Minor and in the *norito* or formal recitation which accompanies the Japanese expiation ceremony of Ohoharahi.

Ashkenazic Jews recite the entire list of offenses literally from *A* to *Z*. The Sephardim, however, reduce it to a few sentences, not even arranged alphabetically; and it would seem that there was also an ancient version consisting of but *eight* verses.

Neither the Minor nor the Major Confession is attested before the Gaonic Age, which began in the seventh century C.E., but there is reason to believe that they were in fact composed during the preceding epoch of the Amoraim (fifth century). Even then, however, they hark back to a more remote antiquity, for we have protoypes of them in the Bible. Isaiah 59:12 ff., for example, is probably to be read as a quotation from a liturgical catalogue of sins ·

Our transgressions abounded before Thee,
    and our sins bore witness against us.
Verily, our transgressions were ever with us,
    and as for our iniquities—they were our familiars:
transgression and deception against Jehovah,
    backsliding from our God,
giving utterance to oppression and rebellion;

conceiving and emitting from our hearts
    words of falsehood.

    Similarly, the afflicted Job, protesting his innocence
before God, recites a kind of "negative confession" (Job
31) which would appear to reproduce (with poetic elaboration) a contemporary ritual formula:

I made a covenant with mine eyes
    that I would not think upon a virgin.

. . . .

I have not consorted with vanity,
    neither hath my foot hasted to deceit.

. . . .

My step hath not swerved from the path,
    nor my heart followed mine eyes,
    nor corruption clung to my palms.

. . . .

I have not been enticed by a woman,
    nor lain in wait at my neighbor's door.

. . . .

I have not refused justice to my servant
    nor to my handmaid, when they contended with me.

. . . .

I have not withheld the poor from their need,
    nor beclouded the eyes of the widow.

. . . .

I have seen no wanderer without clothing,
    no beggar without covering,
but that his loins have blessed me,
    and he hath been warmed with the fleece of my sheep.

. . . .

I have not looked on the sun when it shone,
    or the moon walking in brightness,
and allowed my heart to be secretly enticed
    to blow kisses thereto,
and thereby commit a penal sin
    by denying the God Who is above.

. . . .

No stranger was left to sleep the night outdoors;
  I opened my doors to the traveller.

Such "negative confessions," it may be added, appear to
have been well known in the Near East from earliest
times. Egyptian texts dating back as far as the sixteenth
century B.C.E. contain a form of protestation believed to
have been uttered by the deceased before the tribunal
of the netherworld, and the offenses of which he claims
to be innocent are, in many cases, precisely those specified in the *Viddui*. e.g., "I have not blasphemed . . .
injured . . . stolen . . . caused perversity . . . lied . . .
trespassed . . . practised usury . . . spoken scandal . . .
lusted."

Modern worshipers often find the whole conception
of punishment underlying the Confession somewhat
crude and distasteful. Thus, the prescription of "forty
stripes" for immorality or for working on the Day of
Atonement seems at once futile and barbarous, while
extirpation for sorcery or, in fact, for many of the offenses listed, appears, to say the least, unnecessarily
harsh and drastic. It must be remembered, therefore,
that in the primitive mind those things tend to be represented in *concrete* form which, in more advanced civilizations, can be apprehended as abstracts. The flaying
of conscience assumes the form of a physical, corporal
castigation; while the sense of separation and ostracism
which accompanies (or follows) any violation of common custom or accepted mores is represented by legal
and physical extirpation. In historical perspective, therefore, the drastic penalties imposed in ancient Hebrew
law are merely a more primitive and more concrete expression of what to us are but the *psychological* consequences of sin. Once again, it is only the formulation
that is primitive, not the underlying concept.

The Kol Nidrei service is, as it were, the first movement of a devotional symphony which increases in mo-
mentum from minute to minute throughout the day. The
dominant note of this service is one of nervous trepidation, tempered by confidence in the mercy and understanding of God, i.e. (in modern terms), in the inevi-
tability of evoking the Divine, once a sincere effort is
made. This twofold mood is reflected especially in the
special poems *(piyyutim)* interspersed throughout the
regular prayers and usually chanted to haunting traditional melodies. The note of hesitant approach, for example, is sounded, as if in a tremulous whisper, in the
medieval and anonymous *Ya'aleh,* which is recited antiph-
onally by cantor and congregation in the Ashkenazic
rituals. In the original, this is an alphabetical acrostic,
but its spirit may be best conveyed in the late Nina
Salaman's famous rendering, which forgoes this literary
virtuosity for the sake of inner intensity:[3]

O let our prayer ascend from eventime,
    And may our cry come in to Thee from dawn,
And let our song be clear till eventime.

O let our voice ascend from eventime,
    And may our merit come to Thee from dawn,
And our redemption be at eventime.

Let our remembrance rise from eventime,
    Let our assembly plead to Thee from dawn,
In glory visible till eventime.

Thus at Thy door we knock from eventime,
    O let our joy come forth for us from dawn,
And may our quest appear till eventime.

   . . . . .

[3] Adler-Davis, *Atonement,* i, 31.

More resonant, on the other hand, is the demand for forgiveness—(in modern terms) for the power of inner regeneration—in the famous poem, *Omnam Ken*, composed by Jacob of Orleans, one of the martyrs of the riot at York which followed the accession of Richard Coeur de Lion to the throne of England in 1189. The following is an excerpt from Israel Zangwill's celebrated rendering:

A y, 'tis thus	Evil us	hath in bond;
B y Thy grace	guilt efface	and respond,
		"Forgiven!"
C ast scorn o'er	and abhor	th' informer's word;
D ear God, deign	this refrain	to make heard,
		"Forgiven!"

. . . .

R aise to Thee	this my plea,	take my prayer;
S in unmake	for Thy sake	and declare,
		"Forgiven!"
T ears, regret,	witness set	in sin's place;
U plift trust	from the dust	to Thy face—
		"Forgiven!"
V oice that sighs,	tear-filled eyes,	do not spurn
W eigh and pause,	plead my cause,	and return—
		"Forgiven!"

By the time the morning service comes around the worshiper has already begun to feel the stirrings of the Divine working within him. But he has not yet reached that point in the process of atonement where he can feel confident of its outcome. He has attained only to a sense of wonderment and gratitude that the Divine is, after all, so readily accessible—that there is, in the final analysis, no real contrast between the cosmic power that animates the universe and the indwelling spirit which

informs his own being. In the more primitive language of
ancient thought, what strikes him most forcibly at this
stage of his atonement is the discovery that God is enthroned not only in heaven but also in the human heart.
As a well-known tenth-century hymn expresses it:[4]

Where *A*ngels through the *A*zure fly,
Where *B*eams of light illume the sky,
Where rides *C*elestial *C*avalry,
Where *D*im, *E*thereal voices cry,
  Is seen the wonder of Thy ways.
  Yet dost Thou not disdain the praise

Of *F*lesh and blood who eager throng
About Thy *G*ates and, all day long,
*H*apless raise their plaintive song,
*I*nvoking Thee to right their wrong;
  And this Thy glory is.

Where, in the clear and cloudless height,
*J*ostle the cherub hosts, and bright
Flaming *L*egions pierce the night,
'Mid all the *M*inisters of light,
  Is seen the wonder of Thy ways.
  Yet dost Thou not disdain the praise.

Of them who, in the here below,
Do *N*aught of bliss and comfort know,
Who, *O*verwhelmed with grief and woe,
Tread their *P*etty *P*ace and slow;
  And this Thy glory is.

Where *Q*uires celestial at Thy side,
And *R*egiments of grace abide,
Where the great Bond of Souls is tied,
And all the *T*hund'rous cohorts ride,

 . . . . .

[4] *Asher Omez Tehillateka,* by Meshullam b. Kalonymos (d. 970). Adler-
Davis, *Atonement,* ii, 68.

Is seen the wonder of Thy ways.
Yet dost Thou not disdain the praise

Of them who, *U*nredeemèd, late
And early in their *V*igil wait,
*W*atching at the heavenly gate,
*Y*earning that Thou wilt mark their fate,
   Zealous that thou wilt purge the stain,
   And take them back to Thee again.
      And this Thy glory is.

The worshiper now feels that he can attest by his own present experience the truth of what is said in Scripture about the inherent compassion and condescension of God:[5]

A ll justice holds He in His open hands,
   And all avow that constant He remains.
B eyond all veils He sees, and understands;
   And all avow: He probes the heart and reins.

C lamorous Death through Him gives up its prize;
   And all avow: no champion is as He.
D wellers on earth are judged before His eyes;
   And all avow: His rule is equity.

E rstwhile "I AM that which I AM," He said;
   And all avow: He was, is, and will be,
F or His renown is as His name widespread;
   And all avow that nonpareil is He.

G od thinks on them who think on Him alway;
   And all avow: He keeps His promise true.
H e portions life unto the living; they
   Avow that He doth live the ages through.

I n His wide covert good and bad find room;
   And all avow: His good on all is thrust.

   • • • • •

[5] *Ha-ohez be-yad middath mishpat.* Adler-Davis, *Atonement,* ii, 152.

K nitting our substance in the very womb;
  Yea, all avow: He knows we are but dust.

L ong is His arm and doth all things embrace;
  And all avow: by Him all things are done.
'*M* id darkness dwells He, in His secret place;
  And all avow: He one is and alone.

N o king there is but He doth him install;
  And all avow: He is the world's great King.
O mnipotent, He rules the ages all;
  And all avow: from Him doth mercy spring.

P atient, from froward man He turns His gaze;
  And all avow: He pardons and He spares.
R emote on high, He guards His servants' ways;
  And all avow: He answers whisper'd prayers.

S inners ne'er beat in vain upon His door;
  And all avow: nor is His hand clos'd tight.
T he wicked seeks He out, says: Sin no more;
  And all avow that He is just and right.

U mbrage with Him comes slow, compassion fast;
  And all avow: He is not soon enrag'd.
V engeance and *W* rath by Mercy are outpass'd;
  And all avow: He swiftly is assuag'd.

Y oung and old by Him are levellèd,
  And great and small are equal in His sight;
One net of judgment over all is spread;
  And all avow that He doth judge aright.

Z ealous is He for blamelessness, and they
  That blameless are do reap His rich reward;
And all with one consent avow and say:
  Blameless in all He doeth is the LORD.

At the same time, he is supremely conscious of the
fact that, however accessible the Divine may be, man

has to make active contact with it in order to achieve regeneration; atonement, as a modern rabbi has expressed it, is at root at-one-ment. The classic formulation of this yearning for communion is the great poem of Jehudah Ha-Levi (1086-1145) which forms one of the most prominent elements of the Sephardic morning service:

Before Thee, Lord, my every wish is known,
Ere that one word upon my lips do lie;
Lord, grant me but one moment of Thy grace,
One moment only, and I gladly die.

One moment, Lord, if Thou wouldst but accord,
Gladly would I commit into Thy keep
All that may yet remain of this frail breath;
And I would sleep, and sweet would be my sleep.

When I am far from Thee, my life is death;
My death were life, if I to Thee might cling;
Yet lo, I know not wherewith I might come
Into Thy presence, nor what service bring.

Teach me, O Lord, Thy ways, and grant release
From Folly's prison and her heavy bond;
Show me to bow my soul, while yet I may,
And when I bow it, spurn to respond,

Now, e'er the day come when unto myself
A burden am I, and my head bends low,
And age and slow corruption take their toll,
And I grow weary, and my feet are slow;

Ere that I go where erst my fathers went,
And reach the final goal, which is the tomb—
A stranger and a sojourner on earth,
Whose only portion is her ample womb.

. . . . .

⁶ *Adonai negdeka kol ta'avathi.* Pool, *Atonement*, p. 128.

My youth hath all in wantonness been spent,
And ne'er have I prepared for my long home;
The world was too much with me, veil'd my sight,
That ne'er I thought upon the world to come.

How now can I my Maker serve, when I
Serve this dull clay, and am the thrall of lust?
How seek the lofty height, who yet may lie
Tomorn a-mouldering in the silent dust?

How can my heart respond to present joy,
Which knows not if the morning will be bright,
When day conspires with day but to destroy
And but to ruin night conspires with night?

My dust shall yet be wafted on the winds,
My flesh into the common earth descend;
What shall I say, who am pursued by lust
From life's first dawning to her bitter end?

What profit lies in time or length of days,
An they be empty of Thy grace? What thing
Have I for guerdon, if I have not Thee?
Naked I am; Thou art my covering.

Yet wherefore words, which are but words alone?
Before Thee, Lord, my every wish is known.

The Scriptural readings in the morning service offer
an inspired blend of the ritual and spiritual aspects of
the day. The Lessons from the Law are taken from Leviticus 16 and Numbers 29:7-11 and describe respectively
the ancient ceremonial of "purgation" *(kippurim)* and
the special sacrifices appointed for the occasion. The Lesson from the Prophets, on the other hand, is taken from
Isaiah 57:14–58:14 and represents, in striking fashion,
the sublimation of the traditional rite through the progress of Jewish thought.

Is such the fast that I have chosen?
The day for a man to afflict his soul?
Is it to bow down his head as a bulrush,
And to spread sackcloth and ashes under him?
Wilt thou call *this* a fast,
And a day acceptable unto the Lord?

Is not this the fast that I have chosen?
To loosen the fetters of wickedness,
To undo the bands of the yoke,
And to let the oppressed go free.
And that ye break every yoke?
Is it not to deal thy bread to the hungry
And that thou bring the outcast poor to thy house?
When thou seest the naked, that thou cover him,
And that thou had not thyself from thine flesh?

The symphony of the Yom Kippur devotions reaches its most thunderous movement in the so-called Additional Service which today serves as a substitute for the extra sacrifices offered in the Temple on this occasion.

The principal feature of this service is the recital of what is known as the *Abodah*, i.e., a detailed account of the atonement ritual anciently performed in the sanctuary. Originally, it would appear, this consisted solely in excerpts from the relevant tractate of the Mishnah. In course of time, however, synagogue poets felt tempted to compose elaborate versified paraphrases of this somewhat prosaic narrative, and these came to be substituted for the original Talmudic text. No less than thirty-five different versions are known to us. Two, however, found special favor. The one, by the fifth-century Palestinian poet, Jose ben Jose, is today the standard form in Sephardic congregations; the other, written by the Italian hymnologist, Meshullam ben Kalonymos in the tenth century, is adopted by the Ashkenazim. Both begin with a brief review of human history from Adam to Aaron, intended to demonstrate the primordial character and divine authority of the priestly ritual about to be described. This is followed by the description itself, the latter adhering closely to the text of the Mishnah while at the same time elaborating it with a number of poetic images and tropes. At the end comes a poem (in various versions) portraying the glory and splendor of the high priest when he finally emerged from the holy of holies.

The recital of the Abodah is regarded as the most solemn moment of the Atonement services, and when the precentor reaches the passage which describes how the high priest pronounced, this once in the year, the ineffable name of God, every member of the congregation follows the ancient gesture of his ancestors and "bows and prostrates himself and falls upon his face," exclaiming in a loud voice, "Blessed be the Name of Him Whose glorious kingdom endures for ever." [7]

It has long been recognized that the final poem of the Abodah, that which describes the radiance of the high priest, bears a remarkable resemblance to a passage in the apocryphal Book of Ecclesiasticus—a resemblance so close, indeed, as to suggest dependence. Here is Meshullam ben Kalonymos' version of that poem: [8]

There shone a splendor on the high priest's face
When safe he came forth from the holy place,

Like as the spangled curtain of the sky;
Like as the sparks that from the angels fly:
. . . . .

[7] The more sedate Sephardim, however, content themselves with a decorous bow.
[8] *Mar'eh Kohen.* Adler-Davis, *Atonement,* ii, 166.

Like as the azure skeins we wear so proud;[9]
Like as the rainbow poised within the cloud;

Like as the sheen which our first parents wore
In Eden's garden in the days of yore;

Like as a rose within a garden bed;
Like as a crown about a kingly head;

Like as the radiance in a bridegroom's eye;
Like snowhite robes in all their purity;

Like courtiers stol'd for audience with their kings;
Like as the daystar when the morning springs.

And here is the passage from Ecclesiasticus:[10]

How glorious was he when he shone forth from the Tent,
    and when he came out from the curtained chamber;[11]
As a shining star from amid the clouds,
    and as the full moon on the festival;[12]
As the sun dawning on the palace of the king,
    and as the rainbow seen, in the cloud;
As the blossoming foliage on the festival,[13]
    and as a lotus by streams of water;
As a flower of Lebanon in summer days,
    and as the glow of frankincense in the censer;
As golden vessels, [basin and bowl,] [14]
    tricked out with precious stones;
As a green olive-tree in full bloom,
    and as a verdant tree rich in leaves.

. . . . .

---

[9] On the praying-shawl; cf. Num. 15:37.
[10] Eccles. 50:5-21. Our rendering follows the Hebrew version, discovered in 1896–1900. This differs in many places from the Greek text, from which the standard English translation was made.
[11] i.e., the holy of holies.
[12] i.e., on Passover or Booths, which commence at full moon.
[13] i.e., on the Feast of Booths; cf. Lev. 23:40.
[14] The text is defective; it is here restored on the basis of Ezra 1:9-10.

When he was clothed in the glorious garments,
  and robed in the raiment resplendent,
When his lustre beamed upon the altar
  and bathed the court of the temple in beauty;
When he received the portions from his brethren,
  himself standing by the dressed sacrifices,
Then (his) sons formed a crown around him,
  like the saplings of a cedar of Lebanon,
And they compassed him round about like willows of the brook,
  even all the scions of Aaron in their splendor,
  with the offerings of the Lord in their hands,
  before all the congregation of Israel.
When he had finished ministering at the altar,
  offering oblations unto the Most High,
Then the scions of Aaron, the priests,
  Blew on the trumpets of beaten work;
They blew, and they cried in a voice majestic,
  to make memorial unto the Lord.[15]
Then promptly all mortal flesh
  fell upon their faces on the ground,
Prostrating themselves before the Most High,
  before the Holy One of Israel.
And the choir gave forth its voice,
  and over the throng made their voices ring out;
And all the people of the land
  intoned prayers unto Him Who is merciful.
And when (the high priest) had finished ministering at the altar,
  and had brought unto it its due,
Then he went down, and he lifted his hands
  over all the congregation of Israel;
And the blessing of the Lord was upon his lips,
  and he was glorified (in pronouncing) the Name of the Lord;
And for a second time
  all the people fell down before him.

This remarkable resemblance has recently inspired the
ingenious theory that the passage from Ecclesiasticus was

. . . . .

[15] Cf. Num. 10:10; I Chron. 16:4.

anciently used in the synagogue as a supplement to the
formal recitation of the Abodah from the text of the
Mishnah, and that the modern poems are but later sub-
stitutes for it. In support of this conjecture, it is pointed
out that the relevant verses of the apocryphal book are
indeed prefaced by a rapid survey of world history
(chaps. 44 ff.), just as is the modern Abodah-service
in the synagogue.[16]

The high point of the afternoon service is the reading
(or chanting) of the Book of Jonah as the Lesson from
the Prophets. The reason for this selection is that the
central theme of the book is the value of true repentance
and the clemency of God toward all who evince it, even
though they be confirmed idolators.

Jonah ben Amittai, a prophet of Jehovah, is commanded to go
to Nineveh, the capital of Assyria, and call upon it to repent its
evil ways. Instead, however, he flees to Jaffa and there takes ship
for distant Tarshish.

During the voyage there is a violent storm. Faced with the
prospect of shipwreck, the sailors start calling on their several gods
and throwing cargo overboard to lighten the ship. Jonah, however,
lies fast asleep in the hold and has to be roused by the captain and
reminded of his duty to pray to God. The crew then casts lots
to determine—in accordance with ancient belief—who has offended
the gods and thereby caused the disaster. The lot falls on Jonah,
whereupon they inquire his identity, provenience and occupation.
The prophet tells them that he is an Hebrew and adds, formally
if not accurately, that he "fears Jehovah, the Lord of heaven, who
made both sea and dry land." At these words, the sailors grow
very frightened, and ask him what might be done to allay the
tempest which is raging more furiously by the minute. Jonah replies that he should be cast overboard, because it is obviously as a
punishment for his disobedience and flight that God has em-

. . . . .

[16] Cecil Roth, "Ecclesiasticus in the Synagogue Service," *Journal of Biblical
Literature,* LI (1952), 171-78.

broiled the waters. The mariners, however, are reluctant to take such a drastic step, fearing that the prophet might perhaps be mistaken and they would then be taking his life without cause. So they first try desperately to row to shore, and only when their efforts prove unsuccessful do they finally throw their passenger to the waves, at the same time offering sacrifices to Jehovah and vowing further gifts should they reach safety.

Meanwhile, Jehovah has prepared a "great fish" to swallow Jonah, and for three days and three nights the prophet remains in the belly of the monster, praying to God for release and promising to make offerings should he be delivered. "They that wait on vain idols," he adds—in a smug, oblique allusion to the mariners —"eventually renounce their pledges, but *I*—I will indeed make offering to Thee and loudly proclaim my thanks. Whatever I vow, I will certainly pay." Thereupon Jehovah orders the fish to disgorge Jonah upon dry land. Then he commands him for the second time to go to Nineveh and deliver his message.

Now, Nineveh is a huge city, and it takes a full three days to cross it. But the prophet has not been walking about in it for more than one day, proclaiming its imminent doom ("Forty days more, and Nineveh will be overturned") when the inhabitants instantly turn to repentance, proclaim a fast and, upon orders of the king, clothe themselves in sackcloth and sit amid ashes. Thereupon God relents his decision and spares them.

At this the prophet is exceedingly annoyed, for he feels that he has been sent on a fool's errand. "Isn't this just what I was saying back home?" he complains to Jehovah. "That was why I fled to Tarshish in the first place. I knew all along that you are a gracious and merciful and longsuffering God, and that you would relent of the fate which you had decreed. Now I am sick to death of the whole business, and if you want to punish me for disobedience—well, I would rather be dead than alive!" But Jehovah merely replies: "So you are as annoyed as all that?" and says nothing more.

Then Jonah departs from the city and, constructing a rude shack some distance from it, sits down in its shade to see what is going to happen. While he is sitting there, Jehovah creates a gourd to grow over his head and shelter him from the heat. But the prophet's joy at this unexpected relief is shortlived, for the very next morning, in the flush of dawn, Jehovah orders a weevil to start gnawing away at the gourd, so that by sunrise it is completely withered. Then he orders a sultry wind to blow from the east, and the sun beats fiercely on Jonah's head until he feels faint and wishes to die. At that moment, however, Jehovah addresses him. "So you are really annoyed about the gourd?" he asks. "Yes," replies the prophet, "I am really annoyed." "Well," rejoins Jehovah, "there you are having pity on a gourd for which you never labored and which you yourself did not rear—a gourd which happened to spring up in a night and perish in a night. Should I not, then, have pity on Nineveh, that great city, wherein are more than sixscore thousand persons who know not their right hand from their left hand, and also much cattle?"

One of the major points in the Book of Jonah is the contrast between the instant trust and piety even of the heathen and the lack of confidence and the infidelity of the servant of God. When the storm rages at sea, the idolatrous mariners immediately call upon their gods; the prophet, however, remains asleep in the hold. When he reveals to them that he is the cause of their misfortune, they nevertheless refrain, out of pity and humanity, from casting him overboard, and do so only as a last resort. Moreover, even then, they will not consent to so drastic an appeasement of Jehovah without themselves acknowledging his power by sacrifices and vows. Similarly, when Jonah eventually goes to Nineveh, the inhabitants of that evil city do not even wait for the completion of his mission before expressing their repentance. Nor is this merely a popular demonstration, a mere outburst of public hysteria; it is an act officially ordained by the king, who himself participates in it (3:6). Nor this alone; in the original text there is a subtle point which, even at the risk of grotesqueness, serves to emphasize the ready piety of the heathen: because they seek deliverance not only for themselves but also for their cattle, even the dumb beasts are obliged to observe the general fast, and they too are clothed in sackcloth (3:7-8) !

Nowhere, perhaps, has this basic lesson of the book found better expression in modern literature than in Father Mapple's sermon at the Whalemen's Chapel in Melville's *Moby Dick:*

As sinful men, it is a lesson to us all, because it is a story of the sin, hard-heartedness, suddenly awakened fears, the swift punishment, repentance, prayers, and finally the deliverance and joy of Jonah. As with all sinners among men, this son of Amittai was in his wilful disobedience of the command of God—never mind now what that command was, or how conveyed—which he found a hard command. But all the things that God would have us do are hard for us to do—remember that—and hence, he oftener commands than endeavors to persuade. And if we obey God, we must disobey ourselves; and it is in this disobeying ourselves, wherein the hardness of obeying God consists.

The ancient rabbis, however, not content with such purely general homilies, sought also to explain why the Book of Jonah had been selected especially for the liturgy of the Day of Atonement and, more specifically, why it was recited in the afternoon rather than the morning service. To both questions they found ready answers. On the Day of Atonement, it was observed, Israel is naturally apprehensive lest, for all its repentance, it fail to receive divine forgiveness. God therefore reassures it, through the Book of Jonah, that if He was ready to accept the penitence of heathen Nineveh, he is all the more ready to accept that of His own people. And the reason why the book is read in the afternoon is that this is a time of day when prayers are especially acceptable; for was not Elijah the prophet answered on Carmel "when noontide was past . . . at the time of the afternoon sacrifice" (I Kings, 18:29, 36) ?[17]

In ages less enlightened than our own, when it was considered blasphemous to see in the stories of the Bible anything but the record of historical fact, commentators and ecclesiastics were often put to considerable pains to "authenticate" the more grotesque and bizarre elements of the Book of Jonah, and wondrous and ingenious were some of the explanations they propounded.

What troubled them most, of course, was the incident of the "great fish," for they knew—or thought they knew —that the more common type of whale or shark does not in fact possess a gullet wide enough to swallow a human being. The creature in question, it was patiently pointed out, was a special kind of whale—the so-called right whale, of which Melville tells us that its mouth "would accommodate a couple of whist-tables and comfortably seat all the players." Indeed, even in the edition of Jonah contained in the *Cambridge Bible for Schools,* published toward the end of the nineteenth century, there is a special appendix citing instances of whales having swallowed human beings, and carefully identifying the species!

Moreover, even if the prophet *was* swallowed, how, it was asked, could he have managed to survive in the belly of the monster for three days and three nights, seeing that its gastric juices would at once have poisoned him? Not so, replied the learned Bishop Jebb, the "great

. . . . .

[17] The English Bible distorts the sense by rendering "at the time of the offering of the *evening* sacrifice." The Hebrew term is *minhah,* "meal-offering." In the Biblical context, all that is really meant is that Elijah was answered at the moment when the smoke of the meal-offering ascended from the altar. But the word came to denote the afternoon sacrifice in the Temple, and it survives as the name of the afternoon service. Hence the rabbinical explanation.

fish" which Jehovah prepared was a *dead* fish, in which
all such noxious elements had already ceased to function.
That, too, was why, at the end of the appointed period, it
was able to disgorge the prophet whole, unchewed and
undigested!

Others found an even more fantastic explanation:
"Great Fish," they said, was *the name of a ship,* which
God provided to rescue His servant, and which eventually landed him on *terra firma,* the "belly of the fish"
being simply the hold or steerage. (This vagary, it may
be added, actually finds place in Ferrar Fenton's curious
Bible in Modern English, likewise published at the end
of the nineteenth century.)

Others again tried to surmount the difficulties of the
narrative by the ingenious supposition that the whole
incident of Jonah's being awakened by the captain,
thrown overboard and swallowed by the "great fish" *was
simply what he dreamed* when he was lying fast asleep
in the "sides of the ship"!

Lastly, if these interpretations failed to carry conviction, there was always another way in which the inspiration of the sacred text could be defended without
embarrassing commitment to its factual truth: the story
could be taken allegorically. *Jonah* is the Hebrew word
for "dove," and—following the allegorical interpretation
of the Song of Songs, in which the beloved is addressed
as "my dove"—this became a favorite symbol for the people of Israel. The whole story, therefore, though told as
if it referred to the historical Jonah ben Amittai, was
really an allegory of Israel's constant disobedience to
God's command and of its vain attempts to flee from His
presence. The "great fish" was simply the personification of that lawlessness and chaos, or perhaps even of
the Exile and Dispersion, in which it would find itself

"engulfed" for a certain span, until finally released by the mercy of God!

Such extravagances are now, by and large, a thing of the past. We now know that the Biblical writers made abundant use of current folklore in order to bring home their message; and the story of Jonah and the "big fish" reveals itself as a skillful Hebrew adaptation of a widespread theme. An ancient Indian tale, for example, relates that once upon a time there lived a princess who refused to marry anyone except the man who had set eyes on the Golden City of legend. The hero Saktidêva accepted the challenge, and proceeded to roam the world in search of that fabulous place. In the course of his travels, he set sail for the island of Usthala, to seek direction from the king of the fishermen, who dwelt there. On the way, a storm arose, and the ship capsized. Saktidêva, however, was swallowed by a great fish which carried him to the island and eventually disgorged him whole. The same story is told in Ceylon about the hero Buhadama; while an ancient Greek legend relates that Heracles was once swallowed by a whale near the port of Jaffa, and remained within the animal's belly for three days. Similar tales, it may be added, are current to this day in the popular lore of Melanesia and Indonesia and among French-Canadians. What the Scriptural writer did, therefore, was simply to take a familiar legend, associate it with a Hebrew prophet, and re-tell it for homiletic purposes —a process later repeated times beyond number by the preachers of the Middle Ages.

Although the Book of Jonah deals with a historical character who lived in the eighth century B.C.E., during the reign of the Israelite king Jeroboam II, it was not written by him, but is simply a folktale later attached to his name. Modern scholars believe, on the evidence

of style and of the author's evident indebtedness to later
Biblical writings, that it was composed at some time between 500 and 400 B.C.E.—that is, in the century following the return of the Jews from the Babylonian Exile. Its
purpose would have been to remind the renegade, "assimilated" elements of the Jewish people that escape from
their ancestral faith and from their duty of bearing
witness to God's presence and of exemplifying His dispensation was, in the long run, impossible and vain. The
choice of Jonah ben Amittai as the hero of the tale would
have been especially pointed, for this was the prophet
who, in olden times, had inspired the renegade and
apostatic Jeroboam to extend and stabilize the confines of
Israel so that those who had been living unprotected on
the fringes of the kingdom might again be gathered
within its fold. As the ancient record put it:

[Jeroboam] restored the boundary of Israel from the entrance to
Hamath even unto the Sea of the Wilderness, in accordance with
the word of Jehovah, the God of Israel, which He spake through
His servant, the prophet Jonah ben Amittai, who came from Gath-
hepher. For Jehovah saw that the affliction of the Children of
Israel was very grievous . . . and that Israel had no helper, and
Jehovah was resolved not to blot out the name of Israel from under
heaven; so he saved them by the hand of Jeroboam.

(II Kings 14:25-27)

The situation would have had a certain resemblance to
that which obtained at the return from the Exile, and
the parallel would scarcely have been lost upon the men
of that age.

For the rest, the afternoon service represents a certain
easing of tension after the tremendous moment of the
Abodah. It is, as it were, a kind of interlude between

that moment and the impending urgency and intensity
of the concluding devotions. But it is not without its moments of poetry, and in this respect the following quaint
lines from Isaac ben Israel's *Prelude to the Confession*
in the Sephardic rite are perhaps worthy of quotation:[18]

Said I to head: Head, do thou plead for me.
Said head: on many heads such plea were vain.
How can I hope His mercy to obtain
Who am lightheaded, full of levity?
How can the head which shame and sin do bend
Be raised to Him Who doth all heads transcend?

.   .   .   .

Said I to lips: Mine innocence relate.
Said lips: that is a thing we cannot do.
For how shall God regard our words as true,
Who nothing know but to dissimulate?
Said I to mouth: Call thou upon His name.
Said mouth: I have no words but words of shame.

.   .   .   .

Said I to heart: O pour forth thy complaint
To Him Who dwelleth in the world on high.
Said heart: here in the slough of sin I lie
And cannot move from evil's hard constraint.
How can the heart which forgeth evil things
Be turned in prayer unto the King of Kings?

.   .   .   .

Said I to hands: Hands, be your palms outspread
To God in heaven, and His mercy seek.
Said hands: the hands that base corruption wreak
Are unavailing, fruitless hands and dead.

Said I to feet: Feet, do ye plead for me.
Said feet: it were a feat to find His grace.

.   .   .   .   .

[18] Pool, *Atonement*, 290 ff. The rendering is free.

How can the feet which e'er to evil race
Now tread the humble path to clemency?

The concluding service of Yom Kippur is call *Ne'ilah,*
which is the Hebrew word for the "Closing of the Gate."
Originally, this appears to have referred to the closing
of the Temple gates at dusk, but by an inspired extension
it is now taken to mean the closing of the heavenly gates
of prayer.

The service commences at the moment when the setting sun seems to be level with the treetops, and it must
be timed to end with the appearance of the first stars.
For the latter reason, it is customary to recite the prayers
without an excessive amount of cantillation, the precentor
refraining from the protracted trills and tremolos which
characterize the other devotions of the day.

Ne'ilah represents the last chance for repentance on
the one hand, and for divine forgiveness on the other.
According to the ancient fantasy, it is at this hour that
the roster of the living, which is compiled on New Year's
Day is finally sealed. Accordingly, in all those statutory
prayers wherein, throughout the day, God is besought
to "inscribe us in the Book of Life," He is now entreated to *"seal* us."

The dominant mood of the service is one of urgent,
nay desperate, insistence. The worshiper feels that he
has now all but exhausted his own inner resources in
order to achieve atonement and regeneration; if these
have not sufficed, nothing remains but reliance on the
clemency of God. This mood is caught to perfection in
the stirring poem by Moses ibn Ezra (*ca.* 1070–*ca.* 1138)
which introduces the service in the Sephardic ritual:[19]

. . . . .

[19] *El Norā.* Pool, *Atonement,* p. 294.

LORD, though every power be Thine
    And every deed tremendous,
Now, when heaven's gates are closing,
    Let Thy grace defend us.

Few we be yet, trembling, cry:
    Lord, Thy mercy send us.
Now, when heaven's gates are closing,
    Let Thy grace defend us.

Lord, we pour our hearts to Thee;
    Rend the sins that rend us.
Now, when heaven's gates are closing,
    Let Thy grace defend us.

Be our shield, annul our doom;
    Joy and bliss attend us.
Now, when heaven's gates are closing,
    Let Thy grace defend us.

Shew us pity; bring to end
    All our foes horrendous.
Now, when heaven's gates are closing,
    Let Thy grace defend us.

Lord, renew the days of old;
    Our fathers' deeds commend us.
Now, when heaven's gates are closing,
    Let Thy grace defend us.

In quieter vein, this spirit of resignation likewise finds expression in the short poem, *Yahbienu*, by a certain Isaac ben Samuel, which is chanted to a haunting melody in the Ashkenazic service:[20]

Now, folded in the shadow of Thy hand,
Now, coverted beneath Thine outspread wings,

    . . . . .

[20] Adler-Davis, *Atonement*, p. 262.

O Lord Who probest hearts, now let us stand
Made clean of all perverse and froward things!

Lord God, arise! In all Thy strength arise!
Lord, bend Thine ear and hearken to our cries!

Like all the other services of the day, that of Ne'ilah
works up to the crescendo of the great public confession;
but even this is but a prelude to the tremendous final
moments. When the evening twilight is finally merging
into night, and the incessant devotions are nearing their
end, a solemn hush falls upon the congregation, and the
cantor, covering his head with the prayer-shawl, cries out
in a loud voice, "Hear, O Israel, the Lord is our God, the
Lord is One" (Deut. 6:4), following this immediately
with a threefold repetition of the words, "Blessed be
the Name of Him whose glorious kingdom endures for
ever," the words which were anciently uttered by the
attendant worshipers when the high priest pronounced
the name of God in the Temple. Then, beginning in a
whisper and progressively increasing the volume of his
voice, he declares seven times, "The Lord, He is God"—
the cry of the people when they beheld the miracle
wrought by Elijah on Mount Carmel (I Kings 18:39).
These are the three declarations which every Jew is
expected likewise to utter at the moment of his death,
and which have received a special sanctity in Jewish
tradition from the fact that they have so often proceeded
from the lips of those who have "gone through fire and
water for the hallowing of God's name."

When the last notes of the chant have died away, a
long blast is sounded on the ram's horn (shofar), and
the Fast of Kippur is at an end.

But immediately, without a break, the normal evening

service begins, introducing the new day. For the devotion and commitment of the Israelite are continuous.

Modern scholars believe that the Day of Atonement
on the tenth of Tishri did not become a regular institution in Israel until after the time of the Babylonian Exile,
and that the passages in the Pentateuch which refer to
it[21] really date from that relatively late epoch. The reasons for this view are the following:

(a) The Day of Atonement is not mentioned in the
so-called "ritual decalogue" of Exodus 34:14 ff.—generally regarded as one of the oldest portions of the Pentateuch—whereas the seasonal festivals of Passover, Pentecost and Booths are indeed specified.

(b) Neither is it mentioned in the ancient "Book
of the Covenant" embodied in Exodus 23-24, although
there too the seasonal festivals are duly prescribed (23:
14-19).

(c) The law of Leviticus 25:9 enjoins that the year
of jubilee is to be reckoned from the tenth of Tishri.
This, it is contended, proves that the latter date was
originally regarded as New Year's Day rather than as a
Day of Atonement.

(d) The prophet Ezekiel, writing during the Babylonian Exile, signalizes the tenth of Tishri as New Year's
Day, but says nothing about its being the Day of Atonement (40:1).

(e) The same prophet, in sketching a new religious
order for Israel, designates the new moon of the first
and seventh months[22] (i.e., Nisan and Tishri) as the

. . . . .

[21] Lev. 16:29-34, 23:26-32; Num. 29:7-11.
[22] There is an error in the traditional Hebrew text of Ezek. 45:20. In place
of the words, "So also shalt thou do *on the seventh of the month*" we

two dates in the year when the sanctuary is to be purged
(kapper). This, it is contended, implies that a statutory
Day of Atonement was not yet in existence.

(f) Nehemiah, describing the events which took place
in Jerusalem in Tishri, 519 B.C.E., when the exiles returned from Babylon, duly mentions the holy first day
of the month and the Feast of Booths, but says nothing
whatsoever about a Day of Atonement on the tenth. Nor
this alone; he tells us expressly (9:1 ff.) that the people
convened especially *"on the twenty-fourth day* of the
said month, with fasting and with sackcloth and with
earth upon them." This, it is maintained, would have
been well nigh absurd, if there had indeed been a full-
scale ceremony of penitence and atonement only two
weeks earlier!

These arguments, however, are by no means so con-
clusive as might appear at first sight; each can be readily
answered.

First, the laws of Exodus 34:14 ff. and 23:14-19
are concerned only with the *seasonal* festivals (Hebrew,
hagim), so that their silence on the subject of the Day
of Atonement, which does not fall into this category, is
no proof that it did not exist at the time.

Second, the law of Leviticus 25:9, far from proving
that the Day of Atonement did not exist at the time,
in fact proves just the opposite. The jubilee year, we are
informed (Lev. 25:10, 12), was regarded as a *holy*
period; accordingly it could not begin until the annual
ceremony of purgation and resanctification had taken
place; otherwise it would have been beset from the start
with all the unshriven impurity of the preceding year.
The fact that it is reckoned from the tenth of Tishri thus

---

should read (with the Greek Septuagint version): "So also shalt thou **do**
on the first day of the seventh month."

implies that on that day the required purgation indeed took place, i.e., that Tishri 10 was the Day of Atonement!

Third, it is by no means certain that Ezekiel 40:1 has been correctly interpreted. What the prophet says, in literal translation, is that "in the twenty-fifth year of our exile, *at the beginning of the* year, on the tenth day of the month, . . . the hand of Jehovah was upon me." Now, although the expression "beginning of the year" (Hebrew, *rosh hashanah)* came to be applied to New Year's Day, the prophet need not have been using it in so precise a sense; the tenth day of a year can surely be described, without abuse of language, as "at the beginning of the year."

Fourth, Ezekiel's reference to the *two* days of purgation, on the new moon of the first and seventh months respectively, is no evidence of current practice, and does not prove that the Day of Atonement on Tishri 10 did not exist in this time. For the fact is that the prophet *is deliberately suggesting a new and reformed system—* somewhat like that of the Japanese Ohoharahi ceremonies —whereby the purification of the sanctuary is to be undertaken not only before the autumnal Feast of Ingathering but equally before the vernal harvest festival of Passover. The point of the reform is, in fact, to repeat in the spring what was already standard practice in the fall; and (although the prophet shifted the date) this implies, rather than denies, the existence of at least some sort of Day of Purgation in Tishri.

Fifth and last, it is difficult to see why the narrative in the Book of Nehemiah should be taken to imply that there was at the time no Day of Atonement on Tishri 10. The reason why it was not celebrated on that particular occasion is easily explained. A major feature of the

day was, as we have seen, the purgation of the sanctuary
from the impurities of the past year. In this case, however, the sanctuary had only just started functioning, so
that there was virtually nothing to purge, and the rite
had perforce to be abandoned or postponed. (Indeed, if
any general conclusion is to be drawn, the more logical
one would surely be that the Day of Purgation was
necessarily suspended throughout the period of the
exile.) As for the fast on the twenty-fourth of the month,
this was in no sense a day of atonement. The sanctuary
was not purged, and the crucial word *kapper* is nowhere employed. The purpose of the fast was simply and
solely to express the remorse of the returning exiles
over the religious laxity and defection which had characterized their lives in Babylonia. Ezra, we are informed (Ezra 9:1 ff.) likewise fasted when he heard of
the extensive assimilation and intermarriage that had
taken place. Moreover, the reason why the fast was held
on the twenty-fourth of the month was that this was the
earliest opportunity of doing so after the close of the
festal season on the twenty-second. One day had to inter-
vene because the twenty-second was a festival (the Day
of Solemn Assembly), and preparations for a fast could
not be made on a holy day.

Thus, all the arguments for the relative "modernity"
of the Day of Atonement prove vulnerable. On the
other hand, there are at least two good reasons for
believing that it was really ancient. The first is that the
scheme of seasonal festivals all over the world provides that the moment of joy be preceded by one of
mortification and austerity, expressing the decline of
vitality—the state of "suspended animation"—before the
commencement of a new lease of life. On general
grounds, therefore, the existence of a solemn day of

purgation and abstinence before the autumnal feast of Ingathering is extremely likely.

The second reason is that the scheme of the Hebrew festal cycle in autumn corresponds in general with that of the festal cycle in spring. In both cases, the first new moon is regarded as New Year's Day and in both cases the first full moon introduces the harvest festival (Ingathering and Passover respectively). It is therefore logical to suppose that there was something on the tenth of Tishri corresponding to the selection of the expiatory paschal victim on the tenth of Nisan. The dispatch of the scapegoat and the ceremony of purgation would readily have constituted such a counterpart.

In short, the Day of Atonement would have been originally but one element in a continuous festal program extending from the new moon of Tishri until the close of the Feast of Ingathering.

For the modern Jew, the real difficulty about Yom Kippur lies in the fact that what we now regard as an *internal* process is traditionally presented as an *external* one. God is portrayed as working upon us rather than in us, and this leads to an overemphasis upon atonement and forgiveness at the expense of the more advanced conceptions of self-purgation and regeneration. Once it is realized, however, that the difference is in the final analysis, simply one of idiom and expression, it becomes evident that the process involved is indeed the supreme spiritual experience of which man is capable, and that it is by virtue of this fact, and not of the mere solemnity of its ritual, that Yom Kippur justly ranks as the holiest day of the Jewish year.

IV

Days of Sorrow

THE FOUR FASTS

Fasting is a universal custom; there is scarcely a people in the world among whom it is altogether unknown. Yet its ultimate origin and purpose have proved a puzzle to scholars. A favorite view is that it was designed at first as a means of preparing the body for a ritual meal or for the consumption of sacred food. This view is based on the fact that, in the majority of cases, fasting does indeed form a prelude to feasting. Thus, among many primitive peoples, it is the custom to observe a fast—sometimes for several days—before the great banquet of the harvest-home. Among the Cherokees and Choctaws, for example, no food may be tasted for two nights and one day before the eating of the new crops in August; in New Guinea, a rigorous fast is observed before the gathering of the new yams. The custom prevailed also in the ancient world. In April, the Roman festival of Ceres, the goddess of crops, was preceded by a fast; and in October, a nine-day austerity was ordained in her honor. Moreover, even at the present day, the fast of a bridal couple before the wedding feast and of mourners before partaking of "funeral meats" are familiar usages in many countries.

The objection to this theory is, however, that in most of the cases cited, fasting is merely one aspect of a wider, more comprehensive abstinence. Before harvest, for instance, most primitive peoples prescribe a rigorous communal "lent" or period of austerity. Not only may no food be eaten, but no ordinary work may be done, and no business transacted. Law courts and communal offices are closed; nobody is allowed even to set foot out of doors; strangers are shut out; sexual relations, sometimes even personal ablutions, are prohibited; and all behave as if they were dead and defunct. Obviously, then, it is this more comprehensive austerity, not the mere abstention from food, that really requires explanation.

And the explanation is very simple. Among primitive peoples, life is regarded primarily as a *succession of leases,* each of which is determined by the length of a natural or agricultural cycle. Accordingly, at the end of every such cycle, the community is, so to speak, "at the end of its rope"; its vitality is on the wane and, until the new lease begins, it is in a state of suspended animation. It is this state, this "evacuation" of normal being, that the periodic fasts and abstinences are intended to represent. Moreover, even individual (or private) fasts are explicable on this basis. Thus, in the case of fasting before marriage, what is thereby expressed is that each partner to the union abandons something of his or her single

identity, the two together becoming a new joint person—
"one flesh"; while the fast of mourners symbolizes the
fact that death, though it happens *to* an individual, happens *in* a group, so that the demise of any single member of that group impairs the corporate vitality of the
whole, and all are in a state of temporary eclipse or suspended animation.

When, therefore, we find fasts instituted at regular
periods of the year, the chances are that the latter
originally marked the ends of natural or agricultural
cycles—occasions characterized, as we have seen, by communal mortification.

At the same time, however, it must be borne clearly
in mind that, like every other popular institution, fasting
tends to outgrow its origins and comes in time to be
employed as a purely artificial device to indicate what is
not a natural but a deliberate curtailment of activity. In
practice, therefore, we have always to inquire whether a
particular fast represents a natural or an artificial mortification; and a useful test is whether or not it occurs on a
crucial date of the natural or agricultural year.

Apart from the major Day of Atonement, there are
four minor fasts in the Jewish year. These, however, are
not ordained in the Law of Moses, and therefore do not
rank as sacred days. They are first mentioned by the
prophet Zechariah (518 B.C.E.), who describes them,
somewhat vaguely (8:19), as *the fast of the fourth
month, and the fast of the fifth, and the fast of the
seventh, and the fast of the tenth*. It is therefore commonly supposed that they were instituted only at the
time of the Babylonian Exile.

Jewish tradition associates each of these fasts with an
event connected with the siege and fall of Jerusalem

under Nebuchadnezzar. Taking them in chronological, rather than calendarical, order, the scheme is as follows:

(a) *The fast of the tenth month*—on the tenth of Tebeth, commemorates the commencement of the siege;

(b) *The fast of the fourth month*—on the seventeenth of Tammuz, commemorates the first breach in the walls of the city;

(c) *The fast of the fifth month*—on the ninth of Ab, commemorates the destruction of the Temple;

(d) *The fast of the seventh month*—on the third of Tishri, commemorates the assassination of Gedaliah, the governor of Judah appointed by Nebuchadnezzar (II Kings 25:23-25; Jer. 41:1-3).

It is clear, however, that this scheme rests on something less substantial than historical fact. In the first place, no Biblical source dates the destruction of the Temple on the ninth of Ab. Jeremiah says (52:12) that the Babylonians did not even enter the city until the *tenth* of the month,[1] while the author of Second Kings (25:8-9) relates that they stormed in on the *seventh* and burned the House of the Lord and all the principal mansions. Secondly, there is no Scriptural authority for the statement that the first breach in the walls took place on the seventeenth of Tammuz.

In view of these discrepancies, it is far more probable that the fasts really go back to popular "pagan" observances which the Jews picked up during the period of the Exile and which they attempted to justify by carefully

.....

[1] As a matter of fact, the Talmud (*Ta'anith* 29ª) frankly admits and discusses the discrepancy; while for this reason the sect of the Karaites observed the fast on the *tenth* of Ab.

connecting them with events in their own history. Unfortunately, we cannot yet determine with certainty just what those observances were. Modern scholarship, however, has been able to advance some interesting conjectures.

It has been pointed out, for example, that among the Babylonians, the month of Tebeth possessed an especially gloomy character as being that in which the dead were believed to ascend from the netherworld and stalk the earth, and that it is stated expressly in a Babylonian calendar that on the tenth day it is dangerous for this reason to walk in the streets. The Jews living in exile in Babylonia would almost certainly have become familiar with this institution, and it would have been but natural for the more assimilated elements among them to have taken it over and to have sought to give it an acceptable Jewish complexion.

Similarly, it has been observed that the seventeenth of Tammuz ("the fast of the fourth month") coincides with the time of year when (as the very name of the month implies) the Babylonians performed their annual wailing for Tammuz, the god of fertility, who was believed then to disappear from the earth.[2] These wailings are parallelled in many parts of the ancient and modern world. In Syria, for example, this was the season of the passion of Adonis

Whose annual world in Lebanon allur'd
The Syrian damsels to lament his fate
In amorous ditties all a summer's day;[3]

    • • • • •

[2] A Neo-Babylonian text states specifically that the god sank into the netherworld on the eighteenth of Tammuz. *Zeitschrift fuer Assyriologie,* VI, 244:32-34.

[3] Milton, *Paradise Lost,* I, 447-49.

while in Rumania, little girls stage a mock funeral (and subsequent regeneration) of the spirit of fertility in mid-August.

As for the fast of the ninth of Ab, it is noteworthy that in the ancient Babylonian calendar the month of Ab was known as "the month of torches" and was distinguished by the celebration of a "festival of firewood." The torches appear to have been lit in connection with a kind of Feast of All Hallows, and it was precisely on the *ninth* of the month that deceased heroes were said to ascend through the gates of the netherworld and temporarily rejoin their living kinsmen. These ceremonies, it has been suggested, were picked up by the Jews during the period of the Exile and were skillfully reinterpreted as a memorial of historical events. The flares thus came to symbolize those flung by the soldiers of Nebuchadnezzar into the precincts of the Temple at Jerusalem; and to account for the discrepancy that the Babylonian ceremonies took place on the *ninth* of the month, whereas the Temple was destroyed only on the *tenth,* the rabbis promptly explained that the firebrands were in fact tossed in on the former day, even though the building was not burned out until the latter![4] Nor, indeed, was this the only way in which they transmogrified the ancient fire festival of the season, for they also converted the fifteenth (i.e., the full moon) of Ab into a memorial of the day when their ancestors used to bring firewood for the altar!

Three out of the four fasts might thus very well go back to Babylonian origins, and this would explain why they are first mentioned at the time of the restoration from the Babylonian Exile and why the returning Jews

. . . . .

[4] Talmud, *Ta'anith* 29ᵃ.

specifically sent a delegation to the priests of Jehovah to
enquire whether the austerity "in the fifth month" need
still be observed (Zech. 7:2-3).

There is, however, an alternative view. It has been
pointed out by Professor Julian Morgenstern that, according to the Talmud,[5] the feast of the firewood on the
fifteenth of Ab was celebrated as a rustic festival, so that
the fast which occurs exactly a week previously may have
been originally the beginning of a Lenten period of
mortification and austerity like those which, as we have
seen, usually precede seasonal festivals in most parts of
the world.

A similar explanation, says Morgenstern, will also
account for the "fast of the tenth month," on the third of
Tishri. The traditional view that this commemorates the
assassination of Gedaliah encounters the difficulty that,
during the time of that governor's administration, he
seems to have been considered by many as a kind of
Pétain (cf. II Kings 25:22 ff.; Jer. 40-41), so that it is
a little hard to see why the anniversary of his death
should have been observed as a national fast. The fact is,
however, that the so-called "Fast of Gedaliah" likewise
occurs exactly a week before a great rustic celebration
which, so the Mishnah informs us, coincided in ancient times with the Day of Atonement. Accordingly,
this fast too may originally have marked the beginning of
a seasonal austerity.

If Morgenstern is right, two at least of the fasts would
thus go back to a Palestinian rather than a Babylonian
origin, though it would have been during the Babylonian
Exile that they were perforce reinterpreted on seemingly
"historical" lines.

. . . . .

[5] *Ta'anith* 4:5.

Except for that of the fifth month (which we shall discuss presently), it cannot be said, in all honesty, that these minor fasts have been developed in Judaism to teach any particular transcendental truths. True, the ancient sages sought, in some cases, to divorce them from any single particular event and to present them as generally "unlucky" days on which not one, but several different disasters had in fact befallen the Jewish people during the course of its history. It was said, for example, that the seventeenth of Tammuz was not only the date on which the walls of Jerusalem had been breached in 586 B.C.E., but also that on which the first tablets of the Law had been broken by Moses, on which the daily whole-offering had been suspended during the siege either of the Babylonians or of the Romans, and on which a certain Posthumus (of whom nothing further is known) had burned the sacred scrolls and set up an idol in the sanctuary. Nevertheless, the fasts remain to this day on the level of purely historical commemorations, and for that reason they have fallen into desuetude except among strictly orthodox Jews. They are not even formally observed in Reform congregations, since Reform Judaism regards the destruction of the Temple and the dispersion of Israel throughout the world not as a disaster reparable only with the coming of the Messiah, but as the beginning—tragic as it may have been at the time—of another and even more important stage of Israel's historic mission to mankind.

In Judaism, however, all history is a revelation of the purpose of God, and Israel's history exemplifies also the vicissitudes of its peculiar relationship with Him. Disaster is therefore a sign of God's displeasure—a tenet of faith which means simply, in modern language, that a person or nation which violates the inherent moral order of the universe pays for its misdeeds in inevitable calamity. Accordingly, these three (assumed) anniversaries of national disasters all sound the common note of divine displeasure on the one hand and of human supplication for mercy on the other.

This is brought out in the traditional liturgy by the reading in each case of the same Lessons from the Law and from the Prophets.

The Lesson from the Law is Exodus 32:11-14 and 34:1-10. The first portion describes how Moses interceded with God when He purposed to destroy Israel as a punishment for the sin of the Golden Calf:

Wherefore should the Egyptians say, With evil intent did He bring them forth, to slay them in the mountains, and to consume them from the face of the earth? Turn from Thy fierce wrath, and relent of this evil against Thy people. Remember Abraham, Isaac, and Israel, Thy servants, to whom Thou didst swear by Thine own self and didst say unto them, 'I will multiply your seed as the stars of heaven, and all this land that I have promised will I give unto your seed, and they shall inherit it for ever.' And the Lord relented of the evil which He had said that He would do to His people.

The second passage then continues with the story of how God demonstrated His mercy by replacing the two tables of the Law which Moses had broken in his anger:

And the Lord came down in the cloud, and stood with him there, and he called the Lord by name. Then the Lord passed before him, and he cried: "The Lord, the Lord is a god merciful and gracious, slow to anger and abounding in lovingkindness and truth, maintaining lovingkindness unto them of the thousandth generation; yet doth He by no means acquit the guilty, visiting the iniquity of fathers upon children and upon children's children, even upon them of the third and fourth generation. . . ."

The Lesson from the Prophets is Isaiah 55:6–56:8. Written during the dark days of the Babylonian Exile this passage likewise holds out to an anguished people the promise of divine mercy and the assurance of God's constant accessibility to the penitent:

Seek ye the Lord, since He may be found,
Call upon Him, since He is near;
Let the wicked abandon his way
And the froward man his designs,
And let him return to the Lord,
for He will have mercy upon him,
even unto our God, for He is rich in forgiveness.

By righteous conduct Israel may yet win back the favor of God, achieve a change of fortune and a restitution of its ancient glories. Moreover, such conduct will bring an even richer reward, namely, the final accomplishment of her historic mission:

Thus saith the Lord:
Observe justice and do righteousness,
for My salvation is nigh to come,
and My deliverance to be revealed.
.   .   .   .
My house shall be called a house of prayer
                                        for all peoples.
Thus saith the Lord God,
Who gathereth the outcasts of Israel:
"I will yet gather others unto him
besides his own that shall be gathered."

For the rest, on the fasts of Tebeth, Tammuz and Gedaliah, the liturgy is distinguishable from that of ordinary weekdays only by the inclusion in the service of various poetic lamentations and supplications composed during the Middle Ages. These, it must be confessed, are characterized more by virtuosity than by inspiration. Sometimes, however, the verbal dexterity is itself peculiarly effective, and it is possible to extract from the dross of banality a nugget of pure gold, as in the following verses of a seventeenth-century poem chanted in Ashkenazic congregations on the Fast of Tebeth:[6]

Alas! the world's great cornerstone[7] doth lie
A sorry heap of rubble, and the plow
Drags slowly o'er the mounds of Zion; now
Men scorn the heirs of God with obloquy.[8]

.   .   .   .

The seed which none could count [9] for nought is sold,
None counts the price; a widow,[10] 'mid her tears
She plows her lonely furrow through the years,
Who was God's faithful bride in days of old.[11]

.   .   .   .

O ancient God, Who dwellest in the height,[12]
Renew the ancient days of long ago;[13]
Let all our stain be as the driven snow,
And turn our scarlet sins to gleaming white! [14]

or in these lines from a lament over the breach in the walls, written for the Fast of Tammuz by the great Spanish-Jewish poet, Solomon ibn Gabirol (1021-58):[15]

Now send Thou David's scion
To mend the walls of Zion,
And from the thorns pluck Thou the precious rose! [16]

.   .   .   .   .

---

[6] *Eben ro'shah le-'iyyim we-la-hareshah.*
[7] Zech. 4:7. [8] Deut. 32:5. [9] Num. 23:10. [10] Lam. 1:1. [11] i.e., Zion; cf. Isa. 1:21. [12] Deut. 33:27. [13] Lam. 5:21. [14] Isa. 1:18.
[15] *She'eh ne'esar.*
[16] i.e., Israel, in allusion to the allegorical interpretation of Song of Songs 2:1.

Raise up Thy fallen tower;
Let Bashan burst in flower,
While a new glory over Carmel blows![17]

Quite different, and far more important, is the Fast of the Ninth of Ab.

Primarily, the Ninth of Ab is a day of mourning; only secondarily of fasting. The ancient rabbis therefore prescribed for it a series of observances specifically characteristic of funeral rites. "When Ab comes in," they said, "all merriment must go out"; and to this day it is the custom to omit in the case of Ab the special Blessing of the New Moon which, in that of the other months, is recited during the morning service of the preceding sabbath.

From the beginning of the month, the same restrictions must be observed as apply during the period of mourning. Hair may not be cut, and clothes may not be washed except on a Thursday, when the ban is waived in honor of the approaching sabbath. On the eve of the fast, meat may not be eaten, and only one cooked dish may be served at supper; indeed, it is a widespread custom to make the last meal consist only of hard-boiled eggs strewn with ashes—in imitation of that which is traditionally served to mourners on their return from a funeral. Moreover, people are expected to dispense with mattresses and sleep on the floor, a sign of mourning mentioned in the Bible (Jer. 14:2).

In contradiction to the other fasts, that of the Ninth of Ab is observed, like Yom Kippur, from sunset to sunset.

• • • • •

[17] cf. Nah. 1:4.

The lugubrious character of the day is brought out especially in the services of the synagogue. The worshipers sit on the floor, or on low stools, and remove their shoes or wear felt slippers. Prayer-shawl *(tallith)* and phylacteries *(tephillin)* are not donned until the commencement of the afternoon service. All lights are dimmed or extinguished, save that which burns continually before the Ark of the Law. The ark itself, in which the sacred scrolls are deposited, is draped in black, as is also the rostrum from which, throughout the year, the precentor leads the prayers. The tinkling bells which usually surmount the scrolls of the Law are removed, and black wraps replace the embroidered and brocaded mantles with which they are usually covered. As at a funeral, no greetings may be exchanged between members of the congregation.

The principal feature of the service is the recital, to a doleful singsong melody, of the Biblical Book of Lamentations and of special dirges *(kinoth)* composed during the Middle Ages.

The Book of Lamentations, traditionally ascribed to the prophet Jeremiah, is really a collection of five independent dirges over the destruction of the Temple in 586 B.C.E. and the consequent plight of the Jewish people. In the opinion of most modern scholars, these dirges were written either by eyewitnesses of the disaster or by men who lived very shortly after, when it was still a living memory. All of the poems except the last are composed in the form of an alphabetical acrostic[18] and in a peculiar limping meter in which a line containing

. . . . .

[18] The concluding dirge contains, however, the same number of verses as there are letters in the Hebrew alphabet. It is plain, therefore, that it is a later addition modeled upon the general pattern of the acrostics.

three beats or stresses is followed immediately by another containing but two, e.g.,

Outdoórs they lié on the groúnd.
    yoúng men and óld;
My yoúths and maídens áll
    fáll by the swórd.

(2:21)

This meter probably originated in the custom, still observed in the Near East, of performing a limping dance as a rite of mourning.

It is customary among the peasants of Upper Egypt [wrote the great Arabist E. W. Lane], for the female relatives and friends of a person deceased to meet together by his house on the first three days after the funeral and there to perform a lamentation and a strange kind of dance. They daub their faces and bosoms and part of their dress with mud, and tie a rope girdle . . . round the waist. Each flourishes in her hand a palm-stick or a *nebroot,* a long staff, or a drawn sword, and dances with a slow movement and in an irregular manner, generally pacing about and raising and depressing the body.[19]

This usage is attested also in Syria, when it is known as *ma'id,* or "limping"; while a Babylonian document in the British Museum lists the word "limper" or "leaper" as a synonym for "professional mourner." The dirges sung at these ceremonies would, of course, have had to keep pace with the tread of the mourners, and out of this fact there would naturally have arisen the literary convention of composing threnodies in a limping meter.

Another prominent feature of the Book of Lamentations is that the dirges are sometimes put into the mouth of the "daughter of Zion"—a personification of the ruined city and of the people of Israel in the form of a

. . . . .

[19] E. W. Lane, *Manners and Customs of the Modern Egyptians.* Minerva Library edition (London, 1890), p. 488.

professional wailing woman. It is the "daughter of Zion" who weeps at night and receives no comfort, whose friends and lovers have betrayed her, and who is exhorted to "let tears run down like a river day and night" (2:18).

The discovery during the past one hundred years, of considerable portions of ancient Near Eastern literature throws new and fascinating light on the style and content of the Biblical book. From the ruins of the ancient city of Nippur, in Mesopotamia, for example, has come a series of clay tablets in the Sumerian language, inscribed with the text of a long lament over the destruction of Ur, the hometown of Abraham, at some time during the second millenium B.C.E.; and this shows so many similarities to the Book of Lamentations as to leave no doubt that the Hebrew authors of the latter were following a long-established and time-honored literary tradition which they evidently picked up during their exile in Babylon. The Sumerian poem likewise consists of several independent dirges, and many of these are likewise put into the mouth of a female wailer—or even of the goddess of the ruined city. Moreover, there are many arresting verbal parallels. Thus, if the Hebrew writer declares (2:6) that God "has broken down His booth like that of a garden," his Sumerian forerunner makes the goddess complain that "My house, like a booth in a garden, has caved in on its side." If the Biblical poet laments (2:17) that "Jehovah has done that which He purposed, has fulfilled His word which He decreed long ago," the Sumerian asserts that "the god Anu changes not his command; the god Enlil alters not the word which he had issued." So, too, if the former cries mournfully (4:8) that the visage of the princes "is blacker than soot, they are not recognized in the streets," the latter has the goddess complaining that "Dirt has been decreed for them; verily, their appearance is changed." Or again, if the Hebrew poet mourns (5:18) for "the mountain of Zion which lies desolate, whereon foxes walk," he but echoes the words of his Sumerian prototype, "In the canals of my city dust has gathered; into fox-dens are they turned." Lastly, if the Biblical Book of Lamentations ends (5:21) with the desperate plea, "Restore us to Thee, O Lord that we may come back! Renew our days as of old!" the Sumerian concludes with the passionate appeal to Nanna, the patron god of Ur, to "let the city, restored, step forth proudly before thee!"

On another clay tablet, now in the British Museum, is inscribed, both in Sumerian and in a Babylonian translation, the text of a dirge in which, once again, a female mourner—possibly, the goddess Ishtar herself—bewails the destruction of her city and complains that "invaders have entered my chamber," words which echo the statement of the Biblical poet (1:10) that Jerusalem sighs "because she has seen heathen entering the holy place."

Finally, an inscription copied in the reign of Seleucus from a far older original, and now likewise preserved in the British Museum, describes how the "daughters" of various Babylonian cities lament the doom which has befallen them, just as does the "daughter of Zion" in the Biblical Book of Lamentations. They, too, are exhorted to weep because "shame is present" and because "mothers are cut off from their children" (comp. Lam. 1:8, 11, 2:19-20, 4:3).

Yet even if the Hebrew writers followed a long-standing literary convention, they also introduced a special note of their own, and the comparison with the Babylonian laments therefore serves at the same time to point up more clearly the distintively Jewish elements of the Bib-

lical book and hence of the Fast of Ab, the essential
spirit of which it is deemed to epitomize. In the Babylonian poems, the disaster which befalls the city is represented as due to the rivalry of the gods; in the Biblical
laments, to the sin of the people. In the Babylonian versions, the local goddess is defeated and her shrine defiled; in the Hebrew version, God Himself is the agent
of the destruction, and the hostile nations are the agents
of His will. It is He, of His own purpose, who with-
draws His presence from His treacherous and unregener-
ate people. Finally, in the Babylonian conception, it is
the goddess of the city who utters the laments and en-
treats the intervention of her husband, whereas in the
Hebrew version, it is "the daughter of Zion," a personification of the people itself. Like the typical "wailing
woman" at an Oriental funeral, it is the "daughter of
Zion" who weeps and mourns and who is exhorted
(2:19) to pour out her heart like water "before the presence of the Lord." In Judaism, there is no intermediary
between God and man.

The Book of Lamentations ends on a note of despair: "Or hast Thou utterly rejected us? Art Thou exceedingly angry with us?" The Jewish people has realized, however, out of an experience of over two thousand
years, that despair is corrosive and must be tempered by
hope. Accordingly, it is customary, when the Book is
recited in the synagogue, to conclude by repeating the
penultimate verse: "Turn us unto thee, O Lord, that we
may be turned! Renew our days as of old!"

Among the Sephardim, it is customary to recite not only
the Book of Lamentations but also that of Job, several
members of the congregation intoning a chapter each in
turn.

The argument of the Book of Job has been very much misunderstood. To most people, it seems to consist mainly in the impassioned protest of a righteous man against undeserved affliction. On this basis, however, God's ultimate appearance in a whirlwind and His affirmation of omnipotence can appear only as a gigantic, if magnificent, irrelevance and as a somewhat unfair attempt to silence human logic by divine thunder. The truth is, however, that the real point of the book lies on quite another plane. The gravamen of Job's complaint is *not* that he has been afflicted unjustly, but that he has been afflicted without due process of trial, without hearing the charge against him or being given an opportunity to answer it. Jehovah's dramatic reply is thus both pertinent and logical. What He is saying and demonstrating is that the workings of the divine mind—as seen, for instance, in the arrangement of the heavens, the anatomy of animals, or the periodicity of life—are beyond the categories of human thought, so that there is, in fact, no common frame of reference to make discussion possible. Man can but bow to the superior intelligence of God, drawing from his own observation of nature the assurance that that intelligence works both sensibly and beneficially.

On the fast of Ab, Israel regards itself as in the position of Job. The rehearsal of this lesson is therefore at once a discipline and a solace; it complements, rather than duplicates, the Lamentations.

Judaism, however, is not content with the cold comfort of divine inscrutability; it needs also the warm assurance of God's more personal and particular interest. The reading of the scriptural books is therefore supplemented by the chanting of special dirges *(kinoth)* composed largely during the dark ages of the Crusades and the Inquisition. Some of these are mere recitals of woe. The following,

for example, is a dirge chanted in the Ashkenazic ritual
in the event of the fast's beginning at the conclusion of
the sabbath:[20]

From every youth and maiden
  the cry of anguish rings;
No more with song are laden
  our sabbath evenings.

Doomed are we and blighted;
  God's anger burneth bright;
His fury is ignited
  like torches in the night.

Our homes the fire erases;
  soil'd is our daughters' name;
And over all our faces
  there hangs the pall of shame.

Now alien snares enmesh us,
  and Murder stalks abroad,
And Zion's sons so precious
  are fallen by the sword.

The splendor now no more is;
  the altar flame is dead;
Departed are the glories;
  the crown falls from our head.

No more the scent of spices
  perfumes the holy place,
No more the sacrifices
  are set before God's face.

No more the precious pavement
  by pilgrim feet are trod;

     . . . . .

[20] *Ech mi-pi ben u-bath.*

In bondage and enslavement
   now lies the land of God.

From every youth and maiden, . . . etc.

Not infrequently, however, a deeper note is sounded:
the disaster which has befallen Israel is also a disaster for
God, and God should have prevented it, if not for His
people's sake, then at least for His own:[21]

The House Thou lovedst ere creation's morn,
Which with Thy throne of glory didst adorn,
Why lies it at the foeman's hand forlorn,
    While Thou, O Lord, our Shepherd from of old,
    Nought dost but stand aloof and rage and scold,
    As we were lambs that wandered from the fold?

The House which Thou uprearedst firm and fast,
Which feared no foeman in the days long past,
Why is it sacked by siege-men at the last,
    While Thou, O Lord, now moanest like a dove
    Which lonely sits a lonely house above
    And sighs alway: Alas, where is my love?

The House whereof Thou to Thy seer didst cry,
"Abide within this place, for I am nigh,"
Why waste they it who worship but a lie,
    While thou, O Lord, the while that they lay low
    The dwelling which Thou lovedst long ago,
    Turnest toward Thy people like a foe?

The House where clouds of glory wreath'd Thee round,
Where Thou, unsearchable, couldst yet be found,
Wherefore do rebels raze it to the ground,
    While Thou, Whose hand was our delivering,
    Dost stand aside and no redemption bring—
    While Thou disownest us, who wert our King?
        . . . . .

[21] *Ohalî asher ta'abtâ,* by Eleazar Kalir.

The House which Thou didst take to be Thy bower
On earth, to match the dwelling of Thy power,[22]
Why do the *h*aughty *h*arass it this hour,
 While Thou, O Lord, dost like an eagle dart
 Upon the prey, and sayest, "I will depart,
 For here no prophet is nor holy art"?

The House within whose walls Thou didst abide,
Wherefore do *s*trangers o'er its ruins *s*tride
And trample to the dust its lordly pride,
 While Thou, O Lord, art as a potentate
 Who visits all the cities of his state,
 Yet never cometh to our city-gate?

The House which erst Thou chosest as Thine own,
Wherefore by *o*thers is it *o*verthrown,
Forever to remain forlone and lone,
 While Thou, O Lord, dost as a stranger roam
 Through all the world, and hast no place called home,
 Nor hither in Thy wanderings e'er dost come?

The House o'er which the stars of twilight paled
Because through sin and greed our God we failed,
Wherefore do *v*andals keep its radiance *v*eil'd,
 While Thou, O Lord, by reason of our sin,
 Preferest, rather than do dwell therein,
 To lodge a traveller at a casual inn?

O Lord, O Lord, the story of Thy rage
And wrath is written large on every page
Of Destiny's great book; from age to age
 Men read the never-ending tale and see
 That out of all mankind none else but we
 Are ever chosen for Thine obloquy.

Howbeit, though Thou veil us with a cloud,
Yet still Thine ancient promise rings aloud;

 . . . . .

[22] The earthly tabernacle and temple were considered to be the replicas
of those in heaven.

Our healing cometh, e'en as Thou hast vowed:
　"Behold, though weeping tarry for the night,
　Rejoicing cometh with the morning light!" [23]

Sometimes, too, as in the following quaint conceit of a medieval German poet, the destruction of God's earthly habitation is conceived as a cosmic disaster, which even the stars of heavens could not bear to behold: [24]

When for our sins the House of God became
A ruin, and He quenched the altar-flame,

The sun was darkened, and the moon was veiled;
The light of all the constellations paled.

First came the Ram, [25] and bitter tears it shed
For that the sheep were to the slaughter led.

Then lowed the Bull [26] through heaven long and loud
For that our necks beneath the yoke were bowed.

The Heavenly Twins [27] were sunderèd in twain
For that the blood of brethren flowed amain.

. . . .

The Virgin [28] veiled her face and bowed her head
When youths and virgins in the streets lay dead.

The Scales [29] trembled, quivered, shook and swayed,
For that all Life was then by Death outweighed.

The Waterman [30] his tears like rivers shed
For that the waters swirled about our head.

. . . .

Lord, rise for Zion, rise in all Thy might;
Be jealous for her, and relume her light!
. . . . .

[23] Ps. 30:5.
[24] *Az be-hata'ênū harab mikdash.* [25] Aries. [26] Taurus. [27] Gemini. [28] Virgo.
[29] Libra. [30] Aquarius.

But just as the recital of the Biblical Lamentations is not permitted to end on a note of despair,[31] so too the liturgical dirges lead eventually to that triumphant confidence which is possible only, nay inevitable, to those who have drained the cup of misfortune. The final note of the day is sounded in the great Zionide of Judah ha-Levi (1085-1145), the greatest of Jewish poets since the close of the Bible:[32]

Zion, wilt thou not ask if peace's wing
    Shadows the captives that ensue thy peace,
Left lonely from thine ancient shepherding?

Lo! west and east and north and south—world-wide—
    All those from far and near, without surcease,
Salute thee: Peace and Peace from every side.

.   .   .   .

Lo! it shall pass, shall change, the heritage
    Of vain-crowned kingdoms; not all time subdues
Thy strength; thy crown endures from age to age.

Thy God descried thee for a dwelling-place;
    And happy is the man whom He shall choose,
And draw him nigh to rest within thy space.

Happy is he that waiteth;—he shall go
    To thee, and thine arising radiance see
When over him shall break thy morning glow;

And see rest for thy chosen; and sublime
    Rejoicing find amid the joy of thee
Returned unto thine olden youthful time.

. . . . .

[31] See above, p. 201.
[32] From *Ziyyon halo' tish'ali;* translation by Nina Salaman.

V

The Minor Holidays

10

PURIM

The Feast of Lots

Purim, or the Feast of Lots, is celebrated on the fourteenth of Adar in memory of the triumph of Esther and
Mordecai over the machinations of Haman, vizier of
King Ahasuerus (Xerxes)[1] of Persia, who had selected
that day by lot for the extermination of the Jews. The
story is related in the Biblical Book of Esther, which is
read from a scroll *(megillah)* both in the morning and on
the preceding evening.

Purim provides one of the clearest of all examples of
the transmutation of an earlier, non-Jewish festival.
Scholars have long since pointed out that the story of
Esther, as related in the Bible, is simply a piece of ro-

. . . . .

[1] The Bible does not specify which of the several kings called Xerxes is
meant, and the point is disputed by scholars.

mantic fiction and cannot possibly represent historical fact. None of the Persian kings called Xerxes had a wife named Esther, and none had a vizier named Haman. What is more, the whole story of Ahasuerus' marrying a Jewish maiden is factually preposterous, for we happen to know from the Greek historian Herodotus and from other sources that the Persian king was permitted to marry only into one of the seven leading families of the realm, and the pedigree of his bride was therefore submitted to the most searching examination.

Purim, then, must really have originated in some altogether different manner, the Book of Esther being merely a fanciful explanation of it. A number of theories have been proposed.

According to some scholars, Purim goes back to the New Year festival of Babylon. On this day, it is asserted, the gods were believed to determine the destinies of men *by lot,* and the Babylonian word for "lot" was *puru.*[2] The festival—it is furthermore asserted—was characterized by the performance of a ritual pantomime portraying the triumph of Babylon's gods over those of the neighboring countries. The former were represented by Ishtar, the mother goddess, and Marduk, the patron of the capital city; the latter, by Humman, the chief god of Elam,[3] and Kiririsha, his consort. In the fifth century B.C.E., however, after Babylon had passed into Persian hands, the Jews who still remained there instead of returning to Jerusalem, reinterpreted the festival as a memorial of something that had allegedly befallen their ancestors

. . . . .

[2] Originally, *puru* meant "urn" or "bowl"; then (by metonymy), the lot cast into it.

[3] Elam lay east of Babylonia, beyond the Tigris. It was bounded on the north by Assyria and Media, on the south by the Persian Gulf, and on the southeast by Persia.

under the new regime. That interpretation is embodied
in the Book of Esther. Ishtar and Marduk became Esther
and Mordecai; and Humman and Kiririsha were turned
into Haman and his wife, Zeresh!

Unfortunately, this theory is more ingenious than
plausible. In the first place, the Babylonian New Year
festival fell in Nisan (April), not in Adar (March), and
it lasted a full ten or eleven days. Secondly, there is no
evidence whatsoever that it was characterized by a ritual pantomime of the type supposed. Thirdly, the chief
god of the Elamites was not called Humman; we know
only of a minor Khumban, and it is by no means certain
that Kiririsha was his consort. Lastly, while it is true
that the fates of men were believed to be decided at the
Babylonian New Year, it does not appear that the Festival was known popularly as "the Feast of Lots *(purê)."*

Another theory starts from the fact that both the ancient Greek (Septuagint) versions of the Bible and the
historian Josephus call the festival not Purim but *Furdaia.*
This, it is contended, is a distortion of the Old Persian
Farwadigan, a feast held toward the end of the year, in
March. The fact is, however, that the Feast of Farwadigan lasted at least five days and was primarily a commemoration of the dead. Apart, therefore, from a rough ap-
proximation in date, it bears no resemblance whatsoever
to Purim, nor would it be possible to explain, on this
hypothesis, how the latter festival came to be associated
with the story of Esther. Besides, it is not difficult to show
that the name *Furdaia* (which, incidentally, also appears
in the form *Furaia*) rests on nothing more solid than a
scribal error in the manuscripts of the Greek Bible and
of Josephus.

A third theory connects the name *Purim* with the
Hebrew *purah,* "wine press," and assumes that the fes-

tival arose in the Greek, rather than the Persian, period of Jewish history, and that it is an adaptation of the Greek festival of Pithoigia, or Opening the Wine Casks. (The explanation of it by means of the earlier Persian story of Esther would then have been a subsequent afterthought, dating from a time when the true character of the celebration had long since been forgotten.) This theory, however, may be readily dismissed: a wine *press* is not a wine *cask,* and the opening of the latter takes place in the fall, not in spring. Moreover, the plural of *purah* is *puroth,* not *purim.*

In the present writer's opinion, the whole problem has to be approached from quite a different angle. Since the story of Esther is plainly unhistorical, the only reason for associating it with the feast of Purim could have been that the details of that feast were thereby conveniently explained. Accordingly, the original form of that feast must have involved: *(a)* the selection of a new queen, corresponding to the selection of Esther; *(b)* the parade of a commoner *qua* king, corresponding to the parade of Mordecai around the streets of Shushan [Esther 6:11]; *(c)* a fast, corresponding to that ordained by Esther [4:15-16]; *(d)* the execution of a felon, corresponding to the fate meted out to Haman [7:10, 9:25]; and *(e)* the distribution of gifts [9:22]. Moreover that festival must have taken place around the time of the vernal equinox, for it is then that Purim occurs.

Now, all of these conditions are satisfied if we assume that *Purim harks back to some earlier, pagan New Year festival. (a)* At New Year, it is customary in many parts of the world to appoint a new king, queen or governor, in order to symbolize the renewal of communal life and vigor. The European kings and queens of the May are a standard example of this usage; the celebration of a "sacred marriage" in which the parts of bride and groom were played by the king and a priestess was a common feature of seasonal festivals in Egypt, Babylon and Greece, and survives to this day among several primitive peoples and in the May brides of European folklore.

(b) The installation of a commoner as temporary king (interrex) during the period which intervenes, in ancient calendars, between the formal end of one year and the beginning of the next, or during the extra ("epago-menal") days which are often added to harmonize the lunar and solar systems of reckoning, is likewise a com-monplace of ancient and primitive usage. The Babylon-ian priest Berosus (c. 250 B.C.E.), for example, informs us that at the annual festival of Sacæa, it was customary to attire one of the royal domestics in "raiment resem-bling that of the king" and to install him as a temporary sovereign; in Thailand, a special "rice-king" is appointed for the three days of the summer festival of ókya khăo. European survivals of this usage may be recognized in the familiar "Twelfth Night Kings" and "Kings of the Bean." Moreover—and this is especially significant—the Arab historian Al-Biruni informs us expressly that it was customary in ancient Persia to mount a thin-bearded man on a regally caparisoned horse and parade him around the town, with royal honors, shortly before the spring festival, the ceremony being known as "the Ride of the Thin-Beard."

(c) As for the fast, we have already noted in a pre-vious chapter,[4] that an austerity of this kind, coupled with a suspension of normal activity, is a characteristic prelude to New Year and seasonal festivals in most parts of the world. It symbolizes the eclipse of communal

. . . . .

[4] See above, p. 124.

life which is believed to take place at the close of every annual cycle.

(*d*) The execution of a felon or, alternatively, of a misshapen person is a well-attested variation of the more familiar scapegoat ritual—a device for removing evil and impurity before the beginning of a new year. At the Babylonian New Year festival, we are told, a condemned criminal was led in procession through the streets and ceremonially scourged by the populace; and a similar practice, involving a misshapen man and woman, obtained at Abdera during the observance of the Greek festival of Thargêlia, in May. It would seem, indeed, that the famous fifty-third chapter of the Biblical Book of Isaiah really refers to such a usage, for the prophet likens the servant of the Lord to a misshapen man, who "had no form nor comeliness," and who was "smitten for our transgressions, belabored for our iniquities, by whose chastisement we were made whole, and by whose stripes we were healed."

(*e*) The mock combat between two rival parties is likewise a constant feature of seasonal ceremonies. Originally, it symbolized the struggle between summer and winter, rain and drought, Old Year and New; and in many parts of the world—as, for instance, in certain areas of Sweden—the antagonists are dressed up appropriately in green twigs and furs, or armed respectively with scythes and snowballs. In course of time, however, the real significance of the combat tends to be forgotten, and it then comes to be explained as the commemoration of some historic encounter. In ancient Egypt, for example, a mimetic battle staged annually at Memphis during the Festival of Sokar was presented as a contest between rival factions in the city of Buto, the predynastic capital. Similarly, among the Hittites, the ritual combat was taken to

re-enact some early border clash between themselves and
their neighbors, the Mæonians; while the Roman historian
Livy describes a mock combat, led by two royal princes,
which took place at the festival of Xandika, shortly
before the vernal equinox. In the same way, too, a foot-
ball match held annually on Shrove Tuesday at Jedburgh,
in Scotland, is popularly regarded as commemorating
a fierce battle between the Scots and the English at Fer-
niehurst Castle, near Jedwater.

(f) The custom of distributing gifts at New Year is so
universal that it requires no comment. It will suffice to
point out that, to this day, New Year is known in
France as *jour d'étrennes,* a name derived from the Latin
strenæ, the gilded coins and other small gifts made on
January first.

Finally, the New Year in ancient times used to begin
at the vernal equinox. Not only was this the practice in
ancient Persia, but it was also standard usage in Europe
until the sixteenth and seventeenth centuries; and in England, the civil, as distinct from the calendar, year is still
reckoned from March 25!

On the assumption that Purim goes back to the Old
Persian New Year festival, its name, too, can be readily
explained: it would connect with an Old Persian word
for "first" in the sense of *first day* or first season, like the
French *printemps* or the Italian *primavera.* Moreover, it
is worth noting that in colloquial Arabic, the word *phur*
(which has no native etymology) is still used as a term
denoting New Year.

In popular observance, Purim is a Jewish counterpart
of Carnival (with which it roughly coincides) and of
Twelfth Night—the old New Year. The most prominent
feature of the celebration is the *masquerade,* which ranges

in form all the way from crude "guising" to full-fledged theater. The earliest and most rudimentary type is that in which boys and girls dress up in gaudy and outlandish costumes and make the rounds of Jewish homes singing rough and improvised ditties in the Judeo-German (Yiddish) tongue and soliciting cash or refreshment. The favorite "guisers' song" is the well-known

Heint iz Purim, morgen iz aus;
Gib mir a dreier, und warft mich araus
(Purim lasts only a day at a time;
Throw me right out, but spare me a dime!)

Not infrequently, however, the visitors put on a more elaborate performance, entering the house in rapid succession, dressed respectively as Moses, Solomon and Elijah. Moses comes looking for the five books of his Law, buried under a junkpile of rabbinic commentaries! Solomon, garishly appareled in a profusion of gold paper and tinsel, is accompanied by a bevy of harem beauties—young men dressed up in petticoats. Elijah is a dwarfish little man who creeps in blinking, no longer sure of his real name because Jews have so long been accustomed to invoke him in their prayers by recondite and circumlocutory epithets!

Alternatively, the entertainment consists in a burlesque take-off of the rabbi and his disciples. The leader of the troupe plays the part of that dignitary, and a surefire gag is to mimic his recital of the *kiddush*—that is, the statutory benediction over wine on Sabbath and festivals—by reeling off a meaningless jumble of Hebrew words or by chanting as a round-song a series of obscure verses from the Bible which have no logical connection with one another. Sometimes, too, the performers stage a burlesque satire on rabbinical sophistry. The "rabbi" is asked a

number of absurd questions, to which, in a hilarious imitation of Talmudic discourse, he proceeds to render even
more absurd replies.

Often, too, the performance assumes the character of
a genuine, consequential mummers' play. A favorite
theme is the debate between the wise man and the fool
or between members of different professions, each ex-
tolling his own merits to the detriment of the other. The
following free rendering from a play of this type will best
convey its general tone and style:

> FOOL: What's the point of being wise, and being threadbare
> too,
> And sitting in the freezing cold until your skin turns
> blue?
> What's the point of being wise? The only thing
> you get
> Is endless toil and endless moil, and worry, fuss and
> fret.
> What's the point of being wise, and sitting cold and
> stark
> With nothing in your stomach, or sleeping in the
> park?
> What's the good of wisdom or grey matter in the
> head,
> When feather brains can lie so soft upon a feather
> bed?
>
> WISE MAN: No, no, my friend; I rather think, a little common
> sense
> Can go a long way farther than a lot of pounds and
> pence.
> Intelligence looks better on a man than fancy duds,
> And brains make better jewelry than diamond links
> and studs.
> A fool is just a walking corpse; to put it at the least:
> There's nothing to distinguish him from any poor
> dumb beast.

FOOL: My friend, you'll never talk me round to drop my
point of view;
But you've got sense, and I've got pence; so this is
what we'll do:
We'll start a common business; I will set you up
in style,
And you will lend your wits to me and, in a little
while,
You'll be rich, and I'll be wise, and both of us,
I think,
Will reap a tidy profit out of Sense and Folly, Inc.

Another constant stand-by is the *Robber Play*. In this,
the point of the jest is the futility of trying to rob the
impoverished Jew of the East European ghetto. It runs
as follows:

ROBBER: Here a' comes with the big sharp knife
To slit your throat and take your life!

VICTIM: All I've got's a crust of bread;
So look for someone else's head!

ROBBER: Keep your crust, and eat it up;
I haven't come to dine or sup.

VICTIM: Well, then, there's nothing else, by God,
Except a tiny piece of cod.

ROBBER: Keep your bread, and keep your fish;
A seafood dinner's not my dish.

VICTIM: Well, then, there's only sabbath cake,
And *that* you wouldn't want to take!

ROBBER: Keep your measly sabbath *chollahs;*[5]
What I want are crisp, clean dollars.

. . . . .

[5] *chollah* (*hallah*): the special loaf used for the ceremonial blessing over
bread and wine.

VICTIM: Well, then, I guess, you're out of luck;
          All I've got is one lone buck.

ROBBER: Hand it over! Now we're through;
          I'd rather have your buck than *you!*

Out of these more primitive "guisings" there devel·
oped, in the early eighteenth century, the more formal
Purim play. The first printed specimen of this genre
seems to be the Judeo-German *Ahashverosh Spil*
(Ahasuerus Play), published at Frankfort in 1708,
though earlier examples exist in manuscript. The play is
a burlesque elaboration of the Biblical story of Esther,
leaning frankly on rabbinic legends. Heavily stressed are
the vanity and haughtiness of Vashti, the arrogance and
bluster of Haman, and the shrewd astuteness of Mordecai. Vashti is represented as having met her downfall
because she ordered her Jewish handmaids to do needle-
work on the sabbath; and the triumphal parade of Mordecai through the streets of Shushan is tricked out by
the extra "business" of having Haman's daughter watch
the procession from an upper window and accidentally
pour a pot of offal on her father as he passes! Moreover,
to the indispensable members of the cast there is usually
added the character of a buffoon or smart-aleck, who
serves as a cross between a Greek chorus and a Shake-
spearian clown, punctuating the action with moralizing
comments or ribald "asides." The *Ahashverosh Spil* is
also "embellished" by the presence of a *shadchan,* or
marriage broker, who tries to arrange a new "match" for
the king after the dismissal of Vashti.

Sometimes, however, other subjects are chosen for
these presentations. Common in the eighteenth century,
for instance, was a play, written by a certain Baernann
of Limburg, dealing with the sale of Joseph to the

Midianites, while another, portraying the exploits of David against Goliath, is reported to have attracted large audiences at Frankfort.

It will be readily understood that productions of this type are not exactly literary masterpieces and that their humor often degenerates into mere coarseness, the nice distinction between vulgarity and obscenity tending to disappear. For this reason, they were, as a rule, tolerated rather than encouraged by the rabbinical authorities and, in some cases, we hear indeed of their being actually prohibited. A favorite ground of objection was that the practice whereby men played female roles violated the Biblical commandment (Deut. 22:5) against transvesticism. The fulminations of censure, however, fell but lightly on the populace, and even though particular performances may have been suppressed here and there, the custom as such could not be so easily or summarily eradicated.

At the present day, the traditional plays have fallen largely into disuse. The practice of Purim performances is, however, tenaciously maintained by synagogue schools and Jewish community centers, though it must be confessed that in their modern, more sophisticated and didactic form, they have lost much of that rambunctious spontaneity and uninhibited popular self-expression which was their principal charm.

Another traditional custom of the festival was that of electing a Purim King (usually a boy). This seems to have originated in the fourteenth century in Provence and, when Jews were expelled from that region in 1496, thence to have been carried into Italy. A later variation of it was the appointment of a Purim Rabbi in the seminaries *(yeshiboth)* and religious schools of eastern Europe. In either case, the mock dignitary usually held office from the new moon of Adar (or thereabouts) until the close of the festival. In modern times, especially in the United States and at the Purim carnival in Tel Aviv (Israel), his place is commonly taken by a "Queen Esther," chosen in a beauty contest.

Common also in many parts of the world is the practice of burning Haman in effigy. A medieval document found, at the end of the nineteenth century, in the Genizah[6] at Cairo describes how young men used to make a dummy of Haman and expose it on the rooftop for a few days before Purim. Then, on the festival, they would build a bonfire and burn it amid great merriment and jubilation. The same custom is reported also by an eleventh-century scholar as having been current in ancient times among the Jews of Babylonia and Elam. In Italy, a puppet representing the accursed miscreant was paraded around the streets and finally burned at the stake; and among the mountain Jews of Kurdistan, it is (or was) an established Purim usage for housewives to toss into the grate a piece of black wool which they called Haman.

All of these forms of merriment seem to have been borrowed directly from Gentile customs connected with Carnival and Twelfth Night.

The guisers, for example, have their exact counterpart in the children who make the rounds on Shrove Tuesday singing snatches of verse and begging for cakes, candy or cash. Indeed, the familiar *Heint iz Purim* finds an almost perfect parallel in a traditional Shrovetide ditty from Salisbury, England:

. . . . .

[6] Genizah (lit. "hiding-place"): a closet or room in the synagogue to which damaged scrolls of the Law, or tattered manuscripts of religious works, are relegated.

Shrove-tide is nigh at hand,
And I am come a-shroving.
Pray, dame, something
An apple or a dumpling.
Or a piece of truckle cheese
Of your own making
Or a piece of pancake.

Similarly, the more formal Purim plays possess a ready analogy in the "mysteries" which used to be presented in churches at the Feast of Corpus Christi and at Shrovetide, as well as in the revels of Twelfth Night. The former likewise revolved around Biblical themes—usually, the Annunciation and Nativity—while a favorite subject of the latter was a debate between members of rival professions. Nor, indeed, is the Purim *Robber Play* without a parallel, for one of the traditional Twelfth Night mummeries in the Eifel district of Germany deals expressly with the retribution that is eventually meted out to thieves; and we may perhaps suppose that in its original form, the corresponding Jewish piece also ended on this moralizing note.

As for the Purim King or Rabbi, this is, in all probability, a mere adaptation of the Lords and Abbots of Misrule, the Bishops and Archbishops of Fools, and the Mock Popes, which were characteristic of clerical revels at Carnival and Twelfth Night. In France, we are told, it was customary to attire the sham pontiff and his followers "in the ridiculous dresses of pantomime players and buffoons"; while the Boy Bishop who held office, in English usage, from St. Nicholas Day (December 6) to the Feast of Holy Innocents (December 28), was "escorted to church, with the mitre on; . . . and afterwards he and his deacons went about singing from door to door and collecting money; not begging alms, but demanding

it as his subsidy." The Prince of the Carnival is likewise a common figure of popular Shrovetide celebrations
in Germany; while among the municipal records of the
city of Norwich in England, there is mention of a certain
John Gladman who, in the year 1440, "on Tuesday in
the last end of Christmas made a disport with his neighbors, having his horse trapped with tinsel and other nice
'disguisey' things, crowned as King of Christmas . . .
rode in divers streets of the city with other people with
him disguised, making mirth, disports and plays." Scholars believe that these mock kings and bishops arc the last
lingering survivals of the temporary monarchs who were
often installed to hold sway during the brief period which
intervened, in ancient calendars, between the end of one
year and the beginning of the next; and the late Sir
James Frazer has drawn attention to the fact that a similar officer presided over the Roman festival of Satur-
nalia, held at roughly the same season.

Lastly, there is the custom of burning Haman in effigy.
In this it is not difficult to recognize the familiar Shrovetide rite of burning up the old year or—in a moralizing
version—of human sin and corruption. In the English
county of Kent, it is customary for the girls of the village
to burn a straw figure known as the Holly Boy, and for
the boys to retaliate by consigning to the flames a grotesque puppet called the Ivy Girl; and in Germany, a
large doll representing the demonic Frau Holle is cast
into a bonfire.

The spirit of merriment extends even to the services
in the synagogue, the same kind of license being permitted—though to a lesser degree—as obtained in church
on the Shrovetide Feast of the Ass. The reading of the
scroll of Esther is customarily accompanied by loud stamp-

ing and whirring of noisemakers at every mention of Haman. In some parts, it is even customary to wear slippers with the infamous name chalked on the soles; a reasonable amount of stomping and shuffling will thus cause it to be literally wiped out! Furthermore, when the cantor reaches the passage (9:6-9) listing Haman's sons, he reels them off in a single breath!

Purim is thus in every way a pure folk festival. It is, so to speak, the light relief in Israel's serious and solemn commitment, and it leavens the religious year with the necessary element of fun and cheer.

In its original form, the dominant note of the story of Esther was, perhaps, an emphasis on the element of chance in human affairs. By pure chance was Esther chosen as queen; by pure chance did Mordecai overhear the conspiracy against the king;[7] by pure chance did Haman select the day for the extermination of his rival's kinsmen; by pure chance was "the king's sleep disturbed," so that he ordered the chronicles to be read to him;[8] by pure chance did the reader light on the record of Mordecai's loyal service; and by pure chance did Harbonah the chamberlain break in at the critical moment to apprise his master that Haman had already erected the gallows[9] In Judaism, however, what appears to man as blind chance is really but part of the design of God. The whole story therefore serves as an exemplar of the truth that "God moves in a mysterious way His wonders to perform." As the prayerbook puts it:

.....

[7] Esther 2:21-23.
[8] *Ibid.*, 6:1.
[9] *Ibid.*, 7:9.

> When the wicked Haman arose and
> sought to destroy, slay and annihilate
> the Jews . . . on a single day . . . Thou, in
> Thine abundant compassion, didst
> bring his counsels to naught and confound
> his designs, and make them to recoil
> upon his own head. Thus didst Thou
> perform for the Jews a miracle and a
> wonder, and therefore we render due
> thanks to Thy great name.

Nor this alone. Here again we see how the triumphs and disasters of Israel throughout its history are events whose meaning transcends the immediate incident. It is another example of the continuous process of historical interpretation. Haman, therefore, is not simply a Persian vizier; he is essentially Haman *the Agagite,* by which title he is at once identified as a latter-day scion of Agag, king of the accursed Amalekites,[10] whereas Mordecai is represented as a descendant of Kish, the father of Saul.[11] The enmity between them is thus but one incident in the eternal battle of God against the forces of evil; and to drive the point home, the sages prescribed that the Lesson from the Law on Purim should describe the original discomfiture of Amalek and close with the solemn assurance that "the Lord will have war with Amalek from generation to generation" (Exod. 17:8-16). Moreover, the special "anthem" for the festival is the Twenty-second Psalm, which begins on the tearful note of desperation:

My God, My God, why hast Thou forsaken me?

and ends with the ringing acclamation:

. . . . .

[10] See I Sam. 15:7-33.
[11] Esther 2:5.

All that go down into the dust
    Shall make obeisance to Him.
Even if a man be himself not spared to life,
    His heirs shall yet serve God.
The tale of the Lord shall be told to each succeeding age;
To a people still to be born men shall tell how He dealeth aright.

HANUKKAH

The Feast of Lights

Hanukkah, or the Feast of Dedication, is the only important Jewish festival that is not mentioned in the Bible. It is celebrated for eight days, beginning on the twenty-fifth of Kislev (December), to commemorate the victory of Judah the Maccabee and his followers over the forces of the Syrian king, Antiochus IV, and their re-dedication of the defiled Temple in Jerusalem, in 165 B.C.E. The story is told in the First and Second Books of the Maccabees, which form part of the Apocrypha, and in the writings of the Greek historian Polybius (*ca.* 204-122 B.C.E.). It may be summarized as follows:

On the death of Alexander the Great, in 323 B.C.E., his empire was divided among his generals. One of the results of that division was that Palestine remained a bone of contention between the kingdoms of Syria in the north and Egypt in the south. After passing, for several generations, from one to the other, it was finally conquered by the Syrian monarch, Antiochus the Great, in 198 B.C.E.

When, after the assassination of his elder brother Seleucus, Antiochus IV succeeded to the throne of Syria, in 175 B.C.E., he decided almost at once to launch a military campaign against the rival kingdom of Egypt. The purpose of this adventure was not only to extend his dominion but also—and more particularly—to forestall possible reprisals for the seizure of Palestine which his father had accomplished. To prevent subversion at home, however, it was necessary to weld the disparate elements of the population into a single united front, and this the monarch attempted to do by introducing a form of cultural totalitarianism.

A particular thorn in his flesh were the Jews in the recently vanquished land, for these regarded themselves as its rightful owners and persisted in maintaining a distinctive manner of life. Antiochus' first move was therefore to depose their "orthodox" high priest, Onias, and to install in his place his more Greek-minded brother, Joshua. Joshua—who promptly changed his name to Jason—proceeded in short order to inaugurate a radical policy of Hellenization. Under the citadel of Jerusalem he constructed a gymnasium; he persuaded the Jewish gentry to adopt Greek costume; and under his benevolent eye, the junior priests deserted the service of the sanctuary to engage in Greek sports.

These trends and innovations split Jewry wide open, for while the upper classes and many members of the priesthood went along cheerfully with the new drive toward "assimilation," the more conservative elements reacted by organizing a movement called the Pietists

(Hasidim), dedicated to maintaining the traditional patterns of Judaism by passive and—if need be—clandestine resistance.

In 168, however, matters came to a head. Antiochus, about to lay siege to Alexandria, the capital of Egypt, found himself suddenly presented with an ultimatum from Rome, ordering him to desist. Unable to face so formidable an opponent, he was obliged to comply. But this merely strengthened his resolve to achieve a solid front at home and to impose a tighter control on those of his subjects whom he could not but regard as a potential fifth column. In the following year, therefore, he decided to implement his previous measures by the establishment of a "state church" under which the several religions of his subjects were to be subsumed. The god of this "church" was to be the Greek Zeus, with whom all of the national gods were to be promptly identified; and in order to indicate that it was simply an organ of the state, Antiochus claimed, in accordance with a practice common among the Seleucid and Ptolemaic kings, to be that deity's visible incarnation, arrogating to himself the title of "Epiphanes," or "(God) Manifest," and ordering that title henceforth to be stamped upon the coins of the realm. This policy constituted a break with the system of cultural self-determination and pluralism, to use our modern phrases, which had prevailed since the days of Alexander the Great, a system under which the empire had been regarded rather as a union of vassal peoples, politically subservient to a central government, but culturally and religiously independent.

In pursuit of it, Antiochus issued a decree prohibiting, on pain of death, any expression of Jewish distinctiveness, and ordering the Temple services to be accommodated to the new national religion. When his officers visited the small town of Modin (today called al Ara'in) to supervise enforcement of the measure, an aged Jewish priest named Mattathias, of the family of the Hasmoneans, offered resistance. In the words of the First Book of the Maccabees (2:17-28):

Then said the king's officers unto Mattathias: "Thou art a leader, a prominent and important man in this town, strengthened with sons and brethren: now therefore come thou first and do the commandment of the king, as all the pagans and the men of Judah and they that remain in Jerusalem have done; so shalt thou and thy household be reckoned in the royal entourage, and both thou and thy sons shall be honored with silver and gold and many gifts." But Mattathias answered in a loud voice: "Even if all the nations within the king's dominions hearken unto him to fall away each one from its ancestral faith, and even if they choose to follow his commandments, yet will I and my sons and my brethren walk in the covenant of our fathers. God forbid that we should forsake the law and the ordinances. We will not hearken to the king's words, to go aside from our faith, either to the right hand or to the left."
Now, when he had finished speaking these words, there came a Jew in the sight of all to sacrifice on the altar . . . in the manner prescribed by the king's commandment. But when Mattathias saw him, his zeal was inflamed and his passions were stirred, . . . and he slew him beside the altar. . . . And Mattathias cried out in the city in a loud voice: "Whoever is zealous for the Law and would maintain the Covenant—let him follow me."
And he and his sons fled to the hills. . . .

At first, it was difficult for the partisans of Mattathias to find common ground with the alternative movement of the Pietists. The latter tended to regard them as irreligious hotheads more interested in nationalistic chauvinism than in the real defense of their ancestral faith. Later, however, under the pressure of a rising emergency, ideological differences were subordinated to a unified program of militant resistance. Following the death of the aged Mattathias, this combined movement was headed by his third son, Judah, surnamed the Maccabee; and after a succession of singular victories over police expeditions dispatched by Antiochus, the partisans eventually stormed the Temple hill, drove out the garrison, cleansed the sanctuary and re-established the traditional order of services. The event is said to have taken place, by a dramatic coincidence, on the third anniversary of Antiochus' order of desecration. The Maccabees celebrated their triumph with an eight-day festival, and, with the consent of the ecclesiastical authorities, enjoined that it be perpetuated in Israel as the Feast of Dedication.

The festival is today one of the most popular of Jewish observances. At the same time, one may suspect with reason that its current interpretation has thrown it considerably out of focus and obscured much of its real significance.

In the conventional exposition, the central theme of Hanukkah is usually represented as the victory of Hebraism over Hellenism—that is, of Jewish over Greek values. The revolt of the Maccabees against the power of Antiochus IV is considered, as it were, no more than the particular but, so to speak, routine historical setting within which this momentous symbolic triumph happened to be achieved. The antagonists in the struggle are the people of Jehovah on the one hand, and of Zeus on the other, but these chief characters of the drama are only superficially linked with the authentic realities of either the politics or the culture of the period: they are little more than conventional lay figures in the simplest moral fable. The Jews stand for the Torah-bound—that is, morally and religiously bound—way of life, and the Greeks are a collection of hedonists dedicated to the pursuit of physical and esthetic delights and to the cultivation and worship of beauty. The Greeks, we are told, saw religion in beauty, whereas the Jews saw beauty in the divine law; the battle between them was, in fact, a challenge flung from Zion against Helicon, and the victory was that of the synagogue over the gymnasium. Greek culture, in this view, is a heathen abomination, and the cleansing of the temple by Judah and his followers removed defilement not only from the House of God but equally from the lives of men.

What is wrong with this presentation is that it totally adapts both the authentic facts and the true religious meaning to fit a superficial romanticized ideal. It is plain from the record that the Maccabean revolt was not inspired by a mere ideological resistance to Hellenism. Its purpose was deeper and more precise.

First, it was designed to safeguard the actual identity of the Jews. In Israel—as throughout the ancient Near East—church and state were coextensive, religion being not so much a matter of confession and belief as the sanctioned regimen of communal economy. Any interference with the administration of the Temple or with the practice of traditional religious rites therefore involved *ipso facto* an impairment, if not a dissolution, of Israel's distinctive identity.

Second, the resistance was designed to safeguard the constitutional status quo. In this, Mattathias and his followers were championing a cause which, transcending the particular interests of the Jews, extended also to *all* the national groups within the empire. This is apparent from the very words of his defiance, for modern studies have shown that when the aged priest spoke of "walking in the covenant of our fathers," he was using a phrase commonly employed in documents of the Hellenistic period relat-

ing to the conferment of cultural or religious independence, not only upon Jews, but also upon other national
groups. He was therefore proclaiming his intention not
only of remaining faithful to Israel's traditional covenant
with Jehovah, but also of defending the established civic
rights of the Jews against arbitrary abrogation.

An equally serious distortion of history is the prevalent idea that the Maccabean revolt represented a people's
uprising of the Jews against their Syrian overlord. For
while it is true that the movement eventually attracted a
large number of supporters, the record makes it perfectly
plain that the official spokesmen of the Jewish community
were hostile to it and, moreover, that the bulk of the
Jewish population was already so far gone in the process
of assimilation that the championship of Israel's distinctive identity meant nothing to it. The high priest at the
time was a rank "collaborationist," and the accredited
leaders of the Jews were what might be described as
"Hellenes of the Mosaic persuasion." It was only after
Mattathias and his followers had gained the support of
the religious pietists and, by a fanatical vigilantist campaign, had forced the apostates back into the fold, that
they could muster sufficient strength to offer serious opposition to the state. Thus we read in the First Book of
Maccabees (2:45-48): "Mattathias and his associates
went the rounds, tearing down the heathen altars and
forcibly circumcising children upon whom the operation
had not been performed . . . And they pursued after
the sons of pride . . . And they delivered the Law out
of the hand of the kings; neither suffered they the sinner to triumph." As this passage indicates, the Maccabean
revolt was from first to last a minority movement, directed as much against degeneration within as against

oppression from without. And therein, indeed, lies no small part of its true significance, and hence of the permanent lesson of Hanukkah.

Nor is it only on historical grounds that the conventional presentation of the festival is open to objection. Equally assailable is the very antithesis it implies between Hebraism and Hellenism, for this is, as we have suggested, more a contrast between artificial modern stereotypes than between actual cultures as they existed at the time. No balanced person believes today that the Frenchman is necessarily amorous, the Englishman taciturn, or the Jew sly. In the more abstract realm of culture and ideas, however, the stereotype still reigns. To the average American, for instance, Mohammedanism is still a compound of muezzins, sheikhs, the Koran, and a permit to have four wives; while the epic struggle between the democratic and communist theories of society tends to be conceived, in the popular mind, as a trading of blows between a stereotype Main Street on the one hand, and a stereotype Kremlin on the other. The same kind of facile generalization and superficial caricature produces the conventional antithesis between Hebrew and Greek cultures. For while it is true that the Greeks, by and large, preferred speculation to revelation as a means of interpreting the universe, and while it is true that the Greeks were inclined to be less impressed than were the Hebrews with the authority of transcendental law, it is a pernicious exaggeration to regard esthetics as exclusively "Greek" and morals as exclusively "Hebrew," and only an insensitive and unperceptive philistinism can pit the one against the other as opposing values. The issues raised by Greek tragedies and discussed in many of the Platonic dialogues are essentially moral, even if the approach to them is through philosophy

rather than revelation. Such Greek gnomic poets as
Theognis bear ample testimony to the fact that Greek
standards of ethics were inspired by something more than
wordly shrewdness and practical expedience. Similarly,
the prophetic and poetic books of the Bible—the speeches
of God to Job, for example—suffice to show that an
esthetic, even sensuous, appreciation of nature was by
no means foreign to the Hebrew temperament.

Moreover, even if the alleged contrast between Greek
and Hebrew culture could in fact be maintained for the
Classical age of the former and the earlier Biblical periods of the latter, it certainly did not obtain in the time
of the Maccabees. For the so-called Hellenism of the
Seleucid and Ptolemaic empires was no exemplar of the
ideals of Periclean Athens, but a strange, bizarre amal-
gam of Greek and Oriental influences. Indeed, it is significant that the Zeus Olympios whose worship Antiochus
sought to impose and whose statue he imported into
the Temple at Jerusalem, was not the Zeus Olympios of
Classical Greece but a hybrid of both Hellenic and Asi-
atic extraction.

Equally misleading is the presentation of the Maccabean revolt as a resistance to the abstract principle of
totalitarianism. Such a picture has an obvious appeal to
the contemporary mind, but is totally incorrect. For the
fact is that the distinctive Jewish culture which Mattathias and his followers sought to defend and preserve
was itself essentially totalitarian, resting on the theory
that every aspect of life must be governed by the dic-
tates of a transcendental law (Torah) and subsumed
under the contour of a divine plan supposedly revealed
in that law. Nor, indeed, were the Maccabees prepared
to compromise this totalitarian theory through any defer-
ence to individual conscience. The concept of personal

liberty did not enter into their outlook; as we have seen, those who did not conform to their programs were made to do so by force and regimentation.

An alternative popular presentation portrays the Syrian monarch as a kind of early Hitler and his assault upon the Jews as inspired only by virulent hatred of them. This, too, is a caricature. There is no evidence whatsoever that Antiochus was an anti-Semite, and the explanation has been advanced only by a process of ex post facto reasoning or by a desire to account on a psychological basis for Antiochus' sudden break with the more tolerant policy of his predecessors. The fact is that Antiochus was motivated entirely by political considerations.

He had just returned from a costly expedition against the rival power of the Ptolemies in Egypt, having virtually subjugated that country and actually captured its king, Ptolemy VI. But the peace which ensued was an uncertain one. The Egyptians had promptly placed on the throne their defeated sovereign's younger brother, and although Antiochus tried astutely to use him as a puppet, the arrangement did not work. The old captive continued to plot resistance, and the ambitions of Rome in relation to Egypt were providing a further obstacle to the plans of the Syrian king. Moreover, it was an actual fact and not a mere void suspicion that many national groups within his own borders, and among them a goodly portion of the Jews, were partial to the Egyptian cause, so that the possibility of a "fifth column" was ever present. Antiochus was therefore faced with a grave situation, and perhaps the only way to meet it was indeed to impose by force a unity which he could not create by persuasion. Then, too, it must be remembered that the campaign against Egypt had put a strain on his finances, and the treasures of the Jewish Temple in Jerusalem offered a source of replenishment. What he did was simply to commandeer, in the interest of the state, a particular section of the national wealth; and it may even be supposed that a further motive was to prevent the possible use of this wealth to assist his foes.

All of this does not mean, of course, that Antiochus did not treat the Jews with extreme harshness and barbarity; the records state that his confiscation of the Temple treasures (in 169 B.C.E.) was accompanied by a massacre of some forty thousand Jews in Jerusalem alone. The point is, however, that his measures were dictated by political expediency and not by hostility to Jews or Judaism *per se,* so that the conventional portrayal of him as a mere bloodthirsty anti-Semite is, once again, a serious distortion of history. As a matter of fact, the measures which Antiochus directed against the Jews were directed also against other national groups. The Samaritans, for example, were likewise obliged to turn over the temple on Mount Gerizim to the cult of Zeus, while at Daphne even the Greek Apollo had, apparently, to take second place beside the new national god. The policy inaugurated by the monarch was based on what he conceived to be the stern necessities of a political situation, not on a mere racial bigotry, and the proscription of distinctive Jewish practices was motivated not by ideological opposition to them but by the urgent need of consolidating a diverse and polyglot population in the face of a national emergency. It is important to draw a distinction—all too often ignored—between primary and incidental oppression, to avoid judging motives by effects, and to realize that many forms of suffering which Jews undergo are no more the products of discrimination or anti-Semitism than is an epidemic or a railroad disaster which happens to claim Jews among its victims.

If then, the conventional picture is distorted and Hanukkah does not in fact celebrate a victory of Hebraism over Hellenism, or a mass uprising of the Jews against the principle of totalitarianism, or a triumphant resistance to anti-Semitic bigotry, what does the festival celebrate? What is its permanent and universal value, and what relevance has it for the present day? The answer is implicit in the analysis which we have given above, for although our examination of the problem may have seemed, at first glance, unduly negative, it in fact issues in positive conclusions. These may be stated briefly under two heads.

First, Hanukkah commemorates and celebrates the first serious attempt in history to proclaim and champion the principle of religio-cultural diversity in the nation. The primary aim of the Maccabees was, as we have seen, to preserve their own Jewish identity and to safeguard for Israel the possibility of continuing its traditional mission. Though inspired, however, by the particular situation of their own people, their struggle was instinct with universal implications. For what was really being defended was the principle that in a diversified society the function of the state is to embrace, not subordinate, the various constituent cultures, and that the complexion and character of the state must be determined by a natural process of fusion on the one hand and selection on the other, and not by the arbitrary imposition of a single pattern on all elements.

Seen from this point of view, therefore, Hanukkah possesses broad human significance and is far more than a mere Jewish national celebration. As a festival of liberty, it celebrates more than the independence of one people— it glorifies the right to freedom of all peoples.

Second, Hanukkah affirms the universal truth that the

only effective answer to oppression is the intensified *positive* assertion of the principles and values which that oppression threatens. What inspired the movement of the Maccabees was not simply an abstract and academic dislike of tyranny but a desire to safeguard and evince an identity and way of life which was in danger of extinction. It therefore consisted not only in a fight *against* Antiochus but also in a fight *for* Judaism, the military uprising going hand in hand with an almost fanatical crusade for the internal regeneration of the Jewish people.

The combination was not fortuitous nor was it due solely—as some scholars have asserted—to the pressure of the pietists whom Mattathias and Judah rallied to their cause. On the contrary, it was fundamental. For the Maccabees, the Jews were a kingdom of priests and a holy nation, a society of men dedicated to attesting the presence of God and to exemplifying His law and dispensation on earth. It was for the continuance of this religious-ethical mission as God's witnesses that they were primarily fighting, and the struggle for civil rights was merely a means to this high purpose. The real issue at stake was not the right of the Jews to be like everyone else, but their right to be different; and victory meant not the attainment of civic equality (which after all, was what Antiochus was offering!) but the renewal, after its forced suspension, of that particular and distinctive way of life which embodied and exemplified the Jewish mission. The mark of that victory, therefore, was not a triumphal parade but an act of dedication —the cleansing of the defiled Temple. Moreover, when the Jews wished to perpetuate the memory of their achievement, what they chose to turn into an annual festival was not the day of some military success but the week in which the House of God had been cleansed and the fire rekindled on the altar. There is an important meaning in this, one feels, for our own day, and especially in connection with the problem of safeguarding civil rights.

Concerning the actual observance of Hanukkah, there is little to say. The only religious ceremony which attaches to the celebration is the kindling of the lights each evening at dusk. The usual practice is to start with one light and to increase the number by one on each successive evening, the flames being lit from right to left, after the direction of Hebrew writing. Some ancient authorities insist, however, that all eight lamps should be kindled each night. The candle which is used for the actual kindling is known popularly as the *shammas,* or "beadle." The lighting of the lamps is accompanied by an appropriate blessing and by a brief statement in Hebrew to the effect that the ceremony commemorates "the miracles, deliverance, deeds of power and acts of salvation" wrought by God at this season, and that the lights are not to be used for any utilitarian purpose; "they are only to be seen."

After the lamps have been lit, the Thirtieth Psalm is intoned. This bears the title, "A Psalm, a Song for the Dedication of the House," and therefore serves as the appropriate "anthem" of the festival. Ashkenazic Jews also sing—to the same tune as Luther's famous hymn, *Nun freut euch liebe Christen gmei*—a rousing chant, called from its opening words *Maoz Zur* ("Fortress Rock"). This chant, the authorship and date of which are uncertain, recites the various deliverances of Israel from the days of Pharaoh to those of Antiochus, but there is nothing to show that it was originally composed for Hanukkah. The following is a modern adaptation, in the same meter, by the late Gustav Gottheil (1827-1903):

Rock of ages, let our song
Praise Thy saving power;
Thou, amidst the raging foes,
Wast our shelt'ring tower.
Furious they assailed us,
But Thine arm availed us;
    And Thy word
    Broke their sword
When our own strength failed us.

. . . . ,

Children of the martyr-race,
Whether free or fettered,
Wake the echoes of the songs
Where ye may be scattered.
Yours the message cheering,
That the time is nearing
    Which shall see
    All men free,
Tyrants disappearing.

In fulfillment of the commandment not to use the lamps for mere "functional" purposes, it is customary to pass the time while they are burning in spinning tops, called *trendels,* or playing an ancient form of "put and take," in which the die is marked with the Hebrew characters *N G H S.* These really stood for the Judeo-German words *nimm,* "take," *gib,* "give," *halb,* "half," and *stell,* "put"; but they were popularly interpreted as the initial letters of the Hebrew motto, *Nes Gadol Hayah Sham,* "A great miracle took place there."

The services in the synagogue are the same as those on ordinary weekdays, except that the Hallel, or Psalms of Praise (Pss. 113–118) are chanted and a short passage is inserted in the Standing Prayer reciting the victory of the Maccabees. The latter insertion is made at the point where thanks are rendered to God for his "miracles which are ever with us and for His wonders and acts of grace which are wrought at all times, at evening, morn and noon." Moreover, in order to bring home the continuity of Israel's religious institutions, the portion of the Pentateuch describing the dedication of the sanctuary in the wilderness (Num. 6:22–8:4) is read progressively in the mornings of the festivals.

It cannot be denied that Hanukkah possesses certain militant, revolutionary undertones, and these have often conspired to create around it a certain atmosphere of embarrassment. During the time of the Roman administration, for example, there were not wanting those who considered it imprudent, even dangerous, for the Jewish minority openly to observe a festival celebrating rebellion against a ruling power; and it is significant that Rabbi Judah the Patriarch, the compiler of the Mishnah, tried desperately to suppress any reference to Hanukkah even as he sought also to minimize the importance of Purim, another occasion purportedly commemorating victory over an alien sovereign.

A curious reflection of this attitude may be seen in the prominence which has come to be attached to Hanukkah lights. The lights are not even mentioned in the Book of the Maccabees. Modern scholars are therefore inclined to think that they had originally nothing whatsoever to do with the festival, but, like the candles of Christmas represent only an adaptation of the familiar pagan custom of lighting candles or kindling fires at the winter solstice as a means of reluming the decadent sun. The significant thing, however, is that embarrassment over the more militant aspects of Hanukkah caused the Jews to seize upon this purely secular and even heathen

custom, Judaizing it by an appropriate legend, in order
to divert attention into more innocuous quarters. (*Muta-
tis mutandis,* it is as if the Catholic Church, nervous about
the implications of the Christmas story, had officially substituted the Yule log for the cradle in the manger as the
symbol of the day when Jesus was born.)

Nevertheless, with characteristic genius the Jews
made of this originally foreign and heathen custom the
most fitting symbol of the festival's real message; for the
lights were taken to represent the Temple candelabrum
which Judah and his followers had rekindled and thus
came to epitomize the truth that Hanukkah is not simply
the V-day of the national victory of the Maccabees but
essentially a feast of dedication. What had originally symbolized the mere physical regeneration of the sun, or of
nature, from year to year, was thus transmuted into a
symbol of revival on the *spiritual* plane, becoming indeed, as our fathers told us, a brave light in a naughty
world.

Nor is it only the ancient sages who have had qualms
about the Hanukkah story. Modern readers of it have
likewise felt certain awkward and embarrassing incon-
sistencies between the Maccabee's zeal for Jewish rights
and their intolerant persecution of those who happened
to disagree with their outlook; the forced circumcision
of Jewish infants, for example, seems strangely incongruous with the championship of freedom of belief. The
explanation, however, is very simple: we must not read
modern ideas and ideals into an ancient story. At the
time of the Maccabees, the modern concept of personal
liberty of conscience had not yet been developed, and religion was a collective regimen rather than an individual
persuasion. Accordingly, what the Maccabees were out
to defend was not the right of every individual to wor-

ship God in his own way, but rather the mission of
Israel as a collective unit to serve as God's witnesses and
to exemplify His Torah. Those who refused to accept
this obligation were therefore just as much enemies of
their cause as were any foreign oppressors, so that the
Maccabees' policy toward them, however distasteful it
may seem by later standards, was at the time both logical and consistent. Our modern revulsion at this policy is
simply an example of the way the insights and perspec-
tives of subsequent ages often call into question the ideals
underlying traditional institutions.

However it is interpreted, and no matter where the
emphasis is placed, the significance of Hanukkah for the
modern Jew stems from the story of the Maccabees
and depends on the tradition that it was founded by
them to commemorate the triumph of their cause and the
rededication of the Temple in 165 B.C.E. Modern scholars have suspected, however, that the real origin of the
festival may lie elsewhere—possibly even in a more ancient pagan institution which the Jews adopted and then
rationalized by this story.

A favorite starting point for such speculation is the
fact that in the Second Book of Maccabees (1:9), when
the Jews of Jerusalem exhort their brethren in Egypt to
adopt the annual celebration of Hanukkah, they describe
it as "the Festival of Booths in the Month of Kislev."
This has suggested to some authorities that Hanukkah
was in origin simply a "postponed Succoth," and support
for this view is drawn from the express statement in that
same book that Judah and his followers "kept the eight
days with rejoicing in the manner of the Feast of Booths
. . . carrying wands wreathed with green and season-
able branches and palms" (10:7-8). The true explanation of these puzzling phrases would seem, however, to

be quite different. The fact is that both the First and the Second Temples had been dedicated at the Feast of Booths (see I Kings 8:2,65; Neh. 8:13-18), and in order to dramatize the occasion, Judah and his followers made a point of copying the traditional ritual of that festival when they cleansed and rededicated the sacred edifice. Accordingly, when the Jews of Jerusalem described the festival as "the Feast of Booths in the month of Kislev" their words are not to be taken literally but mean simply "the December version of Succoth."

Another view starts from the Hanukkah lights, fanning them indeed into a veritable blaze. This view, which has recently been developed and elaborated, with characteristic brilliance and ingenuity, by Dr. Julian Morgenstern of Hebrew Union College, claims that back of Hanukkah there lies a pagan festival of either the autumn equinox or the winter solstice, both of which occasions were (and still are) marked in many parts of the world by the lighting of candles or fires. In that case, the resemblance to the equinoctial Feast of Booths (when, according to the Mishnah, bonfires and torches were indeed lit in Jerusalem) would, of course, have readily sprung to mind, and this would sufficiently account for the description of the festival as "Booths in Kislev." There is, however, a very obvious objection to this view, and it was stated clearly many years ago by that redoubtable student of ancient religions, Professor Martin Nilsson: Hanukkah is determined by the *lunar* calendar whereas equinoxes and solstices depend, of course, on a *solar* reckoning; accordingly, there is no assurance that Hanukkah will in fact coincide with either event.

Lastly, there is the present writer's theory which, while accepting the historicity of the traditional account, suggests that the peculiar form of celebration which Judah and his followers chose was motivated not only by a desire to imitate the dedication of the First and Second Temples at Succoth but also to satirize the contemporaneous Greek festival of the rural Dionysia. The festival fell towards the end of December and in many centers it was celebrated only every other year. When the appointed season came around, the votaries of Dionysus would dress themselves up in the skins of fawns or foxes, crown themselves with wreaths of ivy, bear in their hands small staves ornamented with foliage and tipped with pine cones, and then rush madly to the mountains, where torchlight revels were held throughout the night. Every so often, the torches would be lowered and dipped for a moment in wine or water, so that the ensuing spurt of flame might symbolize the fiery and luminous character of the god.

The ceremonies instituted by Judah and his followers would have constituted a pointed satire on these rites. In place of the filthy "purifications" of the pagans, these devoted Jews cleansed and purified the House of God. In place of the orgiastic festal parade, they reverently circuited the altar. Instead of the wreathed wands, they carried the *lulab*. Instead of the frenzied shouts, they recited psalms. And instead of waving torches, they relit the sacred candelabrum.

The writer of the account in the Second Book of the Maccabees seems, indeed, to have been aware of the satire. When he speaks of the resumption of the services of God, he subtly stresses that this took place after a *two-year interval,* and in these words we may perhaps detect a sly jibe at the biennial festival of the heathen. Similarly, when he goes out of his way to observe that the participants in the Jewish ceremony were distinctly relieved to be free at last of the necessity of living on the mountains like wild beasts, it is perhaps not too fanciful to recognize in his statement a pointed contrast with the devotees of Dionysus who of their own free will were happy to dress up in skins and simulate animals. Lastly, when he observes casually that the light for the altar fire was furnished by the normal process of striking flints, he may well have been wishing to suggest to his readers how different this was from the bizarre dipping of the torches in the rites of the Greek god!

Whether any of these theories is right cannot now be known; all of them are based on deductions from fragmentary and inconclusive evidence. But they are not mere academic trivialities; for if any one of them is vindicated, it will shed important light on how, in the course of the ages, the festival has developed and been transmuted by the Jewish genius; and that development and transmutation into a religious and humanistic festival of broad universal meaning is an integral part of its significance. At the moment, however, we must simply wait for more light of the kind that comes from further knowledge and commentary, and new insights. Perhaps, after all, there is a profound lesson in the fact that the Hanukkah lights increase from day to day and that their full radiance is achieved only by gradual stages.

Like Passover and Purim, Hanukkah is regarded as the commemoration of a miracle. But, despite the ancient idiom which so portrays it, that miracle is not an act of supernatural grace. Rather is it the working within man of a passion which transcends the momentary and spurns the opportune. Its symbol is appropriately the light which illumines the House of God; and the real miracle is that the light is never extinguished.

12

THE NEW YEAR
FOR TREES

Besides the formal religious festivals, the Jewish year
also includes a number of purely popular celebrations,
distinguished by no special service in the synagogue and
by no particular ritual. One such occasion is the Thirty-
third Day of the Omer, which we have already described;[1] another is the New Year for Trees, on the
fifteenth day of Shebat (February).

The New Year for Trees is mentioned in the Mishnah[2] among the four "natural" new years which punctuate the lunar twelvemonth. The first of Nisan, we are
told, is the new year "for kings and seasonal feasts"—that
is, for calculating the reigns of the Israelitic kings and

. . . . .

[1] See above, pp. 53, ff.
[2] *Rosh Ha-shanah* i, 1.

for determining the cycle of the calendar festivals; the first of Elul is the new year "for tithing cattle," i.e., any animal born before that date may not be offered as a tithe for cattle born after it; the first of Tishri is the new year for reckoning septennial cycles and fifty-year jubilees, as also for husbandry and arboriculture; the first of Shebat is the new year for fruit trees.

Most of these new years have indeed been absorbed into the formal Jewish calendar, even though some of them are no longer marked by religious ceremonies. For legal purposes, for instance, Nisan I ranks as New Year; while Tishri I—originally the "Day of Memorial"—is the religious New Year (Rosh Ha-shanah).[3] The New Year for Trees, however, has been shifted, in accordance with the opinion of the famous Rabbi Hillel (fl. 30 B.C.E.—10 C.E.), to the fifteenth day of the month. The reason for Hillel's divergent opinion is none too clear; seeing, however, that in the late summer the fifteenth day of Ab was likewise observed as a folk festival,[4] and seeing also that the great harvest festivals of Passover and Ingathering similarly occur on the fifteenth day of the month (i.e., at full moon), it is possible that this represents an attempt to merge the observance with a previously existent celebration.

On the fifteenth day of Shebat, so it is said, the sap begins to rise in the fruit trees of the Holy Land. It is therefore customary on that day to partake of such fruits as grow in the Holy Land, e.g., apples, almonds, carobs, figs, nuts and pomegranates. In some parts, it is the practice also to sit up late the previous evening reciting passages of the Bible which deal with trees and

. . . . .

[3] See above, pp. 107, ff.
[4] Mishnah, Ta'anith IV, 9, 10.

fruits or with the fertility of the earth. Such passages
include: the story of how trees and plants were created
(Gen. 1:11-18); the divine promise of abundance as a
reward for keeping the commandments (Lev. 26:3-18;
Deut. 8: 1-10); and the parable of the spreading vine,
which symbolized the people of Israel (Ezek. 17). Added
to them are various extracts from the Psalms, such as
Ps. 65:10-14, in which the blossoming of the earth in
spring is graphically depicted;

From out Thine inexhausted store
    the rain relieves the thirsty ground;
Makes lands that barren were before
    with corn and useful fruits abound.

On rising ridges down it pours,
    and every furrow'd valley fills;
Thou mak'st them soft with gentle showers,
    in which a blest increase distils.

Thy goodness does the circling year
    with fresh returns of plenty crown;
And, when Thy glorious paths appear,
    Thy fruitful clouds drop fatness down.

They drop on barren forests, chang'd
    by them to pastures fresh and green:
The hills about, in order rang'd,
    in beauteous robes of joy are seen.

Large flocks with fleecy wool adorn
    the cheerful downs; the valleys bring
A plenteous crop of full-ear'd corn
    and seem for joy to shout and sing.[5]

.....

[5] Brady and Tate's translation.

or Ps. 72:16, in which the prosperity of a well-governed realm is likened to the burgeoning of nature:

May (the king) be in the land as an expanse of corn
    waving in the breeze upon the hilltops;
May his fruit be as that which in Lebanon grows,
    and out of the city may men flourish like grass of the earth!

Among the Sephardim, a special manual entitled *The Fruit of the Goodly Tree* (cf. Lev. 23:40), is used on this occasion. A Judeo-Spanish (Ladino) edition of this work, first published in Salonica, includes the following quaint lines composed by a certain Judah Kalaʻi.[6] They are designed to be chanted as each of the several fruits is eaten:

Con nostros abonegue, lo tarde y la mañana,
Y el bien nos muchigne come granos de m a n g r a n a.

Esperamos al goel,[7] come luz de la mañana
Relumbrara a Israel, a color de la m a n z a n a.

De mal la alma esta harta; Dio mira que razon es
Mandes ya que se parta esta casca de la n u e z.
. . . .

Cobrare munchos amigos, y el bien se renova;
Se haran sus enemigos secos come la a l h a r u b a.
. . . .

Ya lo vamos esperando al goel de hora en hora,
Los cueros se van haziendo prietos come la a m o r a.
. . . . .

---

[6] M. Grünbaum, *Jüdisch-Spanische Chrestomathie* (Frankfurt am Main, 1896), p. 69.
[7] A Hebrew word meaning *Redeemer*.

[God increase our worldly goods,
    And guard us soon and late,
And multiply our bliss like seeds
    Of POMEGRANATE.

For our Redeemer do we wait
    All the long night through,
To bring a dawn as roseate
    As APPLE'S hue.

Sin, like a stubborn shell and hard,
    Is wrapped around our soul;
Lord, break the husk and let the NUT
    Come out whole!

.   .   .   .

God give us many friends, renew
    Our old prosperity,
And be our foemen shrivell'd up
    Like CAROBS dry.

.   .   .   .

Behold, from hour to hour we wait
    The dayspring yet to be
While all our hearts are dark and black
    As MULBERRY.]

In Jewish traditional lore, each of the fruits possesses
its own symbolic meaning. The roseate apple stands for
the glowing splendor of God, for does not Israel say of
Him in the Song of Songs (2:3): "As an apple tree
among the trees of the wood, so is my Beloved"? The nut
represents Israel, since nuts are of three kinds: hard,
medium and soft, and thereby symbolize the three different types of character to be found among Jews! The
almond betokens the swiftness of divine retribution, for
the almond blossoms more quickly than any other tree,
and when Aaron's rod sprouted almonds (Num. 17:8),
this was intended as a warning to all who might seek to

usurp the priestly office! The fig is a symbol of peace
and prosperity, for is it not written: "Make your peace
with me . . . and eat ye every one of his vine and every
one of his fig-tree" (Isa. 36:16), and again: "They shall
sit every man under his vine and under his fig-tree, and
none shall make them afraid" (Mic. 4:4)? Lastly, the
humble carob is the mark of lowly fare, and therefore
betokens the humility which is a necessary element of
penitence.[8]

In the modern Holy Land the New Year for Trees
has taken on a new complexion. Largely under the influence of the familiar American Arbor Day,[9] it has
become the custom to go out into the fields, on the
fifteenth of Shebat, and plant saplings; and in Zionist
circles outside of the Holy Land, collections are usually
made for the benefit of the reforestation program. Once
again, in characteristically Jewish fashion, we have an
ancient institution transmuted and reinterpreted in terms
of contemporary life.

• • • • •

[8] The carob is known in European folklore as St. John's bread, and is
eaten especially on the feast of that saint (Midsummer Day). Many
scholars have supposed that John the Baptist ate carobs rather than
locusts when he went into the wilderness preaching repentance, for the
Greek word usually rendered "locusts" is indeed used also in the sense
of "carobs."

[9] The American Arbor Day is of comparatively recent origin; having been
first instituted in Nebraska in 1872. An imitation of it was introduced
into Spain by Alfonso XIII some twenty-four years later, and March 26
is observed in that country as the *Fiesta del Arbol* (Feast of the Tree).
As in the Holy Land, the festival is especially popular among children.

VI

Sabbath

13

THE DAY OF REST

The Hebrew word *sabbath* has passed into every European language, and there is no civilized people in the Western hemisphere to whom the institution of the weekly day of rest is altogether unknown. Although, to be sure, the seventh-day sabbath has been replaced, in Christian countries, by Sunday or the Lord's Day—that is, by the day on which the crucified Jesus is believed to have re-risen—the mode of observance is still a direct, if attenuated, heritage from the ancient Hebrew practice.

The curious thing is, however, that nobody really knows how the sabbath began; for the Biblical statement that it commemorates the rest taken by God after the six-day labor of creation is simply a fanciful attempt to rationalize and explain a traditional institution.

A favorite theory is that the sabbath originated among
the Babylonians. The basis of this theory is that in certain Babylonian documents, the equivalent word *shapattu*
is used to designate the fifteenth day of a lunar month.
From this many scholars have concluded that the sabbath
was originally a full-moon festival, the name being then
explained from the Semitic root *sh-b-t*, meaning "to stop,"
i.e., the day when the moon comes, so to speak, to a
full stop, its waxing thenceforth giving place to waning.
Moreover, in further support of this theory, it is pointed
out that in several passages of Scripture,[1] "sabbath" and
"new moon" are in fact juxtaposed, and that in Lev.
23:11,15 the former term is applied to the beginning of
Passover, which happens to fall at the full moon.

For all its popularity, however, this theory is extremely
tenuous, for there is no proof whatsoever that the term
shapattu denoted the fifteenth day of *every* month; all
that the texts imply is that on certain specific occasions
that day happened to coincide with a sabbath (in whatever sense the word be understood). Moreover, it is
difficult to see how, on this hypothesis, the full-moon
festival developed into the present weekly sabbath, for
the latter is entirely independent of the phases of the
moon. Nor, indeed, can anything really be deduced from
the fact that the words *sabbath* and *new moon* are sometimes juxtaposed in Scripture to convey the comprehensive sense of "sacred occasions." For this may be no
more than an example of the figure of speech known as
merism, whereby two contrasted elements of a thing are
mentioned together to indicate the whole, e.g., "officers
and men" for "army." The essence of a merism is that
the two parts belong to different categories; hence, the

. . . . .

[1] e.g., II Kings 4:23; Isa. 1, 13; Hos. 2:17; Amos 8:4-5.

very fact that "sabbath" is juxtaposed with "new moon" might itself be an indication that the former, as distinct from the latter, did *not* form part of the lunar calendar.

An alternative theory sees the origin of the sabbath in the ancient system of reckoning time by *pentacontads,* or stretches of fifty days. According to this view, the term *sabbath* applied originally to the days which were added to two of these stretches in order to accommodate the system to the luni-solar year. These days were regarded as outside of the regular calendar—a kind of vacant space in time—and were therefore marked by a suspension of normal activity, the word *sabbath* meaning "stoppage" in this sense. In the time of Ezra, it is supposed, when the Jews returned from the Babylonian Exile, rebuilt the Temple and re-established its services, a new system was introduced: all the days in each pentacontad which happened to be divisible by seven were deemed "vacant days" and excluded from the regular count; and thus arose the weekly sabbath.

Fascinating as this theory is, we are perhaps on more solid ground if we start from the fact that the sabbath is by no means an exclusively Semitic institution. Regular days of abstention from work are a common phenomenon among primitive peoples. Among several West African tribes, for example, each god has a special day of the week reserved for his worship, and on that day his own particular devotees are required to desist from all manual labor. Similarly, among the Lolos of Southwest China, a sabbath is observed every sixth day, women being forbidden to sew or launder clothes; while in Ceylon, the lunar quarters are regarded as solemn "*poya*-days," and all stores remain closed. The Tshi-speaking peoples of the Gold Coast keep every first and every seventh day as a sabbath; and the same usage prevails also among the

Ga, who call that day *dsu,* or "purification." So, too, it is customary among the Loango of West Africa and among the Ibo of southern Nigeria to divide the month into seven four-day weeks and to begin each with a sabbath *(nsona);* while the Ewe of Dahomey (North Africa) abstain from work every fourth day.

In most of these cases, the institution appears to have arisen out of purely practical considerations, for the sabbaths are, in fact, market days, when the normal routine has perforce to be suspended in the individual villages while everyone is away plying his wares at the central depot.

Sometimes, however, days of rest are determined directly by the phases of the moon. The Bapiri of Bechuanaland, for example, make a point of staying indoors at new moon; while some of the native tribes of Uganda take a week's rest on that occasion. The Kanarese of India will not plow on either new moon or full moon; and in Nepal, both of these dates rank as special holy days, when no work is permitted and no one may cook food or indulge in litigation. Among the Bahima of Southwest Uganda, the king goes into retreat at new moon; while in Thailand, new moon and full moon are considered "major sabbaths," and the first and last quarters "minor sabbaths."

From these examples—a selection out of many—it is apparent that the sabbath, or periodic day of rest, does not belong to any one particular calendarical system, nor is it everywhere inspired by a single uniform cause. It may be occasioned, in one case, by the practical exigencies of market day, and in another, by superstitions about the phases of the moon. When, however, formal calendarical systems are established, they tend to incorporate and exploit the time-honored traditional institution. This, it may be suggested, is what happened in the case of the Hebrew sabbath, many of the earlier ideas and practices being taken over and absorbed when it was later accommodated to the seven-day week. The abstention from work, for example, may well have derived from the purely utilitarian consideration of a market-day sabbath, whereas the prohibition against kindling fire (Exod. 35: 3) links up immediately with a practice observed elsewhere (e.g., in parts of Egypt and in Hawaii) at crucial phases of the moon and therefore stems, in all likelihood, from a "lunar" prototype. Similarly, the injunction (Exod. 31:14) that anyone who profanes the sabbath is to be put to death obviously stems from a type of observance in which it was more a day of taboos than a purely utilitarian institution; indeed, the same law actually obtains in respect to the weekly "sabbaths" observed by the Yoruba on the Slave Coast, and these are of an entirely "superstitious" character, having nothing whatever to do with such functional occasions as market days.

However it may have begun, the sabbath was developed by Judaism along entirely original lines. It became—as the Biblical law expresses it—"a token of the fact that in six days the Lord made the heavens and the earth, and on the seventh day He stopped *(shabat)* and was refreshed" (Exod. 31:17). There is more to this phrase than appears from the English translation. In the Hebrew original, the term rendered "was refreshed" is connected with the word for "breath, spirit, vital essence." What is meant, however, is not that God "breathed freely" or heaved a sigh of relief, but that in the very act of ceasing from His labors He also, as it were, *became inspirited,* and took on a new vitality; and it is this combination of physical rest and spiritual replenishment that characterizes the Jewish conception of the sabbath. The day possesses a positive as well as a negative aspect: it is not merely a memorial; it is an active imitation by man of that which was done by God; and it is observed from week to week because man's life on earth is, in fact, a continuous process of creation.

The Jewish sages brought out the twofold character of the day by carefully codifying its restrictions on the one hand and by continually stressing, on the other, the necessity of utilizing the weekly pause for purposes of mental and spiritual *recreation* (in the literal sense of the word).

Insofar as the restrictions are concerned, the Mishnah[2] specifies thirty-nine actions which may not be performed on the sabbath, viz.—

sowing, plowing, reaping, sheaving;

threshing, winnowing, cleansing crops;

grinding, sifting, kneading, baking;

shearing, blanching, carding, dyeing;

spinning, weaving, making a minimum of
two loops, weaving two threads, separating
two threads;

tying, untying;

sewing a minimum of two stitches,
ripping out in order to sew them;

hunting a gazelle, slaughtering it,
flaying it, salting it, curing,
scraping, or slicing its hide;

. . . . .

[2] Shabbat VII, 2.

writing a minimum of two characters;
erasing in order to write them;

building, wrecking;

extinguishing, kindling;

hammering;

transporting.

This list in turn underwent further refinement; and, as a matter of fact, a large part of medieval and later Jewish literature consists in the replies issued by rabbinical authorities to questions concerning the minutiae of the law.

An excellent picture of the strictness with which the sabbath was observed by Jews of more rigid cast is afforded by a document discovered, in 1896, among discarded manuscripts and damaged copies of the Law, in the old synagogue at Fostat, near Cairo. This document is the manual of discipline of an ascetic brotherhood which existed in Damascus at some time between the first and third centuries of the current era.[3] The regulations concerning the sabbath (many of which are paralleled in the Mishnah) run as follows:

On the sabbath day, no one is to speak of profane or vain matters. No one is to make loans to another. No one is to engage in litigation about property or profit. No one is to talk business. . . . No one is to go about in his field for the purpose of carrying on his

. . . . .

[3] The brotherhood traced its origin to a reform movement instituted in Jerusalem in the second century B.C.E. by certain "sons of Zadok." Other documents emanating from it have recently been found in a cave at Ain Feskha, near the Dead Sea. It should be mentioned, however, that scholars are still in dispute concerning the date when these writings were composed, some authorities believing that they are of far later origin.

normal work. On the sabbath day, no one is to go out of the city beyond a distance of a thousand cubits. No one is to eat anything that has not been prepared beforehand. . . . When on a journey, no one is to partake of any food other than that which he previously had with him in his place of encampment. . . . No one is to draw water. . . . No one is to commission a non-Jew to do his own work. No one is to wear soiled garments or garments which have been worn while working in the garden except he wash them in water and scrub them with lye. No one is to observe a voluntary fast. No one is to follow his cattle to pasture beyond a distance of a thousand cubits. . . . No one is to bring anything into or out of his house. . . . Nurses are not to take their charges out on the sabbath day. No one is to issue orders to his manservant or his maidservant or his hireling on the sabbath day. No one is to assist an animal to give birth. If an animal fall into a pit or snare on the sabbath day, no one is to lift it out; and if a human being fall into a well whence he cannot be extricated by a ladder or a rope or any other instrument, no one is to lift him out. . . .

At the present day, the strictly "orthodox" Jew will not transact business, touch money, write, tear paper, smoke, switch on lights, use the telephone, travel or carry anything on the sabbath. Indeed, in some cases, even handkerchiefs are pinned to the garments and thereby regarded, by a legalistic subtlety, as integral parts of the clothing rather than as things *carried!*

Especially strict is the ban on travel and transportation. According to the Biblical law (Exod. 16:29), no man is to leave his "place" on the sabbath day. The sages, however, attempted by various legalistic devices to modify the rigors of this restriction. A number of houses, they declared, could be temporarily combined into a single common "place" or domain, if the householders formed a kind of *ad hoc* "holiday club" by each contributing something to a common stock of food placed in a room accessible to all. Similarly, they eased the regulation which confined travel on the sabbath to distances within a

radius of two thousand cubits by permitting people
temporarily to transfer their residence from the center to
the circumference of the imaginary circle. This dispensation, however, was granted only in cases where a
man might wish to travel in order to fulfill a religious
duty (e.g., to attend a circumcision), and to qualify for it
he had, before the advent of the sabbath, to transfer a
token quantity of food to the new dwelling.[4]

In contrast to this more liberal attitude is the practice
of the Samaritan community at Nablus. The Samaritans claim to be the descendants of the ancient Kingdom
of Israel. Their religion is based on the Law of Moses
and they reject the authority of the Jewish sages. To the
Samaritans, the law means just what it says; accordingly
they do not stir from their houses on the seventh day,
except to attend services in the synagogue. It is said,
indeed, that the Samaritan teacher Dositheus, who lived
(probably) in the first century C.E., actually commanded
his followers to remain in one position throughout the
sabbath!

For all their legalistic precision, however, the sages
were conscious always that the sabbath was made for
man, not man for the sabbath, and they insisted that any
of the regulations might be—nay should be—broken immediately in case of life-and-death emergency, or of real
danger to health. In support of such relaxation, they
were fond of quoting the Scriptural verse: "Ye shall
therefore keep My statutes and Mine ordinances, which
if a man do, he shall live by them" (Lev. 18:5).

The other aspect of the sabbath—that of mental and
spiritual recreation—was brought out in the injunction
that the leisure hours of the day should be devoted to

. . . . .

[4] An artificially extended "sabbath domain" is known as an *erub*.

study and to discourse about the Torah. The rabbinic classic *Pesikta Rabbathi,* compiled in the ninth century, has a fine passage exemplifying this doctrine:

Said Rabbi Hiyya, the son of Abba: The Sabbath was given for enjoyment. Said Rabbi Samuel, the son of Nahmani: It was given for studying the Torah. There is no discrepancy between the two statements. Rabbi Hiyya was alluding to the scholars who study the Torah all the week and enjoy themselves on the sabbath, whereas Rabbi Samuel was thinking of laborers who toil throughout the week, and on the Sabbath come to study the Torah.

Enjoyment of the sabbath in this positive sense is, in Jewish tradition, an integral part of its observance. "Those who both observe the sabbath and call it an enjoyment," says the prayer book, "will rejoice in the kingdom of God and enjoy the riches of His bounty." The expression does not refer to ultimate rewards in Kingdom Come, nor is it a mere pious promise of "pie in the sky when you die." It means simply that those who on sabbath retreat from mundane things and consecrate the day to study of the Torah will be automatically refreshed and replenished by a growing awareness that behind the passing show of men lie the abiding verity and sovereignty of God.

There are several ways in which this more positive aspect of the sabbath finds, or has found, practical expression. One of them is the custom of meeting together in the synagogue during the afternoon in order to study the Bible (usually the weekly lesson from the Law) and various rabbinic writings,[5] or to hear an exposition of them from the rabbi or from some visiting scholar.

• • • • •

[5] On each of the sabbaths between Passover and Pentecost it is customary to read a chapter from the *Ethics of the Fathers,* a tractate of the Mishnah in which are collected the apothegms of the ancient sages.

Another is the practice of concluding the introductory meal on Friday night with the chanting of religious table songs *(zemiroth)*, the central theme of which is the delight of the sabbath day. These songs—all of comparatively recent date—are a characteristically Jewish counterpart of the medieval monks' and students' songs. Some of them stem from the group of cabbalists who gathered around the illustrious Isaac Luria in Safed during the early part of the sixteenth century; while others are the product of the Hasidim, or Pietist movement which grew up in eastern Europe some hundred and fifty years later. In many of them, the sabbath becomes, as it were, the "toast of the evening," being fêted in the manner of a carnival queen. In others, as in the following famous poem by Luria himself,[6] the imagery is even bolder and God Himself is the guest, come to regale the company, in the manner of a presiding rabbi, with subtle and profound expositions of the Law and with the tales of miracles and wonders:

I spread the board this sabbath eve,
    And now do I invite
The Ancient Sage, the Holy One.
    Now may His radiant light
Shine in our cups, and may His lore
    Illume our feast tonight!

May He His radiant beauty shed,
    And we His splendor see,
The while He whispers soft and low
    His hidden mystery.
And tells us, as we gather round,
    Of wonders yet to be—

• • • • •

[6] *Asadder li-se'udatha.*

Of sabbath feasts which in His courts
    For us shall yet be spread,
When we shall taste His holy meats
    And break His holy bread,
And all the wine of His great pow'r
    Shall rush into our head!

When in a living tether He
    Shall tie the souls of all,
And nevermore shall flower fade
    And never blossom fall,
And all in one great music break,
    All creatures great and small;

And they shall make sweet minstrelsy
    To crown the festive board,
And His great name be on their lips,
    Forevermore adored;
And they at last find words to tell
    The glory of the Lord.

Both the beginning and the end of the sabbath are marked by special ceremonies. These are determined very largely by the fact that the Jewish day commences at sunset, the moment when, in ancient times, the candles or oil lamps were lit. At the beginning and end of the sabbath, this purely utilitarian act came naturally to acquire a special significance, and it thus attained the status of a religious rite.

The lighting of the candles—at least two—on the eve of the sabbath is assigned to the mistress of the house; and popular fancy supposes that neglect of this duty will be punished by death in childbirth. Shortly before sunset the housewife spreads a clean white cloth on the table and usually places the sabbath loaves (covered with an embroidered napkin) upon it. She then lights the

candles and pronounces the blessing: "Blessed art Thou,
O Lord our God, King of the Universe, Who hast hallowed us by Thy commandments and commanded us to
kindle the lamp." Such a commandment, to be sure, is
nowhere mentioned in the Scriptures, but Judaism regards the institutions established by the rabbis and by
the consensus of tradition as equally inspired by God—
that is, as equal expressions of man's contact with, or
apprehension of, the divine and transcendental, and it
therefore gives them the status of commandments. After
pronouncing the blessing, it is customary for the housewife to spread her hands over the flame and then to
place them for a moment over her eyes. The reason for
this practice is disputed, but the most probable explanation is that it symbolizes an actual *use* of the light
and thus validates the blessing; for in Jewish tradition, a
blessing is not pronounced in general and vague terms
but as an act of thanksgiving and appreciation for some
actual and present benefit.

At the expiration of the sabbath, the ceremony is
more elaborate. Known as *Habdalah,* or "Separating," it
is performed by the master of the house after the evening prayers. The officiant takes a special candle made
of two intertwining pieces of wax and yielding a double
flame, a box of spices, and a glass filled to overflowing
with wine or any other beverage. He then recites a
formula which begins with a threefold invocation to
the prophet Elijah bidding him come speedily "with the
Messiah, the scion of David," continuing with a formula
in which God is blessed for "separating the holy from the
profane, Israel from the heathen, and sabbath from weekdays," and concluding with a separate benediction over
each of the three ritual objects. When he blesses the
candle, he makes a point of curving his hand and look-

ing intently at his fingernails, and when he blesses the
wine or beverage, he cups his hands over it and gazes
into it in the light of'the twin flame. At the conclusion
of the ceremony, the candle is extinguished in that
portion of the liquid which has spilled over into the
saucer or silver tray, while the cup is passed in turn to
all the males and children in the company. Women may
not partake of it; indeed, a popular superstition asserts
that if they do so, they will grow mustaches!

The ceremony looks both backward and forward; if
it marks the end of the sabbath rest, it also marks the beginning of a new week of labor. But what that week
holds in store is, of course, as yet unknown, and the
ceremony therefore includes various devices designed
both to divine the future and to forefend evil. To the
former category belongs the practice of gazing at the
fingernails and of peering into the cup. Gazing at the
fingernails and interpreting shadows which light might
shed upon them was, in ancient times, a common method
of reading the future; and Jewish literature contains a
number of references to the spirits who were then believed to appear and who are known as "the prince of
the palm" or "the prince of the thumb." Similarly, the
habit of seeking omens by gazing intently into water or
into the contents of a cup is abundantly attested both in
antiquity and in modern folklore. In Scandinavia, for
example, people who had been robbed during the week
used to repair to a diviner on a Thursday evening to see
the face of the thief revealed in a bucket of water, and a
similar method is adopted among the natives of Tahiti.
Nor, indeed, should it be overlooked that in the Bible
itself (Gen. 44:5), the silver goblet which Joseph orders
to be hidden in the sack of his youngest brother, Ben-

jamin, is described expressly as a vessel from which he
both drank *and divined*.

On the other hand, the use of the spices is a measure
of protection against the perils of the ensuing week.
They are a kind of symbolic "smelling salts," and are
intended to revive and fortify the spirit after the departure of that "extra soul" with which, so it is said,
every Jew is endowed during the sabbath day.

Of the same order, too, is the invocation of Elijah; for
not only is the threefold repetition strongly suggestive of
a magical formula, but the fact is also that, in Jewish
belief, Elijah, besides being the forerunner of the Messiah—who, it is supposed, will arrive at the close of the
sabbath—is at the same time the protector *par excellence*
against demons and "princes of darkness." (He is
credited, for instance, with the power of protecting ex-
pectant mothers from the assaults of the child-stealing
demon, Lilith). It is therefore very natural that appeal
should be made to him at the critical beginning of a new
week, when—according to Jewish superstition—the devils
and demons which have remained confined in hell
(Gehenna) over the sabbath, are again released to work
their mischief upon men.

The lighting of the candles, however, is not the only
ceremony connected with the incoming and outgoing of
the sabbath. Equally important, on Friday evening, is the
rite known as *Kiddush,* or Sanctification. Properly speaking, this is simply a formal hallowing of the sabbath, in
accordance with the Scriptural commandment to "remember [or, observe] the sabbath day to keep it holy"
(Exod. 20:8; Deut. 5:12); and it originally consisted
only in the pronouncement of a benediction praising

God for granting this institution to Israel as a perpetual heritage. Later, however, perhaps as a counterblast to the Roman practice of beginning a meal with a libation to the gods, it became customary to accompany the benediction with the drinking of wine (itself duly blessed), and it is in this form that the ceremony is today observed.

The Sanctification is prefaced by the chanting of the Scriptural passage, Gen. 2:1-3, describing how God "finished His work on the seventh day . . . and rested." Thereby, says the Talmud, the officiant spiritually retrojects himself to the moment of creation and becomes, as it were, the partner of God in that process.

Kiddush is followed immediately by the blessing over bread which precedes every meal in a traditional Jewish home. This, however, lends itself, on the sabbath, to a special embellishment. Not one, but two loaves are used, in commemoration of the double portion of manna which the Israelites received in the wilderness on the eve of the sabbath (Exod. 16:22,29). Moreover, the loaves are covered with a napkin (often ornately embroidered), symbolizing the "fine layer of dew" which covered the manna (*ibid.*, 13–15).

Sabbath bread is called *hallah* (often spelled *chollah*), the term used in the Bible (Num. 15:17—21) for the cake of new dough which every Israelite was required to present as a "gift unto the Lord." Before it is baked, a portion of the dough has to be removed, in accordance with that commandment. The loaves are commonly fashioned in the shape of "twists" popularly known as *berches*. It has been suggested that this name derives from the old German *Berchisbrod*—that is, bread shaped like intertwined braids of hair which women and girls allegedly used to set out for Berchta, the demonic hag of

Teutonic folklore who was believed to make the rounds on Twelfth Night. More probably, however, the name is connected with quite a different German word, viz., *Berchit*, which in turn goes back to the Low Latin *bracellus*, "arm," and denotes a type of loaf shaped like folded arms. Another form of this word (though the meaning is now somewhat different) is the familiar *pretzel*.

It is customary also on Friday night, at the conclusion of the service in the synagogue, for Jewish fathers to place their hands upon the heads of their children and pronounce a blessing over them. In the case of boys, the blessing runs: "May God make thee like Ephraim and Manasseh," and in that of girls: "May God make thee like Sarah, Rebekah, Rachel and Leah." Moreover, as a graceful compliment to his wife, he chants the concluding chapter of the Biblical Book of Proverbs:

A woman of worth who can find?
Her price is far above rubies.

．　　　．　　　．　　　．　　　．

She looketh well to the ways of her household,
    and eateth not the bread of idleness.
Her children rise up and call her blessed;
    her husband also, and he praiseth her:

"Many daughters have done worthily,
    but thou excellest them all."

At the *conclusion* of the Sabbath, the most interesting feature of the service is, perhaps, the recital of the Ninety-first Psalm. That psalm is known traditionally as the "plague psalm," the name being derived from vss. 5-6:

Thou shalt not be afraid of the terror by night,
Of the arrow that flieth by day,

Of the pestilence that stalketh in darkness,
Of the destruction that ravageth at noon.

At first sight, these verses look like a mere blanket formula, as in the familiar Cornish prayer: "From ghoulies
and ghosties and long-legitty beasties, and things that
go bump in the night, good Lord deliver us!" In point of
fact, however, the reference is to specific demons of
ancient Semitic folklore. The "terror by night" is the
hobgoblin, and he is mentioned again in Song of Songs
3:8, where the attendants of the bridegroom (facetiously
identified with Solomon) are said to be armed—as indeed they are in Oriental weddings—"each man with his
sword upon his thigh," in order to ward off that demon's
assaults. The "arrow that flieth by day" is the familiar
"faery arrow" which, in the belief of many peoples, is
the cause both of stitch in the side and of all diseases.[7]
The "pestilence that stalketh in darkness" is the demon
known to the magical literature of Babylon as "he that
stalks abroad at night" *(mutallik mushi);* while "the
destruction that ravageth at noon" is a personification of
the scorching midday heat which may cause sunstroke or
even death. It is apparent, therefore, that this psalm
originally found place in the service because it was
regarded as a kind of charm against the malevolent spirits
released from hell at the beginning of the week. It was,
in fact, a complement to the ceremony of Habdalah; and
it is significant that it also forms part of the burial service, where it serves to protect both the deceased and his
survivors from the ravages of the evil spirits thought to
be especially rampant at a time of death.

It is easy to smile at these beliefs and to adopt a
superior attitude toward them. They are, however,

. . . . .

[7] See above, p. 54.

simply a primitive way of expressing normal and rational
apprehension of the hazards and perils of an uncertain
future. The belief in the extra "sabbath soul," for instance, is simply a fanciful way of saying that retreat
from mundane preoccupations on the sabbath gives a man
a special spiritual serenity which tends to depart the
moment he immerses himself again in the humdrum
routine of the workaday world. By smelling the fragrant
spices he reminds himself, in symbolic fashion, that he
can become immune from the contagion of that world, if,
so to speak, he but absorb by osmosis the constant fra-
grance of holiness. (Significantly enough, the word
osmosis really means "smelling," and thus provides an
exact counterpart in language to the symbolism of the
ritual). Similarly, the demons and evil spirits which are
believed to rise from hell at the moment the sabbath ends
are no more than picturesque personifications of the
hazards and uncertainties which attend the beginning of
each new week.

In taking over these traditional notions, however, Judaism gave them a new and deeper significance. It was now
not only the individual but also the whole House of
Israel that stood in need of protection from the hovering
demons of disaster. If, on the one hand, the Habdalah
service includes such intimate, personal appeals as the
touching Yiddish prayer of the Jewish mother that "God,
Who in the seventh heav'n dwells, May pity me, my
husband, and my babes," on the other, it now called
upon Elijah not for personal deliverance but for national
salvation; as a long acrostic poem has it, he is to lead
Israel "from darkness to light."

This development comes out especially in the preceding evening service. A feature of those devotions is
the recital of sundry Scriptural prophecies relating to

material prosperity. Each, however, is followed immediately by another which foretells national salvation. Thus, the promise of Deuteronomy (7:13—15) that God "will bless the fruit of thy body and the fruit of thy land, thy corn, thy must and thine oil" is capped, so to speak, by Isaiah's assurance (45:17) that "Israel is saved by the Lord with everlasting salvation"; and the prediction of Joel (2:26) that "ye shall eat in plenty and be satisfied" by Isaiah's confident declaration (35:10, 51:11) that "the ransomed of the Lord shall return and come with singing to Zion"; until, in an inspired climax, the immergence of individual in collective deliverance is brought home by the skillful juxtaposition of the two verses, "Blessed is *the man* that trusteth in the Lord" (Jer. 17:7) and "The Lord will give strength unto His *people*; the Lord will bless His *people* with peace" (Ps. 29:11).

The sabbath is personified in Jewish tradition as a bride whose bridegroom is Israel. Rabbinic fancy plays eloquently on this conception. Observing that the Hebrew term for the marriage ceremony really means "hallowing," the sages interpret the Biblical statement that "God blessed the sabbath day and hallowed it" (Gen. 2:3) as meaning that He wedded it to His people.[8]

In the East, weddings usually take place on a Friday evening, and this served as an added incentive for representing the advent of the sabbath as a symbolic wedding festivity. The Talmud tells us[9] that, on the eve of the sabbath, the famous teacher, Rabbi Hanina used to

. . . . .

[8] *Pesikta Rabbathi,* 117[b].
[9] *Shabbat* 119[a].

put on his best clothes and say, "Come, let us go and welcome Queen Sabbath," while Rabbi Yannai used to rise and declare, "Come, O bride; come, O bride."

The custom of going out to "meet the bride" was especially common among the cabbalists of Safed in the earlier part of the sixteenth century, and some of the more poetically talented of them actually composed symbolic imitations of the conventional marriage songs. The most famous of these is the *Lechah Dodi,* written by Solomon Alkabetz, teacher and brother-in-law of the mystic philosopher, Moses Cordovero. This poem, which is now an integral part of the Friday night service, plays on one of the most prominent features of Arab weddings, namely, the procession of the bridegroom from the local mosque to his own home, where the bride awaits him. He is usually accompanied on this occasion by torchbearers, musicians and singers. The latter, however, do not confine themselves to the chanting of wedding songs; they also intone lyric odes of a religious character in praise of Mohammed. All of these elements find place, if only by hint and implication, in the celebrated Hebrew poem. The bridegroom—i.e., Israel—is first bidden to come and meet the bride:

Bridegroom, come to meet the bride;
Let us greet the sabbath-tide!

Immediately, however, in the manner of the Arab singers, the poet breaks off to offer praise to God; and the familiar expression "the Lord is one, and His name one" looks to all the world like a characteristically Jewish imitation of the familiar Arabic cry, "There is no God but One"—a cry which punctuates all public ceremonies. Then, playing on sundry Biblical verses, he predicts the future prosperity of Zion, evidently a parody of the blessings customarily invoked upon the bride. Finally he addresses the maiden herself:

Come in peace, and come in joy,
Thou who art thy bridegroom's pride;
   Come, O bride, and shed thy grace
   O'er the faithful chosen race;
Come, O bride! Come, O bride!

—an invitation doubtless modeled on that addressed to brides at human weddings.[10]

Lechah Dodi, which has been translated into German by both Herder and Heine, is probably the best known of all Hebrew poems, and it enjoys the reputation of having been set to more tunes than any other poem in the world. It is of interest to note, however, that a very similar though now long forgotten poem, employing the same tropes and many of the same phrases, was composed at the same time by the Italian-Jewish poet Mordecai Dato (1527-85), another follower of Moses Cordovero.

Other fancies also are associated with the sabbath in Jewish traditional lore.

Not only the Jewish people but all the God-fearing elements of creation are believed to observe the sabbath day. It is told, for example, that on a certain occasion a cow which had belonged to a pious man, when sold to a

. . . . .

[10] It may be mentioned also that the rhyme-scheme of *Lechah Dodi*—each line ending in -*lah*- conforms to a familiar Arabic type of composition, inspired by the fact that, in popular songs, it is often customary to end the stanzas with a piercing *lalala,* somewhat like the *fal la la* of Elizabethan lyrics. This device, incidentally, is extremely common in Hebrew poetry; see I. Davidson, "Rhymes in Hebrew Poetry," *Jewish Quarterly Review,* XXX (1940), pp. 299-398.

stranger, refused to work on the sabbath. It is told also that there exists in the far reaches of the world a river called Sambatyon (variously located) which ceases flowing on the sabbath. Such an intermittent stream is mentioned, indeed, by several non-Jewish writers throughout the ages, and many are the tall tales of more recent travelers who claim to have seen it. An ingenious explanation of this legend has been proposed. The river, it is suggested, possessed no such miraculous properties as were later attributed to it. It was simply a river of sand. But the Hebrew word for "sand," viz., *hol,* is indistinguishable from another which means "weekday," and hence arose the notion that "the river of *hol*" was one which flowed only on weekdays and rested on the sabbath!

Finally, it is maintained in Jewish legend that even the angels keep the sabbath—an idea which receives its finest expression, curiously enough, not in Jewish literature, but in Peter Abelard's great hymn for Saturday evening:[11]

Oh what shall be, oh when shall be, that holy Sabbath day,
Which heavenly care shall ever keep and celebrate alway;
When rest is found for weary limbs, when labor hath reward,
When everything, for evermore, is joyful in the Lord?

The true Jerusalem above, the holy town is there,
Whose duties are so full of joy, whose joy so free from care;
Where disappointment cometh not to check the longing heart,
And where the soul in ecstasy hath gained her better part.

. . . .
. . . . .

[11] From the translation by Samuel Willoughby Duffield (1843-1887). For other renderings, see *Hymns Ancient and Modern,* No. 313, and Helen Waddell, *Mediaeval Latin Lyrics* (New York, 1938), p. 163.

There Sabbath day to Sabbath day sheds on a ceaseless light,
Eternal pleasure of the saints who keep that Sabbath bright;
Nor shall the chant ineffable decline, nor ever cease,
Which we with all the angels sing in that sweet realm of peace.

EPILOGUE

When this book was about to go to press, a friend who read it through posed the inevitable question. If, said he, the real purpose of the Jewish festivals is to exemplify certain universal ideals, why cannot those ideals be exemplified just as well by more familiar institutions? Why, for instance, cannot Independence Day take the place of Passover, and Sunday of the sabbath? Since many other readers will doubtless be asking the same question, a brief reply is perhaps in order.

First, then, it should be borne in mind that the Jewish festivals are living experiences, and not merely celebrations. They issue out of the distinctive history and consciousness of a particular people. If they exemplify universal truths and ideals, they also exemplify the way in which those truths and ideals came to be apprehended in a specific setting and in which they are being constantly and progressively developed. Observance of them therefore involves active participation in a particular and distinctive cultural process, and for this reason they cannot be sublimated to an abstract plane nor assimilated to other institutions of the same general import without losing their essential character and identity. Independence Day, for example, cannot serve as a substitute for Passover, nor Sunday for the sabbath, because although in each case both institutions are based on the same universal ideal, this fact no more obliterates their particular natures than does the universal prevalence of marriage obliterate the individual quality and significance of each particular union. In a word, the Jewish festivals are a form of Jewish self-expression, and they cannot be dissolved into extraneous patterns without a corresponding dissolution of Jewish identity.

Second: while it is true that many of the ancient Hebraic teachings have long since been absorbed into general Western civilization, it is equally true that many others have not. Hence, to assimilate the Jewish festivals to Gentile institutions would involve a loss of real and distinctive values. If, for example, the festival of Pentecost came to be discarded on the grounds that the existence of Natural or Divine Law can be readily apprehended by modern man without identifying it with the particular Mosaic Code or associating it with the event at Mount Sinai, we should immediately run the risk of losing the unique concept of the Covenant—that is, of the necessary partnership of God and man—which is Judaism's distinctive elaboration of that concept. Similarly, if we used some other symbol than Passover to bring home the message of freedom, we should thereby forfeit the important corollary—implicit in the Jewish story of the Exodus —that freedom entails a journey through the wilderness. The Jewish festivals are, in fact, a method of focusing and dramatizing many values which have still to fight their way to acceptance. To surrender their distinctive features or to melt them into a common blur would therefore be compromising the struggle for the Kingdom of God on earth.

Thirdly, it must be observed that the Jewish festivals are collective institutions, not individual affirmations. Therefore they must needs assume a form with which all Jews everywhere can identify themselves; and this unity would be destroyed forthwith, were every Jewish community to substitute for the common pattern one born of its own particular circumstance and environment. Nor, indeed, should it be regarded as a drawback that many elements of the traditional pattern are in fact antique and exotic; for this very fact serves to bring home the essential truth that what the festivals express and epitomize is not simply a contemporary mood or outlook but rather the cumulative temper of all ages of Jewish history. They are set against a background of continuous time, not merely of the present generation.

Today, it must be confessed, observance of the Jewish festivals faces a major challenge. Since the dissolution of the Jewish state, in 70 C.E., the festivals have existed in a kind of cultural vacuum, expressing far more the spirit of a tradition than the temper of a living and distinctive society. They have become, to a very large extent, a mechanism for conserving artificially what was once a natural and organic cohesion. For the modern Jew, this lends them a certain air of remoteness and tends to make of their observance an act of sentimental piety rather than of positive and inevitable self-expression; more often than not, the modern Jew speaks of "keeping *up*" the festivals rather than of simply keeping them.

How far this state of affairs will be altered by the re-establishment of a Jewish state in Israel and by the consequent re-integration of the festivals into a distinctive Jewish life, it is at present premature to discuss; but the bare fact that such alteration will take place can scarcely be doubted. Moreover, it will issue from a natural cultural development, and not from the fiat of any central authority—a sanhedrin or college of rabbis. For Judaism is not a creed, to be determined or imposed in such fashion; it is the spirit of an entire people attuned to hear a Voice behind the thunders and ready, even while it stands in a wilderness, to answer together: *We will do and we will hear* (Exodus 24:7).

ABOUT THE
TRANSLATIONS

*Except where otherwise stated, all translations
in this volume are by the author.*

*The original texts of the Ashkenazic (German-Polish)
ritual are cited from* The Service of the Synagogue, edited by
Arthur Davis and Herbert M. Adler *(6 vols., London, n.d.).
Those of the Sephardic (Spanish and Portuguese) ritual are
cited from the editions by* David de Sola Pool *(4 vols., New
York 1947-49) and* Moses Gaster *(6 vols., London 1901 ff.).*

It is not easy to reproduce in English the peculiar spirit and flavor
of medieval Hebrew poetry, because it depends, to a very large
extent, on dexterous manipulations of Biblical words and phrases
and on recondite allusions to rabbinic legend and lore. Familiar
as these would have been to past generations, they are likely, more
often than not, to pass over the head of the modern reader. I have
therefore resorted to a number of compensatory devices.

Sometimes, I have used tags from English poetry in place of the
original quotations and allusions. Where, for instance, the Hebrew
poet speaks of Ophanim and Shina'nim—two classes of celestial
beings—I have had no hesitation in speaking, instead, of "angels
and ministers of grace"; where he complains that worldly lusts
have consumed him, I have made him declare (p. 165) that "the
world was too much with me"; and where he sings of earthly
monarchs growing old and decrepit, and sinking, weary and un-
comforted, into Sheol and the netherworld, I have made him

allude (p. 120) to man's inevitable descent, "after the world's spent riot,/Into the grave unquiet."

Sometimes, again, I have substituted an alternative poetic device for the original quotation from Scripture. Take, for instance, Isaac ben Israel's Confession for the afternoon service of Yom Kippur (p. 178). In the Hebrew, the poet appeals to his various limbs to plead his cause with God, and receives from each a negative reply expressed by an appropriate verse from the Bible. When, for example, he appeals to his hands, they decline on the grounds that unclean hands cannot be extended in prayer—an obvious reference to Psalm 24:3-4: "Who shall go up unto the mountain of the Lord? . . . He that hath clean hands." Similarly, when he turns to his feet, they retort that they are "feet which run to do evil"— an equally clear allusion to Isaiah 59:7 and to Proverbs 1:16. Here I have tried to convey the effect by substituting puns for the Biblical verses, e.g., Said I to feet: . . . But feet replied: That were a feat indeed," etc.

Another device to which I have resorted is that of concentrating on the latent undertones rather than the overt overtones of the Hebrew words. A good example of this occurs in the famous *Unetanneh Tokeph* chanted in the additional morning service for New Year and Yom Kippur (p. 118). In the original, the poet, drawing on a passage in the Mishnah, declares that on New Year's Day all creatures pass before God like sheep before a shepherd, the while He "appoints the term" and "decrees the fate" of each. But—and this point does not appear to have been noticed—he chooses his language with exquisite care in order to continue the metaphor of the sheep; for the words rendered "appoints the term" could also mean "performs a shearing" [1] while that rendered "decrees" really means "cuts," and might refer to the same operation or to the incising of a distinctive mark. To obscure this *double-entendre* would be to short-change both the author and the reader. Here, therefore, I have borrowed a familiar phrase from Milton and rendered freely, "God declares and God decrees/When Fate's abhorrèd shears to these/Shall come, and with His mighty hand/Sets upon their souls the brand."

The innumerable puns and word-plays pose a further problem.

. . . . .

[1] See Song of Songs, 4:2.

Where these are of the essence of a poem, and are not mere verbal excrescences, I have tried to preserve them or to provide a reasonable equivalent by means of paraphrase. A peculiarly striking example is Eleazar Kalir's hymn, "Ere that He stayed the heavens in the height" (p. 64). In the original, the point of this poem lies very largely in a sustained word-play on the traditional names of the seven heavens. One of these, for instance, is *Zebul,* a word which means properly "lofty dwelling, edifice." [2] But in a passage of the Book of Genesis (30:20), there occurs a similar word, *z-b-l,* which many interpreters take to mean "honor, dignify, esteem." The poet therefore represents the primordial Torah as declaring that "when God established Zebul as His holy place, I was *zebulah,* i.e., already dignified, by His holy name." Here it seemed possible to convey the nuance by a corresponding pun, viz., "Ere that the sunlit *welkin* was His place, I was *well kin*dled by His holy grace." It must be confessed, however, that in the case of the other six heavens, the pearly gates remained obstinately shut, and the best one could do was simply to skirt the walls and peep over them.

Similarly, in the beautiful *Melek 'elyon,* which is chanted (in the Ashkenazic rite) during the morning service of the First Day of New Year (p. 120), the point lies in a sustained contrast between the "supernal King" in heaven and the "lowly king" on earth. In Hebrew, the former is called *melek 'elyon;* the latter, *melek ebyon;* and the repeated alternation of these like-sounding phrases constitutes the very core and essence of the composition. Here, therefore, I have preferred to reproduce the poet's meaning rather than concentrate on his actual words; accordingly, I have rendered respectively, "King in the world of light" and "King in the world of blight."

Closely allied to the problem of puns and word-plays is that posed by idiomatic expressions. Many of these are taken straight from the Bible. To a reader of the Hebrew, the original context and association spring readily to mind, but in a bald translation they are likely to go unheeded or to need salvaging by the aid of footnotes. My method in such cases has been to find a comparable English idiom, without being unduly pedantic about verbal accuracy. When, for example, Abraham ben Menahem says of Zion that

· · · · ·

[2] See I Kings 8:13; Isa. 63:15.

"her furrow hath been long these many years and days," what he actually has in mind are the words of Psalm 129:3: "Plowmen, as it were, have plowed upon my back, drawn their long furrows thereon." But for the modern reader the point would seem to be conveyed more adequately by a slight change in the metaphor, viz., "She plows her lonely furrow through the years" (p. 199). Similarly, when Meshullam ben Kalonymos describes mankind as "of few days, forgotten by bliss, full of trouble, grieved of soul," he is manipulating a series of Biblical phrases (Lam. 3:17; Job 14:1; 30:25) which a modern reader would probably miss. Here, again, an approximate idiom seems the best rendering, and I have therefore spoken (p. 161) of men "who, overwhelm'd with grief and woe,/Tread their petty pace and slow."

Then, too, there is what may be called the question of background. Some of the poems presuppose a particular setting which, though implicit enough in the original, has to be spelled out in translation. Thus, the famous sabbath hymn of Isaac Luria, translated on p. 275, plays upon the age-old custom whereby the disciples of rabbis and sages gather around their master at the Friday night meal while he regales them with novel interpretations of Scripture or other pearls of his peculiar wisdom. The poet asks God to play this role to His people—to celebrate with them just such a "great kiddush" and to impart to them the secrets of heaven and of the world to come. The sustained allusion, apparent enough in the original, has had to be brought out for the modern reader by a certain amount of paraphrase and expansion. Those who object that this puts into the mouth of the poet words which in fact he never uttered, forget that the business of a translator is to reproduce, so far as he can, not only what is on an author's lips but equally what is in his mind.

Lastly, there is the obstinate problem of form and style. A favorite device of the medieval Hebrew poets was the acrostic, and this took various and wondrous forms. Sometimes it was purely alphabetical—"from *A* to *Z*"; sometimes it spelled out the author's name; and sometimes again it consisted in the alphabet in reverse —from *Z* to *A*—or was enforced, even to grotesque extremes, by "apt alliteration's artful aid." Where this virtuosity is a primary element of the poem, I have tried to reproduce it, believing that such *bizarrerie* as this process necessarily involves might indeed

convey something of the tone of the original. At other times, however, in fear of the inevitable "zealous" in the last line—what else
can one do with Z?—I have felt that to preserve it would be
merely to tighten a shackle already sufficiently constricting; and I
have therefore let the English rhyme scheme serve by itself as a
reasonable substitute.

Insofar as the style of the translations is concerned, this, in the
final analysis, is simply a matter of taste—and association. My
reaction to Moses ibn Ezra's *El Norà 'Alilah* (p. 178), for
example, is inevitably influenced by the rousing tune to which it
is sung in the Spanish and Portuguese synagogue in London, and
this has made it impossible for me to see it as anything other than
a kind of spiritual marching song, and to render it accordingly.
On the other hand, the same author's "Not in the casual caravanserai" (p. 131) conjures in my own mind the picture of a
weary traveler dragging his feet to the hospice of God, anxious
to lay down his heavy load, and this association has inevitably found
its way into the rendering. Anyone who is at all experienced in
the task of translation from poetry will realize at once that such
subjective considerations cannot be avoided; a translator can merely
transmute into the forms of his own vision. As the Talmud puts it:
"He that translates a verse literally is a liar."

INDEX OF POEMS TRANSLATED

INDEX OF FIRST LINES

FOR FURTHER READING

This bibliography is by no means exhaustive. It is intended only to guide interested readers to scientific studies on the various topics discussed in this book.

A. THE SEASONAL FESTIVALS

Passover:

T. H. Gaster, Passover: Its History and Traditions (1949). This book includes a bibliography covering the several aspects of the festival. The rabbinic laws concerning Passover are set forth in the treatise of the Mishnah entitled Pesahim; this may be read in the translation by H. Danby (1933).

Omer Days:

On the belief that marriages in May are unlucky, see: H. Gaidoz, Mélusine VII (1894), pp. 105 ff.; F. Thistleton-Dyer, English Folklore (1880), p. 187; P. Sartori, Sitte und Brauch, vol. ii (1910), p. 60; P. Toschi Il Folklore (1952), p. 46; D. L. and L. B. Thomas, Kentucky Superstitions (1920), p. 64. For the belief in ancient Rome, cf. Ovid, *Fasti* V, 487; Plutarch, *Quaestiones Romanae*, 86. For its prevalence among Jews, see: I. Abrahams, Jewish Life in the Middle Ages, Second edition (1932), p. 200.

On the custom of shooting arrows against demons, see J. G. Frazer, The Golden Bough, vol. xi, p. 291; Sartori, *op. cit.*, vol. iii, pp. 68, n.2; 158; 171.

On the Robin Hood revels, see Chambers' Book of Days (1886), under May 1.

On the kindling of bonfires on the first of May, see: Frazer, The Golden Bough, one-vol. edition, pp. 614 ff.; P. Saintyves, Essais de folk-lore biblique (1922), pp. 42 ff.

Pentecost:

The Psalm of Habakkuk: The traditional Hebrew text of this psalm appears to be corrupt in several passages, and there are significant variations in the ancient Greek (Septuagint) Version. For a modern critical text, see: R. Sinker, The Psalm of Habakkuk (1890). The translation offered in the present volume incorporates some of the emendations proposed by modern scholars, and therefore differs from that to be found in standard English Bibles.

The Book of Ruth: the most serviceable commentary for English readers is that contained in The Cambridge Bible for Schools.

On the relation of Whitsun to Pentecost, those who can read Latin may consult the article by U. Holzmeister in Verbum Domini XX (1940), pp. 129-38.

On the custom of eating cheese and other dairy dishes at this season, see T. H. Gaster, Thespis (1950), pp. 243 ff.

The reference to the Canaanite rite of "seething a kid in milk" occurs in line 14 of the so-called Poem of the Gracious Gods recently discovered at Ras Shamra (ancient Ugarit) on the north coast of Syria; see Gaster, *loc. cit.*

On the phrase, "the morrow of the sabbath" in Lev. 23:15, see: Morris Jastrow, American Journal of Theology II (1898), pp. 312-52; J. and H. Lewy, Hebrew Union College Annual XVII (1942), pp. 78 f.; W. F. Albright, Journal of Biblical Literature LXIV (1945), pp. 289-91.

The Feast of Booths:

For modern views on the origin of the festival, see: P. Volz, Das Neujahrsfest Jahwes (Laubhüttenfest) (1912); A. J. Wensinck, "Arabic New Year and the Feast of Tabernacles," in Verhandelingen der K. Akad. van Wetenchappen, Afd. Letterkunde n. Reehs, XXV, 2 (1923).

The rabbinic laws concerning the festival are set forth in the treatise of the Mishnah entitled Sukkah. This may be read in H. Danby's translation. An interesting edition of the treatise is: F. B. Dachs, Succa, sive de Tabernaculorum Festo (Utrecht, 1726).

The succah: According to some modern scholars, the succah originated in the leafy bower in which the "sacred marriage" between the god and his consort (impersonated by the king and a priestess) was consummated annually at some earlier Canaanite festival of ingathering. But in that case, we should expect it to survive as a sacred edifice within the precincts of the Temple, not as a private structure in individual homes! Moreover, Tosefta, Sukkah i, 4 refers specifically to the wattled cabins erected in the fields during the ingathering and vintage; for their modern form, see G. Dalman, Arbeit und Sitte in Palästina, vol. i (1928), p. 565.

The Water Libation: R. Patai, Man and Temple (1947), pp. 24-53; J. Hochmann, Jerusalem Temple Festivities (1908); I. Scheftelowitz, Altpalästinensischer Bauernglaube (1925), pp. 93, 95; D. Feuchtwang, Monatsschrift für Geschichte und Wissenschaft des Judentums LIV (1910), pp. 535 ff.; J. de Groot, Theologisch Tijdschrift, 1918, pp. 38 ff.; S. A. Cook in W. Robertson Smith, The Religion of the Semites, Third edition (1927), pp. 580 f.; J. G. Frazer, The Golden Bough, vol. i, pp. 248 ff.; id., Aftermath (1936), pp. 68-73.

An analogous ancient Syrian rite is described by Lucian, The Syrian Goddess (ed. H. A. Strong and J. Garstang, 1913), chaps. 3, 48. For a similar practice at Ispahan, in Iran, see Robertson Smith, *op. cit.*, pp. 231, n.2; 232, n.3; Journal Asiatique II (1842), p. 135.

On the subject in general, see: M. H. Morgan, "Rain Gods and Rain Charms," in Transactions and Proceedings of the American Philosophical Society, XXXII, pp. 83 ff.

The Fire Rite: A. Geiger, Wissenschaftl. Zeitschr. für jüd. Theologie III (1837), p. 417; Frazer, The Golden Bough, one-vol. edition, ch. lxii; E. Westermarck, Pagan Survivals in Muhammedan Civilization (1933), pp. 148, 169 ff.; J. Brand, Observations on the Popular Antiquities of Great Britain (1810), p. 304; T. F. Dexter, Fire-Worship in Britain (1931); T. H. Gaster, Thespis (1950), p. 167 (with full bibliography).

The Lulab: For parallels, see: Sartori, *op. cit.*, vol. iii, p. 173; Gaster, Thespis, p. 376.

On the custom of beating with branches of willow to induce fertility, see: W. Mannhardt, Wald- und Feldkulte (1904), vol. i, pp. 251 ff., 280, 285; Scheftelowitz, *op. cit.*, pp. 91 f.; E. Fehrle, Die kultische Keuschheit im Altertum (1910), pp. 139 ff.; G. Murray, The Rise of the Greek Epic (1907), pp. 253-58.

B. THE SOLEMN DAYS

New Year:

On primitive methods of reckoning time, see: M. Nilsson, Primitive Time-reckoning (1920); S. H. Hooke, New Year's Day (1922).

On the ancient Hebraic New Year, see (but with caution) N. H. Snaith, The Jewish New Year Festival (1947).

Rabbinic laws concerning New Year are set forth in the treatise of the Mishnah entitled Rosh Ha-Shanah. This may be read in H. Danby's translation.

For the concept that New Year is a new creation, see M. Eliade, Le mythe de l'éternel retour (1949), chapter ii, pp. 81-136.

On the Babylonian New Year festival, see: S. A. Pallis, The Babylonian Akîtu Festival (1926); C. J. Gadd in Myth and Ritual, ed. S. H. Hooke (1933), pp. 47-58; H. Zimmern, Das babylonische Neujahrsfest (Der Alte Orient, XXV/3: 1926). The main ritual is translated by A. Sachs in Ancient Near Eastern Texts . . . ed. J. B. Pritchard (1950), pp. 331 ff.

The shofar: On the blowing of the shofar as a means of scaring demons, see I. Scheftelowitz, Archiv für Religionswissenschaft XV (1912), pp. 485 ff.; A. Eberharter, Zeitschrift für Katholische Theologie LII (1928), pp. 492-518. See also: H. Feilberg, Archiv für Religionswissenschaft IV (1901), pp. 170-77; pp. 274-89.

The word shofar is probably related to the Assyro-Babylonian *shuparu,* "horned sheep."

The Babylonian Epic of Creation ("The War of the Gods") and the Canaanite Poem of Baal are retold by the present writer in his volume, The Oldest Stories in the World (1952). Literal renderings of the former may be found in A. Heidel's The Babylonian Genesis (Second edition, 1951) and in Ancient Near Eastern Texts . . . , pp. 61 ff.; of the latter, in T. H. Gaster, Thespis (1950), pp. 115-224; Ancient Near Eastern Texts . . . , pp. 129 ff. (by H. L. Ginsberg); and in C. H. Gordon's Ugaritic Literature (1949), pp. 9-55.

On New Year as the model of the Last Day, see A. J. Wensinck, Acta Orientalia I (1927), pp. 158-99.

Tashlich: On the custom of consigning evil to the depths of the sea, or to running water, see: L. Radermacher, "Das Meer und die Toten," in Anzeiger der Oesterreich. Akad., Phil.-Hist. Klasse, 1949, pp. 307-15; H. Schmidt, Jona (1907), pp. 158 ff.; A. Smythe Palmer, Babylonian Influence on the Bible and Popular Beliefs (1897), pp. 48 ff. The idea is common in Classical literature, e.g. Aeschylus, *Supplices* 529; Sophocles, *Oedipus Tyrannus* 193; Euripides, *Hercules Furens* 649; Tibullus IV, 4, 7.

On the subject in general, see I. Scheftelowitz, Archiv für Religionswissenschaft XVII (1914), pp. 353 ff.

On the Tashlich-ceremony in particular, see J. Z. Lauterbach, "Tashlich: A Study in Jewish Ceremonies," in Hebrew Union College Annual XI (1936).

The Kapparah Rite: See I. Scheftelowitz, Das stellvertretende Huhnopfer (1914). It is interesting to note that in Scottish folklore, "chanticleer is a carrier of bad luck, and is thrown out of the house by the window before the bride leaves for the last time, carrying with him the bad fortune which might attach itself to her"; M. M. Banks, Folk-Lore XXXIX (1928), p. 294.

Yom Kippur:

The Biblical ritual (Lev. 16): See: M. Lohr, Das Ritual von Lev. 16 (1925); S. Landersdorfer, Studien zum biblischen Versöhnungstag (1924); R. Pettazzoni, La confessione dei peccati, vol. iii (1936).

On the custom of changing garments in penitential rituals, see: Pettazzoni, *op. cit.;* E. Crawley, Oath, Curse and Blessing (1934), pp. 90 ff.

On fumigation as a means of expelling demons, see: S. Seligmann, Der böse Blick (1910), vol. i, p. 318; I. Scheftelowitz, Altpalästinensicher Bauernglaube (1925), pp. 82 ff.; A. Wiedemann, Das alten Aegypten (1920), p. 154.

The scapegoat: J. G. Frazer, The Scapegoat (part of The Golden Bough) deals exhaustively with this institution.

Confession of sins: See Pettazzoni, *op. cit.* For the formula "witting or unwitting" (Hebrew, *be-yode'im u-be-lô' yode'im*) as a regular cliché in confessions, see Pettazzoni, *op. cit.,* vol. ii, pp. 107-09; vol. iii, p. 112.

The ancient Egyptian "negative confession" is contained in chapter 125 of the Book of the Dead; cf. C. Maystre, Les déclarations d'innocence (1937); J. A. Wilson in Ancient Near Eastern Texts . . . , p. 34.

The Babylonian protestation is translated by R. Pfeiffer in Ancient Near Eastern Texts . . . , p. 435, lines 25-31.

The Book of Jonah: We sorely need a good English commentary on Jonah—especially from the standpoint of comparative literature and lore. Hans Schmidt's Jona (1907) contains much of interest, but goes too far afield and is highly speculative. The edition by Perowne in The Cambridge Bible for Schools is old-fashioned and ignores comparative material.

C. THE FOUR FASTS

On fasting in general, see T. H. Gaster, Thespis (1950), pp. 7 ff. On fasting in ancient Israel, see S. Friberger, Das Fasten in alten Israel: eine bedeutungsgeschichtliche Studie (Agram 1929).

The Babylonian analogies to the four fasts are discussed in S. Langdon, Babylonian Menologies and the Semitic Calendars (1935). Morgenstern's alternative theory is presented in Hebrew Union College Annual I (1924). See also Pick, Orientalistische Literaturzeitung (1908), col. 513.

Rabbinic laws concerning the fasts are set forth in the treatise of the Mishnah entitled Ta'anith. This may be read in H. Danby's translation, or in that of A. W. Greenup (1921) or H. Malter (1928).

The Sumerian parallel to the Book of Lamentations is translated by S. N. Kramer in Ancient Near Eastern Texts . . . , pp. 456 ff. (where, however, the similarities are overlooked).

The best English commentary on the Book of Job is that of S. R. Driver and G. B. Gray in The International Critical Commentary.

D. THE MINOR HOLIDAYS

Purim:

T. H. Gaster, Purim and Hanukkah (1950); S. Doniach, Purim (1933); P. Goodman, ed., The Purim Anthology (1949).

Hanukkah:

T. H. Gaster, Purim and Hanukkah (1950)—with bibliography; O. S. Rankin, The Origin of the Festival of Hanukkah (1935).

[A novel theory to account for the fact that Hanukkah is described in II Maccabees 1:18 as a "feast of booths" is propounded by R. Leszynsky in Monatsschrift für Geschichte und Wissenschaft des Judentums LV (1911), pp. 400 ff. On Hanukkah, he suggests, it was customary to carry festive bunches. The Hebrew name for these was *sokkoth,* and this was confused with *sukkoth* in the sense of "tabernacles, booths"! This theory, however, is more ingenious than plausible, for the fact that the rededication of the Temple was deliberately patterned after the original dedication, *which took place on the Feast of Booths,* suffices to explain the expression.]

The New Year for Trees:

On the American Arbor Day, see W. S. Walsh, Curiosities of Popular Customs (1898), s.v.

On the folklore of plants, much interesting information will be found in the relevant chapter of A. H. Krappe, The Science of Folklore (1930).

E. SABBATH

On the possible connection of the Hebrew sabbath with the Babylonian *shapattu,* see: S. Langdon, Babylonian Menologies and the Semitic Calendars (1935), pp. 89-90; B. Landsberger, Der kultische Kalender der Babylonier und Assyrer, vol. i (1915), pp. 131-36; H. and J. Lewy, Hebrew Union College Annual XVII (1942-43), pp. 78 ff., 105 f., 117 f., 137; T. G. Pinches, Proceedings of the Society of Biblical Archaeology, 1904, pp. 51-56, 162-63.

On the sabbath as originally the full moon, see: J. Meinhold, Sabbat und Woche im Alten Testament (1905); E. Mahler, Zeitschrift der Deutschen Morgenländischen Gesellschaft LXII (1908), pp. 40, 46 f.; K. Marti, Religion of the Old Testament (1907), pp. 150 ff.; M. Jastrow, Hebrew and Babylonian Traditions (1914), pp. 154 ff., 185.

For other views concerning the origin of the Hebrew sabbath, see: J. Hehn, Der israelitische Sabbath (1909); S. Reinach, Cultes, mythes et religions (1906-12), vol. ii, p. 444; W. A. Heidel, The Day of Yahweh (1929).

On the sabbath among primitive peoples, see H. Webster, Rest Days (1916).

Rabbinic laws concerning the sabbath are set forth in the treatise of the Mishnah entitled Shabbath. This may be read in H. Danby's translation.

On the prohibition against travel, see especially A. Kahlberg in Festgabe für Claude Montefiore (Berlin 1928), pp. 78-82.

On the observance of the sabbath in the first and second centuries C.E., see J. Mann, Jewish Quarterly Review, New Series, IV (1914), pp. 433-56.

On the practice of the "Damascus Covenanters," see G. F. Moore, Harvard Theological Review IV (1911), pp. 346 ff.

Samaritan laws are set forth in the ritual and dogmatic compendium entitled Dulail (The Guide), variously ascribed to Jacob ben Aaron and Pinehas ben Isaac, both of the nineteenth century. The text is still unpublished. The statement about Dositheus is made by Origen, *De principiis* IV, i, 17.

The Hebrew text of the sabbath songs may be found in: *Seder Berachoth ve-Hoda'oth* [Order of Blessings and Praises], Florence 1760; *Zemiroth shel Shabbath* [Songs of the Sabbath], Lemberg 1851. An English verse rendering, with musical notations, was published by Herbert Loewe under the title of Medieval Hebrew Minstrelsy (1927).

On the ceremonies at the beginning and end of the sabbath, see I. Elbogen, Festschrift zu Israel Lewys 70ten Geburtstag (Breslau 1911), pp. 173-87.

On the sabbath candle, see: M. Friedmann, Jewish Quarterly Review III (1891), pp. 707-21; B. M. Lewin, Linda Miller Memorial Volume (1938), Hebrew section, pp. 55-68.

On the custom of looking at the fingernails in the Habadalah ceremony, see: S. Daiches, Babylonian Oil Magic in the Talmud and in later Jewish Literature (1915), p. 52; S. Finesinger, Hebrew Union College Annual XII-XIII (1937-38), pp. 347-65; M. Gaster, Encyclopaedia of Religion and Ethics, IV, p. 807[b]. [The view that this is a magical practice, connected with so-called onychomancy, is denied by M. Güdemann, Monatsschrift für Geschichte und Wissenschaft des Judentums LX (1916), p. 137 and by J. Trachtenberg, Jewish Magic and Superstition (1939), p. 308, n.26.]

Mordecai Dato's composition resembling the Lechah Dodi of Solomon Alkabetz will be found in the edition of his poems by A. W. Greenup (London 1910). The similarity has passed unnoticed.

Sabbath legends: The story about the cow which refused to work on the sabbath is told in Pesikta Rabbathi XIV; Midrash Decalogue IV, 5; Maaseh Buch 209. See M. Gaster, The Example of the Rabbis (1924), No. 312.

On the legend of the River Sambatyon, see: M. Gaster, Exempla, Nos. 15, 369, 445; Stith Thompson, Motif-Index of Folk-Literature (1932-36), D 915.4.1. See also: I. Markon, "Land Schabat in den Reiseberkungen des Athanas Nikitin (1466–1472)," in Jüdische Studien Joseph Wohlgemuth . . . gewidmet (Frankfurt 1928), pp. 31-46.

On stories of absolute repose on the sabbath, see R. Basset, Revue des traditions populaires VIII (1893), pp. 250-54. Analogous is the Christian legend that animals remain still during the ringing of the Angelus.

On sabbath and Sunday, see: J. A. Hessey, Sunday: Its Origin, History and Present Obligation (1889) ; H. Meinhold, Sabbat und Sontag (1909).

On sabbath in Islam, see I. Goldziher, Gedenkbuch zur Errinerung an David Kaufmann (Breslau 1900), pp. 86-105.

On the Jewish sabbath as seen through the eyes of the Romans, see: P. Lejay, Revue de l'histoire des religions VIII (1903), pp. 305-35; M. Wolff, Theologische Tijdschrift XLIV (1910), pp. 167-72.